FREDERICK DORIAN, for many years Professor of Music at the Carnegie Institute of Technology in Pittsburgh, was born in Vienna in 1902 and studied at the University of Vienna. He conducted operatic, concert, and broadcast performances in Europe and the United States and was music critic of the *Berliner Morgenpost* (1930-33) and the *Frankfurter Zeitung* (in Paris, 1934) before coming permanently to the United States. His publications in English include: *The History of Music in Performance* (1942); *The Musical Workshop* (1947); and *Commitment to Culture* (1964).

"THE CONCERTO" By GIORGIONE (*completed by Titian*)

DETAIL SHOWING FINGER POSITION

The
HISTORY *of* MUSIC
IN PERFORMANCE

The Art of Musical Interpretation
from the Renaissance to Our Day

By

FREDERICK DORIAN

New York

W · W · NORTON & COMPANY · INC ·

Publishers

W. W. Norton & Company, Inc. is the publisher of current
or forthcoming books on music by Putnam Aldrich, William Austin,
Anthony Baines, Philip Bate, Sol Berkowitz, Friedrich Blume, How-
ard Boatwright, Nadia Boulanger, Paul Brainerd, Nathan Broder,
Manfred Bukofzer, John Castellini, John Clough, Doda Conrad,
Aaron Copland, Hans David, Paul Des Marais, Otto Erich Deutsch,
Frederick Dorian, Alfred Einstein, Gabriel Fontrier, Harold Gleason,
Richard Franko Goldman, Noah Greenberg, Donald Jay Grout,
James Haar, F. L. Harrison, Daniel Heartz, Richard Hoppin, John
Horton, Edgar Hunt, A. J. B. Hutchings, Charles Ives, Roger
Kamien, Hermann Keller, Leo Kraft, Stanley Krebs, Paul Henry
Lang, Lyndesay G. Langwill, Jens Peter Larsen, Jan LaRue, Maurice
Lieberman, Irving Lowens, Joseph Machlis, Carol McClintock,
Alfred Mann, W. T. Marrocco, Arthur Mendel, William J. Mitchell,
Douglas Moore, Joel Newman, John F. Ohl, Carl Parrish, Vincent
Persichetti, Marc Pincherle, Walter Piston, Gustave Reese, Alexander
Ringer, Curt Sachs, Denis Stevens, Robert Stevenson, Oliver Strunk,
Francis Toye, Bruno Walter, J. T. Westrup, Emanuel Winternitz,
Walter Wiora, and Percy Young.

IN MEMORY
OF
MY MOTHER
1871–1939

Foreword

MUSIC and the theater have in common one element that distinguishes them from the other arts. As Dr. Dorian points out in his own analysis, both require the intervention of outsiders to set before us the patterned ideas of the composer or playwright. Masterpieces may be created by a painter or poet for his own delight, unseen or unsung by any besides himself. But a symphony, like a drama, does not fulfil its meaning unless it is projected by performers before an audience. The printed score of the Brahms First Symphony, or the pregnant pages of Shakespeare's *Macbeth*, are merely blueprints of the creators' intentions, of full value only to exceptionally skilled and imaginative readers. They do not come to life without performers and without audience.

The pertinent problem of musical interpretation has been happily epitomized in an observation made by Arturo Toscanini. Not so long ago in my home, the maestro listened with me to the broadcast of an orchestral performance. He sighed and quoted a remark that the Italian composer, Arrigo Boito, once made to him: "Blessed are the arts that do not need interpreters. They cannot be poisoned by histrionic mountebanks, as is too often the case with the divine art of music."

Toscanini and those of us who subscribe to the principles of interpretative loyalty find in the following words of Verdi a clear-cut expression of our convictions:

> As to conductor's inspiration and as to creative activity in every performance, that is a principle which inevitably leads to the baroque and untrue. It is precisely the path that led

7

music to the baroque and untrue at the end of the last century
and in the first years of this, when singers made bold to
"create" (as the French still say) their parts, and in consequence made a complete hash and contradiction of sense out of
them. No: I want only one single creation, and I shall be quite
satisfied if they perform simply and exactly what he [the com-
poser] has written. The trouble is that they do not confine
themselves to what he has written. I deny that either singers
or conductors can "create" or work creatively. This, as I have
always said, is a conception that leads to the abyss.*

Yet music for the public has always been dependent upon
the performer. Never too much in the background, his
position in the present organization of concert-giving is so
emphasized that he often overshadows the composer himself.
Yet who is to say him nay? What, besides inborn instinct
and good taste, is to set the limits beyond which he may not
go? Tradition, handed down from one generation of musicians to another, is often distorted in passage; yet how else,
after the composer's death, are his wishes to be translated into
sound? Since a composer is often notoriously not his own best
interpreter, by what standard is one reading of his work better
than another?

Through all the years of my professional life, this problem
in its various aspects has been to me the most intangible and
troublesome. One's technique is a definite thing that can be
demonstrably adequate or not. Since I have had the honor
of being leader of one of the world's most skilful and re-
sponsive orchestras, such technicalities have been matters of
routine. But the question of interpretation is never so clearly
right or wrong. Nor is it ever likely to be.

My first vague awareness of the problem of interpretation
came when I was about eight years old (my concertgoing had

* Translation by E. Downes.

begun at three). I then heard the famous Russian conductor, Vasili Safonov, in works with which I was already familiar through performances of good musicians resident in Budapest. Why, I asked myself, do these symphonies that I know so well sound so different with a strange man conducting? I have listened ever since with the greatest care to performers of all sorts, gleaning what I could from the good, learning from the bad what not to do. Fifteen years' familiarity with the simple, natural approach of Toscanini has convinced me that the most difficult (and the most honest) procedure is that which submerges the personality of the performer and reveals only the wishes of the composer.

But how are we to understand and to follow out the wishes of the composer? The instruments of the orchestra are not what they were in Bach's day; conditions of listening have basically altered since the Vienna and London of Haydn; what was an emphatic dissonance for Mozart has become a commonplace harmony for us, destroying his intended climax; our social background is not that of Beethoven. All of these elements affect the question at issue. Those of us who are public performers must all be targets for criticism, friendly and unfriendly, private and in the press. We are told that this movement was too fast, that one too slow; that here we have missed the true inwardness of a passage, and there we have overstressed another. By what standards, I often wonder, are these opinions formed? And are those comments always the result of the same kind of patient study and listening and comparison that go into an honest performance?

The researches and conclusions that Dr. Dorian has gathered into the present volume constitute the first attempt, within my knowledge, to systematize the material pertaining to this extremely variable but vitally important branch of musical study. The author is a musician as well as a musicologist, who brings to his task a rare combination—his practical experiences as an accomplished conductor, blended with the scholarship of his science of music. From old treatises and textbooks, from the scores of the masters and voluminous comment on them by the composers themselves and by their contemporaries, Dr. Dorian has built up his evidence. He has concentrated on the art of the performer in all its aspects—historical, technical, spiritual. From contemporary sources he has learned of Italian *bel canto*, of the Elizabethan virginalists, of baroque organ playing. He has gone into the matter of the acoustic conditions for which the music of the past was planned. He has compared accounts of Beethoven's piano playing, and has sought to duplicate Chopin's use of rubato. He has traced the rise, with Paganini and Liszt, of virtuosity for its own sake. Phrasing and dynamics have been considered historically, as has exactness of tempo in relation to the development of the metronome. He has digested the theoretical writings of Berlioz and Wagner. Of especial interest, in this day of individualized expression on the part of each new performer, is his discussion of the revision and "correction" of classical scores. His book closes with a glimpse of future possibilities—electrogenic scores, music for the films and for television.

If only for its collection and ordering of this valuable material, Dr. Dorian's book will prove enlightening and provocative to performers and to scholars, to the critic and to the lay listener. It will open up new perspectives to the professional and bring new discernment to the concertgoer. It will make for clearer understanding of the just relation between the creative and the interpretative artist. It provides both basis and stimulus for further thought and work toward the discovery of what is the truth in interpretation.

Eugene Ormandy

Contents

PART III: ROMANTICISM

PART IV: THE OBJECTIVE PRESENT

═══════Illustrations═══════

Introductory Note and Acknowledgments

This book is addressed to the music lover, whether listener or performer, amateur or professional, who desires to orientate himself in the specific differences that prevail in the styles and interpretative ideologies of the various musical epochs. The theme of the book is interpretation. Its chapters deal with the spiritual and technical aspects of the performer's approach to masterworks. For a guide, the author has used the scores and documentary statements of composers, as well as other available material, through which an authentic insight into the styles of performances and their background may be obtained. With the emphasis on performance, this volume, while following the historical evolution, shows a disposition and standard of evaluation not necessarily identical with those of a musical history of works and personalities.

The great composers have not contributed equally to the clarification of the various problems of interpretation. Palestrina and Bach, bestowing on humanity the spiritual wealth of their works, left little evidence other than the scripts of their scores as to the proper execution of their music. In contrast, Berlioz covers in an almost encyclopedic manner the entire territory of interpretation. But it is perhaps only in the case of Wagner that creation and commentary are equably balanced, in scores and theoretical discussion. And so Wagner's name flows through the following chapters like the *cantus firmus* in a contrapuntal composition.

The trends of interpretation are traced not only from the shining stars of the musical firmament; sometimes lesser lights prove to be of greater value for our purpose. Treatises and scholarly textbooks are of utmost help in the reconstruction of the old performance, along with study of those great scores that made history. In addition, contemporary literature and philosophy, in every epoch, appear as truly dominant forces behind the musical ideology and interpretation of their times. The reader, then, must not be disappointed if his favorite Rossini or Tchaikovsky is not appraised in space or words according to his merits as an opera or symphony composer. To reiterate: This book is not a history of music. It describes techniques, ideas, experiences, from the specific viewpoint of performance.

In a measure, this volume has grown out of an attempt to harmonize for the senior and graduate classes of the Carnegie Institute of Technology the spiritual and technical aspects of interpretation in their reciprocal role in music. These classes presented an opportunity to explore, in a laboratory manner, the interaction between the aesthetic, historical, and technical questions of performance. And so I hope that my book may prove to be valuable not only as a source of reference but also as a guide in the study of the fascinating historical interrelationship of style and interpretation.

My first word of acknowledgment is addressed to Dr. Curt Sachs. Generously giving of his time, he has guided me with his vast experience and scholarship in the preparation of the manuscript. Dr. Sachs most kindly offered me the opportunity of consulting with him on many problems that arose during the years of planning and writing. His contribution has proved of substantial value for my work. I am deeply indebted to him.

I am also obliged to Mr. Glendinning Keeble, director of the College of Fine Arts of the Carnegie Institute of Technology, for his encouragement in my work and for suggestions concerning the manuscript. The material for this book was provided by the Library of Congress in Washington, the New York Public Library, and the Carnegie Library and the Carnegie Institute of Technology in Pittsburgh. I wish to thank the various members of these organizations for their courtesy, and to mention especially the assistance of the Misses

Irene Millen, Ella Poindexter, Esther Fawcett, Mildred Lawton. My colleague, Professor Charles Pearson, has kindly helped me in the reading of the proofs. Dr. J. Vick O'Brien, head of the music department of the Carnegie Institute of Technology, was most co-operative in planning my classes on Interpretation.

Last but not least, for their interest, patience, and fatigueless help, I am most grateful to my wife, to my friends Elizabeth Gilbert-Koskoff and Dr. Yale David Koskoff, and to Dr. Max Schoen, head of the Department of Psychology of the Carnegie Institute of Technology. Dr. Schoen rendered special service discussing with me questions on the borderline between psychology and music, and graciously spent countless hours re-examining my thoughts and findings. I am most appreciative of this help.

For permission to quote and reprint, acknowledgment is made in regard to the following: excerpt from the Fourth String Quartet of Arnold Schönberg, reproduced by permission of the publisher, G. Schirmer, Inc.; quotations from an article by Edgar Istel, "The Secret of Paganini's Technique," in the *Musical Quarterly* reprinted for January, 1930, by permission of the publisher and the author; quotations from *Stravinsky: An Autobiography*, by permission of the publishers, Simon and Schuster, Inc.; quotations from articles by Olin Downes (concerning Shostakovich and his arrangement of *Boris Godunoff*) and by Howard Taubman (concerning the recording of Caruso's voice), by permission of the *New York Times*.

Grateful acknowledgment is due to the entire staff of W. W. Norton and Company for their kind assistance and wholehearted co-operation. Valuable help also was given by Mr. Joseph Breitenbach who photographed the manuscript and pictures appearing in this volume.

═══ Prologue ═══

INTERPRETATION: APPLIED MUSICOLOGY

MUSIC lives through interpretation. Between a musical work and the world stands the interpreter who brings the score to life by his performance. The relationship between the performing and the creative artist, however, has changed profoundly in the history of music and continues to do so. This situation in music, as compared with the other arts, is unique. Paintings in the gallery speak to the visitor without the help of a mediator; this is true similarly of the works of sculpture and architecture. In reading poetry or prose, we act, as it were, as our own interpreters. But in music, the score of the St. Matthew Passion, as such, has meaning only for the intellect of the trained musician. The large mass of music lovers, in order to hear masterworks, is dependent upon actual performance of them. Thus it becomes obvious that in music, in contrast to the other arts, the interpreter is of paramount importance—a factor *sine qua non.*

Our musical life has become more and more a cult of the interpreter. It is the singers, a dramatic soprano and a high tenor, and not Richard Wagner, who receive the praise for *Tristan und Isolde.* Audiences worshiping at the feet of a "divine" conductor easily forget Beethoven's contribution to his own score, and eulogize the grandeur of a particular director's rendition of the Ninth Symphony. This present overemphasis on the interpreter's role is sharply contrasted by the disregard of it in former periods. The ecclesiastical spirit of the

Middle Ages did not acknowledge interpretation in our modern sense, as the individualized expression of the performer. The picture has gradually changed in the last four hundred years, so that the interpreter, who was formerly very much in the background, has now become the star of the performance. Small wonder, then, that the musical world is disturbed by heated arguments over the rights and limits of interpretation. What are the interpreter's rights? Where are these limits?

The nature of the main issue can be demonstrated by the question of the interpretation of the first measures in Beethoven's Fifth Symphony. This best-known example takes us to the very core of the problem.

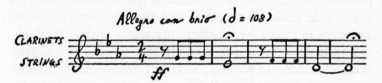

Suppose an interpreter has never heard the symphony and is not acquainted with the programmatic implication of the opening motif: "Here Fate knocks on the door!" How will he, in his performance, play the music of the famous bars? The answer is obvious. Since the only instructions in the score are *allegro con brio* for the tempo (the metronome being set at ♩ = 108), and *fortissimo* as to the dynamics in all instruments, the interpreter, adhering to Beethoven's script, will probably proceed somewhat along the following lines. He will set the slider of the metronome at 108, and see that in his performance the time value of one half note will be equal to one pendulum beat. He will play the introductory measures precisely in time, without any special emphasis on each eighth note, without retardation of the main tempo or special accentuation, giving the *fermata* no more than its conventional value. Such a performance, however, is frequently not what we hear in listening to a performance of the Fifth Symphony. Because of the allegory of "Fate knocking on the door" (which we read about in any of Beethoven's biographies), interpretation has been influenced and conditioned. And so, until the sixth measure, it is frequently played in considerably slower tempo than the indicated *allegro con brio;* special dynamic emphasis is given to each eighth note, and the pauses are prolonged.

Who is to decide? The composer is dead and has not left any clue to the problem, other than the score and the words quoted. Beethoven cannot be consulted by any conductor; but Richard Wagner's imagination, invoking him in spirit, makes the composer's voice call from the grave to the conductor of the Fifth:

> My pauses must be long and serious ones. Hold them firmly, terribly. I did not write them in jest or because I was at a loss as to how to proceed. I indulge in the fullest, the most sustained tone to express emotions in my adagio; and I use this full and firm tone when I want it in a passionate allegro as a rapturous or terrible spasm. Then the very lifeblood of the tone is to be extracted to the last drop. I arrest the waves of the ocean, and the depth must be visible; or I stem the clouds, disperse the mist, and show the pure blue ether and the radiant eye of the sun. For this I put *fermatas*—sudden long sustained notes—in my allegros. Ponder them here on the first announcement of the theme. Hold the long E flats firmly after the three short tempestuous quavers and learn what the same thing means when it occurs later in the work. [Essay *On Conducting*.]

Thus spoke Wagner. Dare anyone question so supreme a judge? Yes; famous conductors play the Fifth in exactly the way that aroused Wagner's anger. They curtail the pause on the E flat too soon, holding it as a rule "no longer than a forte produced by a casual bow stroke might be expected to last." Others, however, still hold to Wagner's precept. There is also a trend to compromise—to offer a hint of what Wagner advocated, and yet not make the listener wait for the entry of the faster tempo until after the second pause. In whatever way the beginning of the Fifth is played, the question of its interpretation remains a perplexing one. And it is noteworthy that the whole problem did not start with the performance of the finished score, but in the brain of Beethoven himself, who was in doubt regarding the most suitable characterization. On his manuscript, he has scratched out a word after *allegro* that might have been *molto*, and replaced it with *con brio*, written at a later time with different pen and ink.

INTERPRETATION: OBJECTIVE OR SUBJECTIVE?

Richard Wagner's poetic and powerful interpretation of the opening of the Fifth cannot be tested by objective standards, that is to say, by musical clues provided in Beethoven's score. No matter how fascinating we find his explanation, it must be classified as subjective, as it brings to the fore Wagner's views on Beethoven rather than the actual interpretative criteria for the music as we understand them from the reading of the script. In any case, the *subjective* approach reflects the interpreter's individuality more than it does the world of the masterwork—not only in details like those that have just been demonstrated, but also in the delineation of the composition as a whole.

In opposition to such a subjective reading stands the *objective* treatment, where the interpreter's principal attitude is that of unconditional loyalty to the script. Setting aside his personal opinion and detaching himself from his individual feelings, the objective interpreter has but one goal in mind: to interpret the music in the way the author conceived it. Logically, the objective interpreter of the Fifth will perform the opening measures according to metronomic and other objective determinations, as indicated by the score and not by his personal feelings.

If we turn from the particular case of the Fifth Symphony to any classical score, in fact to a score of any period, the inevitable question arises as to whether the score should be interpreted literally or whether the performer should have carte blanche in general interpretation, on the ground that, besides the script of the score, its background must also be freely taken into consideration. If all this could be answered by a simple formula, the continual argument about interpretation would not exist. We should hardly see one particular performer singled out as the omniscient one, as the one to whom enigmatic texts have opened their hitherto concealed meanings, whereas other interpreters have not been selected by Fate to become initiates into the mysteries of the sphinxian score. It would be simply a question of reading and knowing the score, which in any case would speak for and explain itself.

However, this problem of objectivity or subjectivity in musical interpretation is one of great complexity. First of all, interpreters are all different human beings. Each one's natural impulse toward one and the same score is bound to differ. Each one's personal background, education, culture, and human and artistic experiences, are likewise different. In spite of this, it would still be conceivable to insure what we call authenticity of interpretation, namely, the *objective* realization of the author's wishes, if the score as such were explicit enough to protect the composer's intentions against any misrepresentation on the performer's part.

NOTATION CANNOT EXPRESS
INTANGIBLES

Even the modern score, however, frequently admired as one of the highest achievements of the human spirit, is far from perfection. Of course, great composers have superbly transformed their ideas into scores, making the best possible use of musical notation. But it is this very notation that is imperfect and may remain so forever, notwithstanding remarkable contributions to its improvement. There are certain intangibles that cannot be expressed by our method of writing music—vital musical elements incapable of being fixed by the marks and symbols of notation. Consequently, score scripts are incomplete in representing the composers' intentions. No score, as written in manuscript and published in print, can offer complete information for its interpreter.

The farther we go back in the different periods of history, the more difficult it becomes to read and know the score, to understand its graphic marks and symbols, and to supplement its meager directions, if any—all of which is necessary for the faithful performance of the work. Instructions of a type considered indispensable today, such as those for the main tempo of a composition, were frequently omitted in early scores. This means that, from the very start, the interpreter has to supplement the material of the score with his own good judgment. Consequently, even the interpreter of truly objective spirit is bound to find himself occasionally on subjective terrain, irrespective of his loyal inclinations.

The performer's first task, that of setting the main tempo, becomes mere guesswork unless he is thoroughly acquainted with certain fundamental facts concerning the style of the period concerned. After all, time is relative in music, as elsewhere, and so the purport of the different designations, from

adagio to presto, has to be adjusted according to the peculiari-
ties of the composer and his work. And there are still numerous
other questions confronting the interpreter. In the scores written since the end of the eighteenth century, these are partly
answered by the marks of dynamics or phrasing.

INTERPRETATION LIVES
THROUGH STYLE

Sketchy as the old score may seem to the modern performer,
it fulfilled its function by offering the necessary information
in its own day, when the composer and the interpreter were so
often one and the same person. Palestrina conducted his own
Masses, Handel his own oratorios, Mozart his own operas,
and Bach himself sat on the organ bench of the St. Thomas
Church in Leipzig, playing his fugues and chorales. Even as
late as the beginning of the nineteenth century, it was rather
the exception when the composer was not his own interpreter.
Chopin dreamed his nocturnes at the piano; and Paganini displayed his demoniacal virtuosity in the rendition of his music
on a priceless violin.

The composer knew what he wanted. He could afford to
write the score according to his fancies and to design the pictures of his own script in lines that appear vague to us. Should
we infer from facts like these that the old master had greater
trust in the capacity of his fellow-interpreter to read and render
his works? After all, the composer could not have expected
to be his own interpreter forever. One thing is certain: modern
composers do not have such faith in their interpreters. This
becomes clear by comparing the manuscripts of the scores of
old and modern times. Today, the interpreter of contemporary
works frequently has little or no personal choice, as he is
forced to follow the very strict directions of the composer.

Starting with the instructions of the Classicists, and increasing with those of the Romanticists, we reach the height of direction in the modern score. In a work like Mahler's Second Symphony, written at the turn of our century, the composer has given instructions complete enough for a scenario. Players in the finale are told exactly when to enter and when to leave the podium for the backstage music; they are also told in which position to hold their instruments for better tone production. Again, in significant contemporary scores, particularly in those of Schönberg, letters help the performer to understand the polyphonic texture by pointing out the relationship between principal part and accompanying part.

Stravinsky does not hesitate to compare a good conductor with a sergeant whose duty it is to see that every order is obeyed by his player-soldiers. The question arises whether through such a point of view the interpreter is not demoted to the role of nothing more nor less than a musical traffic policeman. He might find solace in this statement of Sibelius: "The right tempo is the one the artist feels!" This dictum of Sibelius again opens the door to subjective interpretation. What the artist feels becomes the decisive factor in the rendition. Obviously, one cannot expect to set an inflexible, mathematical standard in art; if ideas of composers are subjective and their directions relative (in spite of such mechanical aids as the metronome), the interpreter's knowledge is likewise subjective, and therefore his ways of performance are subjective too. We conclude, then, that the ego of the interpreter and the score of the composer provide the very combination through which creative inspiration may be translated into musical reality.

With such different convictions on the part of the composers, the problem of interpretation increases in complexity. As things are, performers can roughly be divided into two groups. They

are, according to their attitude toward the score, either objective or subjective executants. And any interpretation, at its
very beginning, has to be one or the other. Suppose an interpreter—as many of the best of our day have already done—decides in favor of objective interpretation. If his task is the rendition of a new score of the elaborated type he may secure
sufficient clues for his goal of work-fidelity. If he interprets an
old work with few or no instructions, then a most difficult task
confronts him. He must, because of the elasticity of the old
score, reconstruct the work in terms of its musical background.
As every score is an integral part of the age in which it is
created, every detail of its performance depends upon knowledge of the manners and customs of a particular period. In
listening to modern performances of Bach, we are seldom if
ever aware that the composer had some twenty singers and a
similar number of players assembled around him for the rendition of his great vocal scores, and that he had to fight for the
small salary of a third viola player to "enlarge" his orchestra.
Yet some of his scores at times require nine voices to be heard
simultaneously. Is not the great modern performing vehicle
better adapted to take care of such inspired polyphony?

Nothing is more difficult than this task of rethinking the old
works, on the basis of the original elastic score script, in terms
of the great masters who wrote them. There are three paths
that will lead the interpreter out of this labyrinth. First, he
must learn how to read the script and to understand its language. Second, his fantasy must discover the musical essence,
the inner language behind the written symbols. Finally, the
interpreter should be fully acquainted with the background and
the tradition of a work—with all the customs surrounding the
score at the time of its creation.

This end can be accomplished only if the interpreter leans

on the accumulated knowledge of the trained historian as the true guardian of the authentic style. Of course, style is not the only requisite for fidelity of performance, but it is certainly the framework. If music lives through interpretation, then true interpretation can live only through the genuine style.

PART ONE

THE BIRTH OF MODERN INTERPRETATION

I. From Renaissance to Baroque

INTERPRETATION is as old as the art of music itself. Yet, as the musical expression of personalized emotions and individual feelings, interpretation could not unfold its power as long as the medieval spirit recognized and controlled the arts only as servants of liturgy. Thus certain types of musical performance, essential today, originated as by-products of what the sixteenth century called *la découverte de l'homme*—the discovery of the human being. As Láng points out, the search for a new type of humanity appeared in literature before it was clearly perceptible in the other arts. However, the "scientific and critical spirit of humanism led art to methods which resulted in the discovery of linear perspective, anatomic studies, the construction of the human body according to mathematical measurements, and in music to the modern principles of harmony." Such departure from medievalism was bound to affect strongly the realm of musical interpretation: individualism appeared as the growing force in musical performance. It is with the clash between the ideals of tradition and those of progress that we start our investigation into the different style periods of interpretation in the sixteenth century.

ECCLESIASTICAL SPIRIT

Music is merely liturgy's humble handmaid.—PAPAL DECREE

UNIVERSALITY OF EXPRESSION

On Good Friday, 1555, the newly elected pope, Marcellus II, left the Sistine Chapel, troubled in spirit about the worldly attitude of the papal choir. Upon reaching the Vatican he summoned the singers to his presence. "Whatever is performed on these holy days when the mysteries of the Passion and Death of the Saviour are celebrated," Marcellus enjoined the members of the chorus, "must be sung in a suitable manner, with properly modulated voices, and so that everything can be both heard and understood properly."

The conductor in whose hands rested the great responsibility of properly rendering the music of the Holy Week services was Palestrina. He had been chosen for this distinguished position in the Sistine Chapel in spite of his being not only a layman but a married man. However, upon the death of Marcellus, and with the accession of the severe, uncompromising Paul IV, Palestrina, because of his status, was summarily dismissed. Yet it quite soon became evident that the great conductor's services were indispensable, and he was reinstated.

A grave situation had arisen, demanding special attention at the Council of Trent, where the cardinals found themselves engrossed in the problem of musical performance in the churches. The ecclesiastical spirit of the services was in jeopardy. Performing habits had deteriorated into obvious worldliness. Popular tunes were being fashioned into sacred hymns, by simple expedients, such as doubling the values of the notes. But churchgoers were as familiar with many of these secular melodies as Americans are today with *The Star-spangled Ban-*

ner, and easily recognized their notes even in the guise of double duration. Undeniably the terrestrial had encroached upon the celestial.

Luther's great reforms of church music called for counteraction on the part of the Catholic cardinals. At the Council of Trent some of them insisted upon proscription of all polyphonic music. Others were willing to tolerate this type, provided its rendition would keep the listener mindful of the sacred text and not divert his attention by embellishments.

Clearly, such premises for the proper material to be used in church could not be divorced from those for execution. Palestrina was not only a superb composer of scores in the ecclesiastical spirit, but also their ideal interpreter. The classically balanced vocal polyphony of his compositions is eminently suited to the ideals of the sacred service, particularly because of its concordance with the principles of the Gregorian chant, considered the prototype of all church music. His type of interpretation expressed the collective spirit of the community, excluding the aspect of individual feeling from musical performance. Palestrina achieved universality of expression as the ultimate objective in sacred music—a spirit "catholic" in the true etymological sense of the word.

MAESTRO DI CAPPELLA
PALESTRINA

The performance in the pontifical choir demanded primarily a reverent quality suitable to the liturgy. No one could conform with all these demands as ably as Palestrina. Therefore, in spite of all objections to his station in private life, the year 1571 found him again in Rome, as *maestro di cappella* at St. Peter's, a post he retained until his death in 1594.

Could we have had the opportunity of watching Palestrina

at work with his chorus, we would have found only male singers there. The question of celibacy, which had proved of such consequence to the *maestro* himself, affected all the members of his chorus. Women, being ineligible for any liturgical office, were not permitted to take part in the performance. The principle *Mulier taceat in ecclesia*, enjoining silence on women in church, necessarily applied to Palestrina's chorus. Consequently, a modern Palestrina performance can recapture the essential sound of the Palestrina group only by employing boys for the high parts. Naturally their voices have a decidedly different timbre and expression—naïve, chaste, childlike—a spiritual quality that has been employed in modern scores seeking to evoke the old ecclesiastical spirit. (The boy chorus in Gustav Mahler's Eighth Symphony, which combines the old hymn *Veni Creator Spiritus* with the final scene of Goethe's *Faust*, is an example.)

Palestrina adhered strictly to the unaccompanied type of choral performance, called *a cappella*. On the other hand, the contemporary Florentines sought expression, more and more, through the medium of instruments. It is true that Palestrina's personal choices did not always exclude the orchestra. His performances at the Villa d'Este involved the use of viols, lutes, trumpets, and trombones, as well as two organs and a choir; but there is no evidence that this in any wise affected his preference for the music of the human voice. Though Palestrina was himself an organist, and though instruments eventually found their way into the sacred service, he remained to the last a guardian of the *a cappella* style.

Research in recent years has gradually brought to light a participation of instruments in church services much greater than generally supposed. However, the *a cappella* nature of the Palestrina performance may safely be assumed. His mastery of *a cappella* rendition, and his realization of all the vocal beauties in pure choral music, made his renditions glorious. A superlative choral conductor in spite of his notoriously weak voice, he accomplished with his singers wonders of tonal beauty, fulfilling the idealistic conception of the great theorist Zarlino, who put *un harmonia et un concerto de voci* higher than any combination of instruments.

More than four centuries have elapsed since the birth of Palestrina. Yet the memories of his performances still linger as the model of permanent musical values in the Catholic church. This fact is clearly demonstrated in the *Motu proprio* given from the Vatican in November, 1903, when Pius X joined Gregory and Marcellus II in the procession of great music-loving popes who stand out in history as the reformers of church music. This document, on the threshold of our century, once more conjured up the spirit of the Palestrina performance. As the greatest master of church music was himself a traditionalist, so the conservation of his style and of his interpretations has remained the safeguard of ecclesiastical spirit throughout the ages.

A CAPPELLA STYLE

FREE DECLAMATION

"With the exception of the melodies proper to the celebrant at the altar and to the ministers, which must always be sung in Gregorian chant and without accompaniment of the organ, all the rest of the liturgical chant belongs to the choir of levites, and, therefore, singers in church, even when they are laymen, are really taking the place of the ecclesiastical choir. Hence the music rendered by them must, at least for the greater part, retain the character of choral music."

These lines from the *Motu proprio* disclose the reason for the permanency of the *a cappella* style in liturgy and reveal its background. Thus directions for this type of rendition may be taken from the *Motu proprio* as well as from documents written four hundred years prior to it. We learn that the singers must maintain rhythmic precision and evenness of execution in all the parts. A symmetrical style of singing is required, also special skill in the rendition of dynamics. Since there were no hints in the manuscript, such as "piano" or "forte," only very well-educated and capable singers could recognize the dialogue and echo effects from the music itself, and incorporate all the contrasts suggested by the polyphony. The primary rule was: Dynamics must be analogous to the text, must deepen the content of the underlying affection—a law from which very fine dynamic shadings of the performance may be deduced. The modern interpreter of the old *a cappella* music faces a difficult problem in the dynamics, and must also realize that conducting with a regularly recurring accent has no place whatsoever in performances of this style. Instead of this, a free declamation with accentuation of words and motifs, contrary to the modern conception of the regular measure, is the aesthetic goal.

This aim, however, is rarely realized in modern readings. We must remember that our notation cannot cope with the true atmosphere of the *a cappella* music. As a result, it has been suggested by Schünemann and others that we should abolish bars and perhaps resort to other symbols as they were sometimes employed in old manuscripts. The historical score picture, compared with the modern one, is merely a sketch; the detailed execution of the design was left to the conductor's artistry and instinct. In the case of well-known music, such as Masses, the text was written out for the singers' convenience only in certain parts, and had to be distributed according to the general laws of good rendition—that is to say, without offenses against accentuation and always with the aim of beautiful tone quality.

The Palestrina or Orlando di Lasso performer of today must bear in mind that there was no such thing as regular subdivision of the parts into bars. The measure (*tactus*) had no good and bad accents as we know them today. Consequently, word accents and motif accents must be taken freely, without regard to their actual position in modern notation. It is best to direct the old works with an even, quiet yet firm beat in order to insure a precise rendition of the polyphonic voice web. As to the tempo designation, the interpreter must gather his information from the affection of the score, from its spiritual and poetic content. Tempo modifications are possible, although too many of these tend to weaken the expression. For words and vocalization, the original rules of Zarlino and Vicentino are best.

SETUP OF CHORUS

How were the choruses grouped in this classical time of *a cappella* singing? Zacconi, in his *Prattica di musica,* writes in 1596: "The singers must not stand too close, but so arranged that they can hear one another well and control their voices individually." Some other practitioners want the voices so distributed that soprano and tenor, alto and bass, are brought together. The principle is clear: high and low voices, respectively, were joined for better blending. The choruses were not written in score, but studied and performed from individual parts or choir books. Parts belonging together did not appear one under the other (as in modern arrangements); this makes old manuscripts difficult to read today. But they presented no bewildering problems to the performers of that time; their education included such independent reading of chorus parts. As Kinkeldey explains, the keyboard musician learned his score in playing from chorus books; he was required to execute on the organ or cembalo all the voices written apart from one another. The conductor, who was obliged to follow the course of the music from the chorus book *prima vista,* had to be adept in the same method.

According to our standards, this method is quite complicated. But we must remember that musicians of that time were able to read even the complex mensural notation very readily. All performers had to pass through a long period of probation that schooled them in this intricate notation, as well as in the aesthetic rules of singing. Things are made far more comfortable for the performer today. Unquestionably, there has been a downward trend as regards what the average musician must know. The general present-day level of his training is, in many respects, far lower than that set for his earlier colleague's ambition in his craft.

As to the *a cappella* conductor's special duties, Zacconi, in *Prattica di musica,* warns that the beat must never flutter, even if singers introduce embellishments, and that only an even, precise beat can insure clarity in direction. The beat was given evenly as a necessary means of orientation in performance. No change of tempi within pieces was permitted, the rhythmic dispositions being indicated through notes and measures. Thus, acceleration and retardation were normally avoided, and exceptional changes of tempi in the course of a composition were specifically indicated by changing the time signature. However, when Schneegass, in his *Isagoges musicae,* 1591, suggests that certain modifications of tempo are advisable, we already have a foreshadowing of the later technique of time variation. Gradually instruments came into use for the accompaniment of so-called *a cappella* music. To judge from pictures, the players were relatively few, but the small instrumental groups that participated represent a transition to a new style.

LE NUOVE MUSICHE

*Una certa nobile sprezza-
tura di canto.*—CACCINI

ANCIENT IDEALS

The year 1600—turning point of two centuries as well as of two musical epochs—was marked by a great spectacle: the invention of the opera. Paradoxically, an innovation that proved of paramount importance to music was not the work of musicians. It was but the art product of theoretic speculation in a circle of aristocrats, poets, and philosophers, *literati* who met in the Florentine palace of Count Bardi and called themselves *camerata*. Interpretation turned first to the sung word. After all, it was the old classical word drama that the *camerata* hoped to restore. Thus, the Greek singer's performance of the poet's words, to the accompaniment of stringed instruments, guided the seventeenth-century musician's imagination. By reason of his dramatic goal, musical performance likewise became an expression of language and rhythm in the first place, and of vocal beauty in the second place. Inevitably, these new ideals clashed with the performing practice of the preceding polyphonic era, which had these points reversed to a complete predominance of the music over the text. But suppression of the poetic idea induced a reaction. Clear-headed, the new opera interpreter subordinated the song: now, the meaning of the word was of first importance.

Such was the artistic program of Giulio Caccini, one of the leading protagonists of the *camerata*. Fully conscious of the revolutionary nature of his style, he proudly called his collection of airs, published in 1601, *Le nuove musiche*—"The New Music." In the preface to this historic work, Caccini says, significantly, that he learned more in the erudite discussions of the *camerata* than in thirty years' labor with counterpoint. In aggregate, his theories provided for posterity the rational program for the true interpretation of this style. It was based on "miraculous devices of the old poets," simultaneously counteracting "the sensuous ear-tickling of the bravura embellishments" in the contemporary vocal execution. Caccini's interpretation attacked whatever seemed opposed to genuine emotional expression. Now, with the humanistic attitude of respect toward the word, the new interpretative goal was to express clearly the true effect of the "tone language," as music was significantly called. This permitted a performance of the new monodic compositions on the basis of a broad subjective treatment of the text as the performer's guide. Emphasis was exclusively on the dramatic meaning of the poem and not on beautiful tone rows.

OLD ITALIAN METHODS OF SINGING

After monodic solo singing had burst into bloom as the first fruit of the new theory, a new technique of singing was bound to follow. The first teachers of solo singing likewise became the first great interpreters. What they taught is correctly epitomized in the "old Italian method," today almost forgotten. For if one alludes today to an "old Italian method," usually the nineteenth-century system of singing is meant. Yet, as Hugo Goldschmidt has already proved, the principles of the *nuove musiche* differ considerably, in many respects, from the later ways. It is a case of aesthetic laws changing from one period to another, as inventions of fluctuating taste. These principles, to be sure, are apart from the permanent laws taken from the very nature of singing, which cannot alter in spite of the progress of periods and centuries. For example, purity of intonation is an unalterable law of singing performance that naturally remains constant through the ages.

In contrast, a change of aesthetic laws is seen in the different treatment of the device called *messa di voce*. Its principle consisted in the vitalizing of every tone of considerable duration. In the eighteenth century, the equal sustaining of longer tones was rejected as unaesthetic, and the *messa di voce* was employed instead. Yet today, as in the seventeenth century, both ways of expression are accepted with or without this change.

Another important difference between the performing style of the *camerata* and later taste is exemplified by the variance in the theories of register. The old Italian school knew two registers: chest and head. The later school acknowledged three registers: chest, falsetto or middle, and head. Caccini recognized only two registers: *voce plena e naturale* (full and natural voice) and *voce finta* (artificial voice). In his interpretation he wished to restrict male singers to the use of the natural voice, rejecting their falsetto as ugly; but sopranos and altos, boys as well as women, were permitted to use both registers. The use of the female falsetto was even considered enjoyable for *esclamazione*, a singing device of the Renaissance that retained its importance for centuries. Originally the term designated the reinforcing of the voice at the moment when it was about to diminish—a crescendo at the *end* of the tone. Metaphorically, not only the final crescendo but the whole figure is called *esclamazione*. Its importance may be judged from the fact that a representative British account of the new style, written as early as 1655, quotes from *Le nuove musiche* as follows:

> There are some that in the *Tuning* of the first Note, Tune it a *Third* under: Others Tune the said first *Note* in his proper Tune, always increasing it in Loudness, saying that this is the good way of putting forth the *Voyce* gracefully. . . . I have found it a more affectuous way to *Tune* the Voyce by a con-

trary effect to the other, that is, to *Tune* the first *Note*, Diminishing it; Because Exclamation is the principal means to move the Affections; and Exclamation properly is no other thing, but in the slacking of the Voyce to reinforce it somewhat. . . .

This explanation from John Playford, which quotes Caccini literally, gives, in its quaint English, a better suggestion of the seventeenth-century Italian than would a modern version.

SUBORDINATION OF SONG

Reviewing other essential features of Florentine song interpretation, we see that falsetto stood exclusively for the false—that is to say, forced—voice, which was synonymous with "head voice" before the three-register theory came into use. The fact that all these references appear at the beginning of Caccini's *Le nuove musiche* shows how much importance was attached to these devices as a principal means of expression. First and foremost, Caccini expressed his main idea of interpretation in the watchword, *una certa nobile sprezzatura di canto*—"a certain noble subordination of the song." The singers' task was to speak musically, as it were. It is with such an aim in mind that *passaggios*, i.e., bravura embellishments, were permitted exclusively in connection with the illustration of the word sense—not for their own decorative sake. Caccini laid great stress on purity of color in choosing the best-sounding vowels. Yet decision as to what vowel was the best had to be made solely in connection with the meaning of the word, and not because of the brilliancy of the vowel itself. Never were words to be altered. Performers were forbidden to indulge in the bad habit of substituting an *a* for an *e*, or an *i* for an *o*. And the open vowels were considered more beautiful than the closed.

While Caccini with his rational program of *sprezzatura di*

canto emerges as the guiding spirit of monodic interpretation, other important writers helped to retrace its proper style. They all present essential similarities of attitude. For the sake of genuine dramatic expression, the singer was given extraordinary freedom. As to the tempo, authorities such as Ottavio Durante, Emilio de' Cavalieri, Ignatio Donati, Gioseffo Zarlino, and Lodovico Zacconi all stress this liberty of movement. In order to produce a dramatically meaningful and aesthetically beautiful crescendo, the singer was permitted to retard; on the other hand, if interpretation warranted, he was allowed to accelerate. The *esclamazione*, according to Donati, was to be executed in a broad, dignified manner. Zacconi warns against too strong a voice, and also against going to the other extreme of pianissimo, since even piano must sound full.

But whatever the individual and technical demands were, the vital function of the musical interpretation was to intensify the spiritual content of the poetry. Full comprehension of the poet's thought was required of the musician, in order to achieve a rendition in the true style of the *nuove musiche*.

MADRIGALS

ITALIAN AND ENGLISH STYLES

"Modern madrigals . . . are sung, now languid, now lively, in accordance with the affections of the music or the meaning of the words." We shall encounter this statement of Girolamo Frescobaldi's again later in this chapter in our discussion of keyboard interpretation (p. 54). It is true that Frescobaldi's fame as one of the greatest interpreters of his century was based chiefly on his organ readings. Yet he was at the same time one of the keenest observers of contemporary vocal art. And he rendered instrumental music in a specific singing style.

The distinguishing tuneful character of his performances enchanted the melody-loving Romans; according to Baini, no less than thirty thousand people flocked to the square of St. Peter's hoping to find entrance to the cathedral to hear Frescobaldi's magic organ playing—a *bel canto* performance on the keyboard!

The interrelationship between vocal and instrumental styles becomes more understandable from the fact that in 1614, when Frescobaldi's toccatas were published, madrigal performance was blossoming as never before, not only in Italy, but also in other European countries. At the same time the madrigal reached the height of its popularity in England. Here, too, masters of the keyboard appear also as masters of the madrigal. This dual virtuosity is shown by the great Tudor virginalists such as Byrd or Gibbons.

Gibbons, regarded as the greatest keyboard performer of the Elizabethan era, published his famous set of madrigals in 1612. Though Italian madrigals were known in England probably a half century before that event, the English madrigals of that period show little resemblance to the southern model. Naturally interpretation of the two national types will have to differ according to their respective characteristics. The performance of the Italian madrigal must depend primarily on the text; that of the English madrigal is strongly guided by the specific musical laws of proportion and form. Even if unmistakably Italian models were used by the British, and the music was set to Italian words (as Byrd's *La Verginella*), it does not follow that the interpreter's style of rendition was to be in the Italian manner. Today's madrigal performer, in addition to careful discrimination of the individual national styles around 1600, must bear in mind that the Italian type significantly referred to as "modern" madrigal by Frescobaldi has little or nothing to do with the madrigal of the thirteenth century, or with that of the *ars nova* of the fourteenth century.

STILO RAPPRESENTATIVO

The difference between the old and the new style of madrigal is demonstrated by Sachs:

> The sixteenth-century composer dealt with love through the medium of a madrigal in several parts. No one found any fault in the basses playing the role of a young girl or the sopranos that of a wooer. The music did not try to achieve illusion. In the seventeenth century the singer was merged with the imaginary character to whom the poet's verses were ascribed. The singer had to identify himself with him whose joys and sorrows were depicted in the words. Hence music itself more or less abandoned vocal polyphony. And the monody, freed from the bonds of polyphony imposed on its voice parts, was not only inspired by the actual meanings of the words, but even by the speech cadence of the orator or actor. After the polyphonic style of the past, *les jeunes,* around 1600, aspired to a *stilo recitativo* or *rappresentativo,* imitating natural diction and expressing even the most delicate and secret emotions of the soul. Composers and singers were not satisfied to amuse or to delight their public; they wanted to move and allure it. This was a style to which the public was quite unaccustomed. We find proof of this in contemporary chronicles which point out as fact worthy of record that—in 1607—in Monteverdi's opera *Arianne,* the forlorn heroine's lament caused listeners to melt in tears.

The modern interpreter of the Italian madrigal must first concentrate on the emotional content of the text. He must, like the seventeenth-century singer, absorb the words as well as the music, if he wants to move the emotions. The Italian madrigal performance is historically correct only when sung with intensely passionate feeling.

The question as to whether the madrigal is to be performed *a cappella*, or accompanied, can likewise be answered only according to the particular styles involved. The feeling that the older ideal of *un concerto de voci*, as expressed by Zarlino, was higher than that of any combination with instruments, still prevailed. Zoilo, Valentini, and Mazzocchi insisted on *a cappella* performance of the madrigal. As late as 1647, Lodovico Cenci, in the preface to his madrigal scores, restates Zoilo's demands. However, with the growing evolution of instruments, both types of performance—accompanied and unaccompanied—came eventually into use.

AFTER-SUPPER SINGING

The conservatism of the English prevails also in their performance of music. Thus they adhered to the *a cappella* style of madrigal singing as long as possible. In fact, it is this kind of rendition they are so fond of even today. That charming textbook, *Plaine and Easie Introduction to Practical Musicke*, by Thomas Morley, gives us a vivid picture of the particular manner in which madrigals were sung in old England. In the dialogue of two friends discussing a "banket" that one speaker, Philomathes, had attended, the other, Polymathes, receives the following description of events:

> Among the rest of the guestes, by chaunce, Master *Aphron* came thether also, who falling to discourse of Musicke, was in argument so quickly taken up & hotly pursued by *Eudoxus* and *Calergus*, two kinsmen of *Sophobulus*, as in his owne art he was ouerthrowne. But he still sticking in his opinion, the two gentlemen requested mee to examine his reasons and confute them. But I refusing, & pretending ignorance, the whole com-

panie condemned mee of discurtesie, being fully perswaded, that I had beene as skilfull in that art, as they tooke mee to be learned in others. But supper being ended, and Musicke bookes according to the custome being brought to the table: the mis- tresse of the house presented mee with a part, earnestly re- questing mee to sing. But when after manie excuses, I pro- tested unfainedly that I could not: eurie one began to wonder. Yea, some whispered to others, demaunding how I was brought up: so that upon shame of mine ignorance, I go nowe to seeke out mine olde frinde, master *Gnorimus* to make my selfe his scholler.

Small wonder that with such social after-supper functions, an Englishman like Frank Howes compares madrigal singing of that day with our modern craze for bridge:

> Just as nowadays to be unable to take a hand at bridge is re- garded by some circles as a sign of barbarian upbringing, so in the days of Elizabeth and James I it was a social solecism to sit out when music books were brought to the table.

KEYBOARD PERFORMANCE

ROYAL VIRGINALISTS

Upon his death King Henry VIII left a remarkable collec- tion of musical instruments, among which were no less than thirty-two virginals. His possession of so large a number of these keyed instruments is not so very surprising when we consider that the virginal was a favorite with royal performers, especially court ladies. The extent to which Queen Elizabeth developed her keyboard ability is entertainingly related in the memoirs of Sir James Melville, a Scotch ambassador to Eng- land. Sir James records the cross-examination to which Eliza- beth subjected him regarding the appearance and habits of

Mary Stuart, asking "which of the queens was fairere, which of them of the highest stature, and which exercises she used." He recounts that "for a queen, Mary played reasonably well"; yet, when Elizabeth demonstrated her own musical abilities on the virginal, Melville, himself an accomplished musician, had to admit the superiority of Elizabeth's performance. In contrast to the custom at the Paris court, we learn from this document that the English queen "was not used to playing for men, but only to shun melancholy when she was solitary." Nevertheless, so pleased was Elizabeth with Melville's compliments that she invited him to remain for two additional days so that "she could dance for him."

In this connection, it might be well to mention that, contrary to some opinion, the virginal was not so called in honor of the Virgin Queen, with whom its history is so intimately connected; as Sachs explains, it derived its name from the medieval Latin *virga*, meaning rod or jack, and was first mentioned at the end of the Middle Ages.

However, the great composers of English virginal music, such as Byrd, Giles, Farnaby, John Bull, Orlando Gibbons, and Phillips, were associated with Elizabeth's times or her court. A great number of their works are found in such important manuscripts as *My Ladye Nevell's Booke*, containing music by Byrd, and the *Fitzwilliam Virginal Booke*, in which Byrd's compositions join company with those of Bull, Farnaby, Phillips, Morley, and others.

While these representative composers and famous interpreters of virginal music are men, virginal playing was essentially a feminine pastime, as attested by many records such as that of Sir James, and also by the rarity of pictures showing men playing this instrument. It might have been in keeping with such a function that virginal playing developed into performances of romantic moods and nuances. Byrd's music conveys impressions of pastoral and lyric scenes; that of Gibbons or Phillips, of elegance and decoration. It goes without saying that in such music the question of ornamentation calls for special study. Effort must be made to reproduce the trills and mordents, which are not only part of the melody but also, as it were, the prolongation of the short-lived virginal tone. (For a fuller discussion of ornamentation in general, cf. chap. ii.)

FINGERING

Important documentary sources for our information on performing are the prefaces to printed editions of masterworks. The virginalists, however, left us only handwritten manuscripts. In these, some clues may be derived from the fact that phrasing and fingering were employed in a mutual and well-defined relationship. And fingering is well marked in the scripts of the English.

There were two schools of keyboard performance—the English and the Italo-German. They had one idea in common: to use good fingers for the accented notes and weak fingers for passing tones. But the two schools differed in their viewpoints as to what constitutes "good fingers" and "weak fingers." This may appear curious to the modern pianist, as the fingering problem seems to be one of anatomy of the hand in relation to a certain technical task. Be this as it may, the English virginalists considered the first, third, and fifth fingers as good, while the continental school, in a contrary outlook, decided in favor of the second and fourth digits. The consequence can readily be discerned from any practical example. In runs, passages, or skips, the English technique resorted more to the little fingers and less to the thumbs, since the thumb was considered more a handicap than an asset in achieving their ideal of velocity. The system of denoting the fingers does not start, as it does today, with the thumb of each hand as the first. The English virgin-alists' first finger of the left hand corresponds to our fifth, but the right-hand fingers were numbered in accordance with present practice, the thumb being used as first.

The English technique is convincing to the pianist of today, because it exploits the natural resources of the hand, and because it enables the player to cope with the considerable difficulties of the old virginal music. Its masters employed virtuoso technique in an almost modern sense, their scores presenting problems of manual independence comparable to those of the scores of Chopin. One of the principal demands on the performer in the Elizabethan era was that of impeccable digitation. Unquestionably, this style shifted the emphasis of musical evolution, for the first time, from the Continent to England. The contemporary Italian performers had contributed little, if anything, to the virginal. Significantly, they were called merely *sonatori di balli*—dance players. The great Italian keyboard scores were devoted to the organ. Thus, the refined type of interpretation on the virginal, demanding a softer, delicate technique, remained in England, whereas for the Italian dance accompaniment of the *sonatori di balli* a more robust and earthy execution was the rule.

FRESCOBALDI'S ORGAN PLAYING

Girolamo Frescobaldi, in the preface to his *Toccate* published in Rome in 1614, gives a most comprehensive description of organ interpretation. A digest of his rules follows.

1. First, this kind of performance must not be subject to strict time—as in modern madrigals, which are sung, now languid, now lively, in accordance with the affections of the music or the meaning of the words.

We learn, thus, that Italian madrigals were sung with liberty of tempo, "now languid, now lively." Obviously, the vocal style influenced the instrumental music. A singing *bel canto* performance on the instrument was the ideal.

> 2. In the *Toccate*, I have attempted not only to offer a variety of divisions and expressive ornaments, but also to plan the various sections so that they can be played independently of one another. The performer can stop wherever he wishes, and thus does not have to play them all.

This almost dangerous admission on the part of Frescobaldi would seem to open up new vistas for subjective interpretation. However, we must not lose sight of the particular type and time of music to which Frescobaldi's aesthetic directions apply. He certainly did not intend to give license for the treatment of all music with such freedom, attributed by him specifically to the toccata.

> 3. The opening parts of the *Toccate* should be played adagio and arpeggiando; likewise, syncopations slurred and sustained notes, even in the middle of the work. The harmonies should be broken with both hands so that the instrument may not sound hollow.
>
> 4. On the last note of a trill, or of a scale passage, there must be a pause, even if this note is an eighth note or a sixteenth note. Such a pause eliminates confusion of the different phrases.
>
> 5. The cadences, though written as rapid, must be performed quite sustained; as the performer approaches the end of the passage of cadence, he must retard the tempo gradually.

Rules 3, 4, and 5 focus our attention on facts of great importance, not only for music of this period but also for the performing of music of following periods. We see that rubato and phrasing, in interpretation, were not invented with the employment of signs designating these features; the signs did not appear in a more elaborate way until the late eighteenth century.

6. If one finds a trill for the right hand (or the left hand), and simultaneously the other hand plays a passage, one must not divide the trill note for note but only execute the trill quickly. The passage is played less rapidly and affectionately. Otherwise there will be confusion.

7. If one finds any passage of eighths and sixteenths to be played together, for both hands, one must not play them too quickly. The hand that plays sixteenths must play them somewhat dotted, dotting not the first but the second, and so on with all the following notes, one without dot, the other dotted.

This amounts to an alteration of rhythm. Variations in note values are used in specific application and not promiscuously. (How the method of rhythmic alteration works in other details, we shall take up in the section on Lully.)

8. Playing double passages of sixteenths with both hands, one must pause on the preceding note, even if it is a black key (accidental), then resolutely play the passage, so that the agility of the hand will become apparent.

9. In the *partite*, when one finds quick divisions and affectionate passages, it will be advisable to play largo; the same applies to the *toccate*. Those numbers written without divisions may be performed a little more allegro, and it is left to the good taste and fine judgment of the performer to control the tempo, which consists of the spirit and perfection of the manner and style of interpretation. The *passacailles* can be played separately *a piacere*, if the various movements are adjusted to one another. The same procedure holds for the *chaconnes*.

From these rules emerge main principles of interpretation for the seventeenth century that also were to prove basic for centuries to follow: (*a*) subjectivity of reading, as good taste and fine judgment become rulers of performance; (*b*) the special differentiation of types, such as the dances, according to their characteristics; (*c*) a general necessity of individual decision, changing almost with every passage; (*d*) the impossibility of generalizations applicable in more than the broad aspects indicated in rules 1 to 9.

Frescobaldi's testimony is authoritative. He was not only the greatest interpreter on the organ of his time, and one of its greatest composers, but also the teacher of generations of organists who came from other countries to Rome to study his masterful style. Among his followers or personal disciples were Johann Jacob Froberger, Georges Muffat, Caspar Kerl. The influence of this style continued until the severe Baroque of Bach's polyphony changed organ performance into an objective, transparent, specifically instrumental style.

═II. The Baroque═

The Story of the Score

THE STORY of the modern orchestra began after vocal polyphony had reached its zenith at some time in the sixteenth century. Italy again became the show place of an evolution, when aristocratic audiences in Florence followed the mythological librettos of the first operas. The singers were accompanied by an orchestra of various instruments. Its variegated composition may seem strange, even grotesque, today. Yet this conglomerate instrumental make-up was natural to the seventeenth-century musicians. They used it not only for the opera, but likewise as an accompaniment for the oratorio—in fact, for every kind of dramatic music that came to the fore after Monteverdi had contributed, in his *Orfeo*, the first great opera of the new genre. With these new avenues of artistic expression, the accompanying orchestra was destined to achieve more and more significance, and, as history moved on, to attain complete independence.

FOUR STAGES OF EVOLUTION

Four clearly defined stages mark the evolution of the orchestra from its debut with the Florentine opera up to the present. Defining these periods in terms of the great masters, the initial period reaches from Monteverdi to Bach and Handel. The second is the classical period, characterized by the growth of the symphony in the hands of Haydn, Mozart, and Beethoven.

After its unique treatment by the so-called Viennese classical school, the orchestra climbed in successive stages to the late-romantic culmination—marking the third period. This era is most significantly represented by the scores of Richard Wagner and his successors. The most important of them, Richard Strauss, calls Wagner's method the alpha and omega of modern orchestration, but Strauss himself turned from the 113-piece orchestra of his *Elektra* score to the chamber-size orchestra in his opera *Ariadne*. And yet it was not he, but the Latin spirit of Claude Debussy, that rebelled against the element of the colossal in scoring, and inaugurated a highly individualized orchestration. In his music we come to French Impressionism, as it is known today.

The names from Monteverdi to Wagner and Debussy are milestones in the evolution of the orchestra. But it is not always the immortal who makes history. Often he is merely the spokesman of a circle in which the development has centered. Lesser-known figures, unsung and almost forgotten—known perhaps only to the historian—have been the indispensable stagehands on the platform of musical progress through the centuries. It is they who have been responsible for the transition from one style to another. They are the "smaller" and yet, in their inspiring technical function—in contrast to their forgotten work —truly important masters. Such were Stamitz, with his insufficiently recognized vision of the symphony and its dynamic performance; Marschner, forerunner of Wagner as composer of romantic opera; and many others throughout the centuries.

As the function of the orchestra expanded, there was a constant and proportionate increase in the precision, clarity, and dependability of the score. In the earliest stages, just as the role of the orchestra was indeterminate, so the score was ambiguous, offering only vague information as to its performance. However, as the baroque period reached its height, scores began to display that clear and unmistakably graphic character that changed the problem of interpretation from guesswork to knowledge, from dependence on the interpreter's instinct to reliance on the composer's instruction.

The classical score releases the interpreter from the task of a musical archeologist who has to dig for information in dust-laden volumes in libraries. Often enough, even the few available treatises on the old manner of performing are a complete disappointment to the truth-seeking modern interpreter. Then, as it were, he may find himself in a detective's role—a kind of musical Sherlock Holmes, who faces certain facts in the score, but must trace further clues in order to bring the complete truth to light.

MEDIEVAL MANUSCRIPTS

We have, to be sure, been speaking of the orchestra score alone—the "full score," that complete version of a composition in which each instrumental or vocal part is written on a separate staff. It may seem superfluous to offer so pedantic a definition. However, there is so much confusion that it might be well to clarify the term "score" once and for all. One hears the word used for what is correctly called only a vocal score or a piano score (the German *Klavierauszug*). In this chapter we are concerned with the orchestra score alone, the predecessor of which was the historic *partitura cancellata*.

There were scores before the founding of the orchestra. But unfortunately many of these important manuscripts have been lost. Two of the earliest examples, however, can be traced back some thousand years: namely, the famous treatise Musica Enchiriadis (the ascription of which to the monk Hucbald, 840–930 A.D., is now a matter of controversy), and the thir-

teenth-century canon "Sumer is icumen in," one of the musicological treasures of the British Museum.

"The Musica Enchiriadis," as Gustave Reese puts it, "affords
us the first account we have that is sufficiently detailed to give
us an idea of what organum was. More than one type of organum is described in it."

Composite Organum at the Fifth

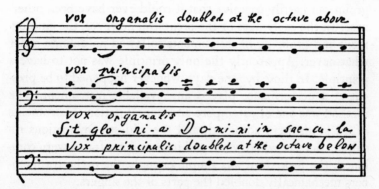

In the case of the other manuscript, "Sumer is icumen in,"
there appears under the English words a Latin text, and instructions to the performers are also written in Latin. Obviously, here is scoring with directions in its embryonic state,
for the interpreters of the famous manuscript are specifically
told how to go about the singing of the canon.

FIRST PRINTED SCORES

Naturally, the examples cited, and those that appeared in the
centuries immediately following, were handwritten. The most
sweeping change occurred in the sixteenth century, when it became possible to print scores. Cipriano de Rore's madrigals,

dating from the year 1577, were probably the first examples of printed scores, and the first printed score for orchestra was the *Ballet comique de la royne*, Paris, 1582.

From the system then adopted to the complicated scores now in use, the way is long and the process is one of logical development. Today it is taken for granted that the orchestra is a group of performers of which each one plays an individually prescribed part. In fact, the young musician who joins an orchestral group can hardly conceive that it could ever have been otherwise. In the early days of the orchestra, however, the employment and grouping of instruments followed no definite order whatsoever. Apparently the only principle was not to have a principle. In those bygone days, whoever happened to be present at a performance played any available instrument. The method was one of extempore and improvisation. Instruments of all kinds were admitted, and the oddest combinations resulted. In cases where vocal and instrumental forces were combined, the procedure was simple enough: the orchestra members mechanically doubled the parts of the singers.

Primitive as was this method, it was the origin of the early system of scoring. Should we attempt today to interpret one of these historical scores, the obvious handicap would be the absence of tonal balance as we know it, since the old audience had no conception of our modern desire for tonal proportion. Instrumental symmetry in the art of scoring belongs to a considerably later period.

ARCHITECTURE CREATES PERFORMING STYLE

The conductor in the early days acted simultaneously as his own arranger. His responsibility was not limited to rehearsing and directing performances. First of all, he had to adjust the *res facta,* that is, the composer's written score and its tone rows, to the vocal and instrumental forces at hand. How such a metamorphosis of an original score into a variety of versions was brought about, is demonstrated in *Syntagma musicum,* a treatise published in 1619 at Wolfenbüttel, Germany, and containing invaluable information in many respects. Its author, Michael Praetorius, did not believe in the pure *a cappella* sound of the Palestrina style as an unalterable ideal of interpretation. Enthusiastic about the new orchestral medium, Praetorius shows the possibilities of arranging vocal scores by changing kaleidoscopically the colors of voices and instruments. His example is the ten-part motet *Quo properas* by Orlando di Lasso. Seven suggestions as to the possible mixed arrangement of the motet are given. We quote from the third volume of *Syntagma musicum:*

First Chorus	*Second Chorus*
1. Varatio: Cornetto vel voce, 4 tromboni	Cornetto vel voce, 4 tromboni
2. Varatio: Solae voces humanae	Cornetto, 4 tromboni
3. Varatio: Solae voces humanae	5 Viole da braccio
4. Varatio: Solae voces humanae	2 Flauti, 2 tromboni, fagotto
5. Varatio: 5 Viole da braccio	Piffari, 4 tromboni
6. Varatio: 5 Viole da braccio	2 Flauti, 2 tromboni, fagotto
7. Varatio: 2 Flauti, 2 tromboni, fagotto	Cornetto, 4 tromboni
	Et cetera

We observe here the method called *varatio per choros,* variations designed for two contrasting choirs. Such an antiphonal setup was widely favored toward the middle of the seventeenth century. Orlando di Lasso himself, in Munich, did not eschew this performing practice. However, it was primarily the architecture of that glorious church, St. Mark's in Venice, that strongly suggested the idea of double choruses for scoring and performing. There are at St. Mark's two organ lofts, one on each side. Inevitably, acoustic conditions resulting from this structure of the church inspired musical fantasy and stimulated composers and interpreters to the use of antiphonal features.

Moreover, when the great Adrian Willaert was appointed to take charge of the music at St. Mark's, he naturally brought with him antiphonal counterpoint as a polyphonic tradition of his native Flanders. Willaert's technique of choral rendition was likewise continued by his successors, who, in keeping with the custom of the period, were chosen from the ranks of outstanding composers. Among them were Cipriano de Rore, Claudio Merulo, and the two Gabrieli—Andrea and Giovanni —uncle and nephew.

Two important facts emerge from this phase in the history of performance. First, we see how musical styles and the form of their interpretation wander from one country to another, from north to south. Second, referring to the Venetian cathedral and the musical activities there, we have a striking example of interaction between architecture and musical performance.

SONATA PIANO E FORTE

As early as 1597, Giovanni Gabrieli published a composition called *Sacrae symphoniae*. This work showed a scoring of instruments independent of the vocal parts—a great step forward. The upper parts were played by two violins, the middle parts by two cornets, and the bass parts by two trombones. The G string of the violin was not used at all, and the upper register was employed no farther than the third position—indicating that for Gabrieli the violin was just a substitute for the soprano. On the other hand, he used the alto clef for the *violino*, and descended beyond G. Apparently, as Sachs explains, "the terminology varies greatly at that period, and in the *Sacrae symphoniae* the *violino* part is clearly a viola part. Lodovico Zacconi, in his *Prattica di musica* (published 1592) includes in the term *violino* both the violin and the viola." Accordingly, the lower registers of instruments stood for tenors or basses. Most new instrumental conceptions of that time originated in previous vocal patterns. Significantly, through the medium of the instrumental inventions of his successor, Gabrieli, we can still see the *a cappella* world of the great Palestrina.

After the violin was established as the soprano of the string chorus, the logical next step was to substitute other members of the string family, which was done according to their range. Thus violas, violoncellos, and double basses were intrusted with the respective parts of alto, tenor, and bass in the chorus. An analogous development took place in the other sections. In his *Sonata piano e forte*, Gabrieli contrasted two orchestras antiphonally, the first consisting of two alto trombones, one tenor trombone, and one cornet, the other of one viola, two tenor trombones, and one bass trombone.

THE ORCHESTRA MAKES ITS DEBUT

MONTEVERDI'S INSTRUMENTAL PALETTE

In present musical activities there remains not even a vestige of the great orchestral scores that made history at the turning point of the sixteenth and seventeenth centuries. The only great figure emerging as an exception is Claudio Monteverdi: his creations have not lost their power, and are occasionally revived by interpreters who have sufficient artistic courage. In Monteverdi's scores we find certain orchestral effects for which no substitutes have ever been found. He was the first to use the tremolo in the strings, which is so important in scores of Wagner, Bruckner, Mahler, and many others. When Monteverdi introduced it in his ballet *Combattimento di Tancredi e Clorinda*, the players were shocked by the novelty and refused to play the passages marked tremolo. Monteverdi also fully realized the potentialities of the violin as the leading melodic instrument of the orchestra. Augmenting its compass from the third to the fifth position, he progressed from the point where the vocal mind of Gabrieli stopped. In other words, he liberated the violin from its function as a substitute for the soprano, and made it an independent orchestral instrument with individual expression.

It does not lessen Monteverdi's lasting contributions if we do not call him the inaugurator of the orchestra. His great accomplishment was that of a reorganization of medieval attempts, a historic fulfillment rather than a new beginning. Thus, if we speak of the debut of the "modern" orchestra, we mean that a state of instrumental emancipation from the vocal setup has been reached, that the art of scoring enters into more definite forms, and, last but not least, that Monteverdi's orchestra displays a beauty of sound we can fully appreciate today.

On the second page of the score of his *Orfeo*, Monteverdi has left a complete list of the instrumentalists used at the *première* of this opera. This is a fortunate cue, since, as has been pointed out before, the question of orchestral personnel at this time depended on circumstances and improvisation. The *Orfeo* list gives an authentic picture of the make-up of Monteverdi's organization. Let us compare the band used at the wedding festival of the composer's patron, the Duke of Mantua, with the colossal opera orchestra of a contemporary composer. The following table will serve to contrast two instrumental bodies

—one at the beginning of the orchestral evolution, and the other at its present numerical maximum.

ORCHESTRA OF MONTEVERDI (*Orfeo*)

2	harpsichords	3	viole da gamba
2	double basses	4	trombones
12	members of the violin family	1	portable organ
1	double harp	2	cornetti
2	violins	1	small flute
2	bass or archlutes	1	clarino
2	organs with wooden pipes	3	muted trumpets

ORCHESTRA OF STRAUSS (*Elektra*)

8	first violins	4	horns
8	second violins	2	B-flat tubas
8	third violins	2	F tubas
6	first violas	6	trumpets
6	second violas	1	bass trumpet
6	third violas	3	trombones
6	first cellos	1	contrabass trombone
6	second cellos	1	contrabass tuba
8	basses	6–8	timpani (2 players)
1	piccolo		glockenspiel
3	flutes		triangle
2	oboes		tambourine
1	English horn		small drum
1	heckelphone		birch rod
1	E-flat clarinet		cymbals
4	B-flat clarinets		bass drum
2	basset horns		tam-tam
1	bass clarinet		celesta
3	bassoons	2	harps
1	contra bassoon		

In both examples, the orchestra is the accompanying instrument for the stage action in the drama of a Greek myth. It is not surprising that in so great an interval of time the palette of the opera composer has changed completely, and even where the choice of instruments remains identical, the proportion is altogether different. Thus Monteverdi employs two violins, and Strauss twenty-four. But the important thing is not the increase in number from Monteverdi's ensembles of chamber-music size to the 113-piece orchestra that Strauss requires for his *Elektra*. The great difference lies in the fact that Strauss had in mind, to put it in his own words, "to allow harmony in three or four parts to be written in an absolutely homogeneous *timbre*." In the Monteverdi score, however, a Venetian artist is at work, a colorist in music who paints his tone picture in transparent hues like Tintoretto or Titian. Each scene was accompanied by the instruments that best reflected its particular character, emphasizing variety of shade and light in every number. The modern way of employing at least a majority of instruments throughout the work is foreign to Monteverdi's conception. It was only in the overture and in a few other places in the score that he called upon all the instruments to play. Sometimes even the singers were obliged to do double duty by performing in the orchestra as well as on the stage. One might wonder how it was possible for the heavily costumed performers to rush from the stage to the orchestra. This, however, was not so difficult as it seems, for the simple reason that the orchestra was invisible, playing from behind the stage.

REFORMER LULLY

Precisely when the orchestra was moved to its present visibility in front of the stage cannot be said with certainty. It is possible that Louis XIV of France and his royal court were the first to see an opera orchestra in performance: for Lully, a master not only in writing his scores but also in presenting them to the world, is by some historians given the credit for having moved the orchestra from its concealment behind the stage to a conspicuous place between the scene and the parquet. Here, in front of his musicians and visible to all, stood Maître Jean Baptiste, pounding the beat with a heavy, decorated stick—a musical commander with military manners, insisting upon instrumental discipline and utmost rhythmical precision.

Effective as this dictatorial method seems, it was somewhat too drastic, surviving Lully, however, in spite of constant opposition. Generations later, Jean Jacques Rousseau protested against the noisy beating of conductors in the theater. Rationalist that this philosopher-musician was, he finally became resigned to the idea that without the noise the measure of the music could not be distinctly felt by the singers and orchestra players. Returning to Lully, we note that his habit of conducting had tragic consequences, for we learn that he struck his foot with the heavy cane, causing an injury that led to an infection and, finally, fatal complications.

The great importance of Lully rests in the fact that it was he who, continuing Monteverdi's task, established the art of orchestral performance in a way that attained permanency. Of course, not he alone was responsible for the new development. Lesser-known figures like Cesti and Cavalli were, likewise, important participants in this evolution. However, their scores, acclaimed in former days, are now reposing unmolested in the libraries. And the picture is incomplete because, unfortunately, much has been lost that otherwise would probably have given significant information. Lully, Italian by birth like his forerunners, found decisive stimulation in the great French dance tradition. The historic ballet orchestra, its traditional treatment of the wood winds and other features, were absorbed splendidly in Lully's opera scores. He replaced the instrumentally elaborate organization of the ballets with typical baroque simplicity, just as Titian's multicolored palette was followed by Rembrandt's great technique of simpler contrasts in the elementary use of light and shade.

The interpreters of today and yesterday find in the Lully score more support than ever before. Thus, the previous ambiguous direction *tutti instrumenti* yields to more definite orders. The use of certain sections is strictly methodical—almost stereotyped—to such an exent that Lully has been suspected of not having taken the trouble to write the parts personally. The nineteenth-century opera composer Halévy pictured Lully sitting in his studio inventing only melodies and *basso continuo*, while two favorite apprentices, Lalousette and Colasse, took one sheet after another from the hand of their master to finish the orchestration—the first assembly-line system in musical history.

In spite of the routine character of the instrumentation, it is not without difficulty that the performer today can understand the instrumental setup of the score. The handicap lies in the fact that many of the orchestra parts look alike. There is little to distinguish one section from another; wood-wind parts resemble string parts, and vice versa. Consequently, it takes considerable experience with Lully's technique before the conductor can decide for which orchestral groups, respectively, the parts are meant. The same difficulty exists also within the string section. For example, when the word "violin" appears below the staff for the first violin, it implies automatically that, in accordance with the use of Lully's typical four-part string orchestra, violas, cellos, and basses are to take the lower staffs in the normal order. This four-part string ensemble is the kernel of the Lully orchestra, and the great majority of instrumental pieces are built around it.

Lully was the first orchestra conductor to gain an international following of interpreters. Musicians from other European countries flocked to Paris, where Lully's activities centered, to discover the secrets of his orchestral magic. After years of apprenticeship, they returned home, transplanting the French method to their native countries. The most distinguished among these disciples was the Alsatian musician Georges Muffat. He has given us the most valuable account we have of Lully's style and interpretation. Muffat published, in 1695 and 1698, two volumes of instrumental pieces, under the title *Florilegium*. It is in the preface of this work that he preserved for posterity detailed reports on Lully's orchestral performances. Muffat characterizes Lully's method as based on trueness of tone and smoothness and evenness of execution, and makes a special point of describing the clean attack of the orchestra. He further asserts that the Lully performance produced the most agreeable combination of vigor and flexibility, of grace and vivacity.

ALTERATION OF RHYTHM

A special contribution in Muffat's *Florilegium* is his display of the different national styles in violin playing. He has conscientiously marked the bowings in order to indicate how the different schools in France, Italy, and Germany, respectively, would have played certain melodies. The following little minuet theme is one of his illustrations.

One can see at a glance that the bowings in this example lead to a difference in accent and rhythm. The upper marks indicate the Italian and German bowing, the lower marks that of Lully. Surprisingly, the German and Italian bowings are identical, and are in contrast to the French manner. At this time, the German and Italian styles of performance had numerous features in common, owing to the constant interchange among the musicians of the two countries. The national barriers that today make for two different worlds of artistic expression gradually grew up as a result of the Latin vocal traits, which the German music was never able to absorb successfully.

In the following illustration Muffat clarifies the considerable contrast that existed between notation and performance.

We see how the rhythm is altered in the performance; script and execution are strikingly inconsistent. Such discrepancies cannot be comprehended from the modern point of view, with its striving for utmost clarity in notation. Yet alteration of rhythm was a common trend in the old practice of music. Therefore, the present-day interpreter, eager to perform these old masterpieces correctly, must reorientate himself in the intricate notation of this music. If the composer wrote those rhythmic patterns as he did—differently from the way they were to sound—he depended on the performer's knowledge of tradition. Every player was able to render such altered rhythm *prima vista*. As time went on, this tradition was weakened and finally vanished. Our reconstruction of these important details does not rely on the evidence of one witness only. It has the corroboration of other sources, eliminating any doubt that might arise in regard to the statement in Muffat's *Florilegium*. There is complete coincidence of other records concerning alteration, including those of a later period. Among the French authorities are Rousseau and Corette. They reaffirm Muffat's conclusion in detail. Among German eighteenth-century documents contributing to this question is the famous *Versuch* of Quantz.

We learn that ordinary sixteenths were played as though dotted, an execution called *pointer* (referring to the principle of prolonging the strong beats at the expense of the weak ones). We are informed, however, that this practice of dotting applied only to sixteenths in the four-four measure, and only to eighths in the three-four measure, in singing as well as in playing.

UNITY OF BOWING

Foreign visitors to the Paris opera or Académie Royale de Musique were stupefied especially by the string section of the Lully orchestra, referring to the unity of bowing as an unheard-of phenomenon. With the strictest discipline in phrasing, Lully had developed the twenty-four *violons du roi* into the finest string orchestra in Europe.

A specialty of the Parisian playing was the renowned *premier coup d'archet* (first stroke of the bow)—a detail of performance as much admired in the seventeenth century as are certain virtuoso accomplishments of some of the great orchestras of our eastern cities today. But in contrast to the general adulation of the French string virtuosity, the Parisian *spécialité de la maison* was belittled one hundred years after Lully by a musician whose competence no one will doubt, since his name happens to be W. A. Mozart. Being the son of a violin pedagogue, he could hardly have failed to report his experience to his father, Leopold, and accordingly wrote him on June 12, 1778: "I did not miss *le premier coup d'archet*. My Lord, what a fuss those asses make about it! However, I find nothing unusual; they begin well together as they do in other places."

Mozart's reaction is easily explained. The century separating him from Lully sufficed to dispel the sensation of the Parisian string attack. The fabulous Mannheim orchestra had already come to the fore. And the Paris orchestra did not retain, after Lully's death, the glamour and precision of performance attained under its master.

The picture of Lully's interpretative endeavors would be incomplete were we to stress only his achievements in rhythm, phrasing, and discipline of the orchestra. He was just as much concerned with the problems of expression, and his scores are full of special instructions to insure delicacy and nuances in performance. The manuscripts contain many admonitions such as: "Play softly, almost without touching the notes"; "Do not take off the mutes until you are told to." Such thoroughness in instructions guaranteed the dependability of Lully's performance, and this, in turn, was the basis of its brilliance.

Lully's orchestra became the prototype of all the later court orchestras and opera orchestras in the musical countries of the world. Thus what the American opera lover sees today when attending a performance of the Metropolitan, the Chicago, or the San Francisco opera—the singers on an elevated stage and the orchestra below, both directed by the conductor from his central podium, the audience in the semicircle behind—is the very arrangement which Maître Jean Baptiste built up almost three hundred years ago in the Paris opera of Louis XIV.

BACH AND HANDEL

TRADITION AND ITS DANGERS

A freak of Nature selected the year 1685—two years before the death of Lully—for the birth of Bach, Handel, and Scarlatti. This marks the turning point of the baroque era in music. However, the general aesthetic meaning of the term "baroque" has caused more confusion than enlightenment so far as the interpretation of the scores of this period is concerned. It seems to be the fate of this word to lend itself to frequently changing meanings, as its very etymology proves. From the original Portuguese *barocco*—the fisherman's word for a small, irregular pearl in contrast to a perfect one—through the generalized application to anything in art that tends toward irregularity, to the final connotation suggesting vastness of proportion and splendor of colors, the road is a long and winding one indeed. And so are the ways of performing those masterpieces in music that today are labeled baroque. Since this term involves so many ramifications into the other arts, there is a need to retrace baroque interpretation to its core, to its origin with the great masters with whom it is historically linked.

The lifespan of Bach and Handel extended to the middle of the eighteenth century, when Haydn took over their mission in the art of scoring and orchestration. In the baroque scores of Bach and Handel, all that had previously been achieved in the France of Lully and in the Italy of Monteverdi reached its culmination. Their baroque works are like two great rivers into which all streams pour as tributaries. Beethoven's pun,

"Bach ['brook' in German] should be called *Meer* ['ocean'],"
is very significant.

Bach and Handel were great both in composing and in interpreting their scores. But Handel in London was more fortunate than Bach in Leipzig in being recognized as the great
creator he actually was. Bach's fame during his lifetime was the
result of his reputation as an interpreter. He was a performer
in various roles—a choirmaster, and an interpreter on many
instruments. He played his own music, as well as the scores of
others. It is essential to realize that Bach's scores were written
for his own use and often rendered under the composer's personal supervision in the various German towns where he was
active as musical director.

But even as an interpreter, Bach's prestige was local rather
than international. Certainly his renditions reached only a
limited circle within Germany. After his death, his music
would have been forgotten had it not been for a limited number of private circles in Berlin that honored his memory with
renditions of his smaller works. The Princess Anna Amalia of
Hohenzollern, Forkel, Kirnberger, and Reichardt were spon-
sors of the music of the late St. Thomas cantor. Reichardt, in
his autobiography, gives special credit to the Bach readings in
the Berlin home of Dr. Fliess.

However, the real renaissance of the great works did not
occur until Mendelssohn, in 1829, revived the St. Matthew
Passion at the *Singakademie* (an event to which we shall pay
special attention in a later chapter). It is since this time that
Bach has really lived in the musical world. Therefore, what
"authentic" German Bach interpretation really was can be only
a hypothesis. The "tradition," as such, covers a span of only
one hundred years—from Mendelssohn until today—whereas
two centuries separate us from Bach. There is clearly a void of
one hundred years in which Bach's scores were rarely played,

and consequently no tradition of Bach performance could be handed down from the eighteenth to the nineteenth century.

This fact contributes to a better understanding of the circumstances surrounding Bach interpretations today. Anyone who has heard a sufficient number of representative Bach concerts in Germany knows that there are two distinctly different schools of Bach interpretation—the objective and the subjective, characterized in accordance with our previous definitions. The objective school, of course, follows with strict allegiance the meager directions of the score for tempo and dynamics. Each detail of the polyphonic texture and instrumentation is adhered to with utmost fidelity. The subjective school, in contrast, allows considerable deviation from the original Bach directions, from what is actually written down in the symbols and marks of Bach's notation. Dynamics and phrasing are added. The Passions are considerably dramatized. The readings of the choruses and especially of the recitatives seem to point more toward the style of opera than that of the religious service. Condemned by the objective performers as profaners of the score, the subjective interpreters, in turn, charge the others with a lack of imagination and failure to see that opera and oratorio in the preclassical period are closely related styles of musical expression.

The abandoning of tradition leads to opposite extremes in interpretation. On the one hand, it opens the door to excessive liberty; on the other, it may bring the interpreter to a slavish adherence to the score exclusively, because he cannot trust tradition as his guide. Again the previously explained viewpoints of the subjective and objective methods appear in these sidelights on tradition. The objective interpreter is like a physician who insists upon his own diagnosis, not relying on the opinions of others.

Facing the task of interpreting the baroque masters, it is

necessary to forget about all vague formulas of a hypothetical tradition and to return to the original scores and all available documents. The material is ample enough. We know precisely the size and setup of the composers' original orchestras. We are, in the case of Bach, fully informed about orchestra and choir personnel, even to the extent of knowing the names of the musicians. In Handel's case we are acquainted with details of his performances through his own accounts, as well as those of others.

BACH: FROM WEIMAR TO LEIPZIG

We turn first to Bach. The lists reproduced below show in chronological order the setup of his performing groups in the different centers of his activity as a music director.

WEIMAR

Bach entered into the ducal service as *Kammermusikus*, in 1708, as a young man of twenty-three. He was later appointed court organist, and finally was promoted to the post of concertmaster. There are three different lists of instrumentalists, from which we can reconstruct the ducal orchestra as follows:

  3 violinists (one of them probably a viola player)
  1 violonist
  1 bassoonist
  6 trumpeters
  1 drummer
12 players in all

In contrast to the list of Monteverdi's orchestra units (p. 67), where the student must acquaint himself with the now obsolete instruments, he will find himself quite at home with the Bach orchestra. An exception is the violone, which was an instrument intermediate between violoncello and double bass, equipped with five strings—F^1, C, G, D, A. The surprisingly light instrumentation of the cantatas written during Bach's years in Weimar was the inevitable consequence of the miniature size of the band that performed them. The court chapel, narrowly built, could not accommodate a more sumptuous body of performers.

CÖTHEN

Bach's position here had become for the first time officially that of a conductor. The orchestra consisted chiefly of strings, plus flutes, oboes, bassoon, trumpets, and timpani. In writing for his own performances, Bach had to take into consideration the limitations of the orchestra which his employer, Prince Leopold von Anhalt-Cöthen, was willing to supply. The visit of two waldhorn players as guests in 1722 proved to be a welcome change, and this is reflected in the Brandenburg Concerto in F, which uses a pair of French horns. Our source is a list of orchestral musicians who served under Bach from 1717 to 1723.

LEIPZIG

In the latter year, in the prime of his life, Bach was appointed cantor of the St. Thomas Church, and remained in this position until his death in 1750. Most of what seems to us immortal in Bach was written here and used for the routine services of the church calendar—the gigantic Passions, the Mass, the great cantatas. In a memorandum dated August 23, 1730, to the city council of Leipzig, Bach declared his needs for the "due rendering of church music" and asked for an apparatus of striking economy:

2 (preferably 3) first violins	2 flutes
same number of second violins	2 (or 3) oboes
2 desks of violas (4 players)	1 (or 2) bassoons
2 violoncellos	3 trumpets
1 violone	1 timpanist

He hoped to secure a minimum of eighteen players. In résumé, we see that, of the total of eighteen to twenty players, nine or ten were available for the wind instruments, and that two or three players took care of each string part.

Referring to his needs regarding vocal performers, Bach asked for a minimum of three singers for each part, if possible four, especially since "singers absented themselves because of illness." Comparing the two groups, we see that the orchestra is larger than the chorus. This fact is of utmost significance for Bach interpretation today. We see that Bach himself wanted more orchestra players than singers. If this were taken into account, one would not constantly hear the modern arrangements of Bach performances in which precisely the reverse is the rule. Today, with a few creditable exceptions, it is taken for granted, nearly everywhere in the world, not only that the Bach chorus should be much larger than the orchestra, but that it may even be doubled or trebled. Such a system makes all kinds of retouching of the original orchestration indispensable. It is impossible to detect in many present-day renditions the fundamental features of Bach choral scores: co-ordination of the vocal and instrumental groups, their equality in contrapuntal and structural importance. Bach's orchestra is never the accompanying instrument, but always the equal partner of the choir.

The correct conception of Bach's linear polyphony is the key to all the interpretative problems, including the dynamics. Bach knew so much better than many present-day interpreters are willing to give him credit for knowing, what he wanted and how to go about it in his scores. Surely there is no necessity for rearranging and retouching his originals, since the master himself took care of the problems as they occurred in his performances. At the same time, to obtain a completely authentic picture of the problems in performing Bach, we must not overlook the facts, first, that today's performances take place in large concert halls and not in the St. Thomas Church, and that therefore the acoustics are different; second, that the master himself might have welcomed an opportunity of increased equipment. The question remains, however, how far he might have gone had he had the facilities of today's conductors. Could he, in his wildest dreams, have imagined the vast orchestral forces that perform today?

Albert Schweitzer, with his infallible insight into the Bach workshop, recommends a happy medium between Bach's limited resources and today's great amplitude. For a chorus of from fifty to eighty voices, Schweitzer suggests an orchestra of:

6 first violins	2 basses
6 second violins	2 flutes
6 violas	2 oboes
4 cellos	

For a chorus of from one hundred to one hundred and fifty voices:

10 first violins	4 basses
10 second violas	6 flutes
10 violas	6 oboes
6 cellos	

Notwithstanding the fact that Schweitzer suggests a chorus that outnumbers the orchestra, he too feels that the latter must play a leading role. For acoustic reasons, he disapproves of the practice of thrusting the orchestra like a wedge into the choir. Instead, he proposes to obtain better effects by placing the strings and wood winds in front of the choir.

If there is no room in present-day Bach practice for orthodox adherence to the master's customs, the least one may ask for is an arrangement in which modern apparatus re-emphasizes all the structural ideas of Bach's setup. This can best be accomplished by studying the original features of the historical renditions. We cite the St. Matthew Passion as the most typical. In this work, Bach uses two orchestras, with at least twelve players in each. Normally, however, his orchestra comprised from eighteen to twenty players, corresponding exactly to the *grosse Cantorei* of his singers, which performed the Sunday cantatas and sometimes concert music as well. Seventeen choristers were listed both in 1730 and in 1744, and we may therefore assume that this was the normal number. In 1744 there were five sopranos, two altos, three tenors, and seven basses.

It is obvious that the strong reinforcement of the melody—especially in the chorals—was designed to secure a correct balance between the *cantus firmus* and its counterpoint. Many of today's choirmasters, in charge of small groups, may find comfort in the fact that Bach was confronted with the same shortcomings of an unevenly balanced group, especially in the middle voices. It is fascinating to note how Bach coped with this situation and how he circumvented the difficulty by frequent instrumental reinforcements of the respective parts.

HANDEL: BAROQUE PROPORTIONS

Handel's orchestra resembles that of Bach: as in Bach's scores, the orchestra centers around the strings, while wood winds and brass are part of the full body of players, forming the ripieno. Instruments used in the solo manner, as obligato, play continuously throughout a whole movement. This, of course, is in contrast to the later method of intermittent solo passages: the technique of furnishing coloristic effects by means of a solo (for a few bars only, after which the performer again joins the full body of the players) was not applied until the time of the Classicists.

Handel's orchestral music comprises the *concerti grossi* —corresponding to Bach's Brandenburg concertos—the operatic overtures, and the instrumental parts of his oratorios, concertos, and "open air" pieces (Water Music, Firework Music).

As in the instance of Bach, we are fortunate in being able to reconstruct the complete picture of important Handel performances, which gives us many clues to the interpretation. We have his list from the original score of the Firework Music, indicating the number of players used for each part. Thus we are able to ascertain the balance of the various instruments, which were:

3 first trumpets	12 first oboes
3 second trumpets	8 second oboes
3 timpani	4 third oboes
3 first horns	8 first bassoons
3 second horns	4 second bassoons
3 third horns	

The number of oboes is extraordinary. Of course, the outdoor setup of the Firework Music called for special emphasis on the melodic parts, but even so the total of twenty-four oboes is a figure thinkable only in the terms of the Baroque. For a present-day performance of this work, a special effort would have to be made to raise from different organizations, and perhaps even from different cities, the number of players required by Handel. While strings are missing in this score, we know through another list, revealed by the archives of the Foundling Hospital in London, their proportion in the Handelian orchestra, which consisted of:

12 violins	4 bassoons
3 tenors	2 horns
3 celli	2 trumpets
2 double basses	kettledrum
4 oboes	organ

While this list (1759) refers to the very last years of the master's life, a wave of Handel performances followed after his death.

One of the most detailed descriptions of any arrangement that has come down to us is that of the historic performance of Handel's *Messiah* in Westminster Abbey in 1784 (facing page 97). Here we have a massive performance par excellence—a group that was tremendous in size but, as we shall see, not too well balanced.

Unquestionably, a setup like this, taking every bit of available space for its hundreds of performers, was truly baroque—stolid, rigid, stupendous, and undeniably out of proportion. Turning the pages of contemporary records on the rendition, we see how little the ecclesiastical spirit of the place interfered with the thorough worldliness of this musical affair. We learn that the church officials, attempting to control at least the appearance of the fashionable audience, warned them that ladies with hats, particularly hats with feathers, would not be admitted—further informing them that only small hoops, if any, would be tolerated. The behavior of the congregation proved to be out of control, as attested by the *Morning Chronicle*, according to which Signor Storace, one of the singers, received storms of applause during the performance. And in addition to the enthusiasm of the audience, the music itself turned out to be on the bombastic side. For even a witness favorably disposed, like Walpole, complained that the "chorus and kettledrums for hours were so thunderful" that they gave him a headache.

In Germany there followed several attempts to emulate the annual Handel festival in London and also the English monster performances in general. The most remarkable of these renditions took place under Bach's son, Philipp Emanuel, in Hamburg, in 1775, and under Hiller in Berlin, in 1786. The number of performers was at first 550, later 600, and finally reached the gigantic total of 1,000. All this happened in the eighteenth century. When Gustav Mahler, in our century, called for the apparatus which gave his Eighth Symphony its appellation *Symphony of the Thousand*, he did not ask for something unprecedented in the history of performance, as frequently assumed.

Summing up, we must realize that the task of restoring the correct proportions in the case of the Handel performance is somewhat more involved than in that of Bach. There are in Handel's works definite features that demand expressive simplicity and interpretative asceticism. On the other hand, the majesty of the Handelian themes and the brilliancy of his scoring lent themselves more readily than did Bach's superpersonal, intrinsic, strict part-writing, to the splendor of baroque performance. In spite of all the grandeur that certain Handel interpretations connote, the finest musicological minds of our day protest against external, pompous manifestation of Handel's works. Romain Rolland claims that Handel's compositions, when executed on such a stupendous scale, are degraded to a "monumental tiresomeness similar to that of the very conventional Christ of Le Brun."

As everyone following routine symphony programs knows, we are living in an era of transcriptions for orchestra, particularly of Bach and Handel scores. It should not be denied that the modern orchestra and its potentialities are a convincing medium for expressing the inspired polyphony of the Baroque. Yet, unfortunately, there is an overabundance of inferior arrangements that dress up the spiritual, linear counterpoints of the Baroque with supervirtuoso orchestral glitter, in a display of showy brilliance conceived in late-romantic notions. There could be no greater misunderstanding of the baroque scoring! While we shall further discuss this contemporary problem of interpretation in the chapters on modern performance, it cannot be pointed out emphatically enough in connection with the baroque masters that they used the palette of the orchestra much as the organist employs register: one combination for the principal theme, others for the counterpoint, the changes being made at certain definite points. Contrary to the tendency of numerous arrangements, the baroque masters did not orchestrate in the modern individualistic manner. The sudden shifts from one particular timbre to another for coloristic purposes is a misrepresentation of major aspects of their old style. The thinking of Bach and Handel along contrapuntal lines is completely reflected in their art of scoring. It is only in exceptional instances that, for the sake of intensified expression or dramatic effect, they appear concerned about color in their orchestras. Neither Bach nor Handel gave predominance to any special instrument, unless it was designated specifically for solo function.

The interpreter of baroque music must never try to "improve" the harmonies and instrumentation of the Handelian score, or the "want of balance" in Bach's choral compositions. Genuine Bach or Handel performances must be strictly in keeping with the old style, without any attempt to assimilate the historical sound with the acoustic ideal of our modern time.

III. Rococo and Enlightenment

ORNAMENTATION

Graces are indispensable, but if ill-chosen they may do much harm.—PHILIPP EMANUEL BACH

THE MUSICAL child, in his daily practice, is seldom if ever aware of the more intricate questions of style—he hardly knows what interpretation means. But there is sure to be one problem that the little girl at the piano and the boy with his violin will stumble upon. Inevitably, children are confused by the *ornaments* that occur in their first classical readings, following the introductory phase of their studies. As soon as the youngsters are able to play the simpler sonatas of Haydn and Mozart, or the two-part inventions of Bach, they are confronted with the grace note and its manifold problems, and with a variety of signs denoting different patterns of ornamentation. Then the teacher comes to the rescue, often with the help of the edition on the music stand, supplying his pupil with the necessary information as to how to execute the graces. Naturally the teacher follows, in most cases, the opinion of the editor, who in turn has depended upon some musicological research for his knowledge. We see, then, that the road to the correct playing of graces may easily lead to confusing detours.

FUNCTIONAL AND ORNAMENTAL
GRACES

Of course, the main reason for the performer's confusion is the ambiguity of notation. Ornaments are designated by a method of musical stenography. In its more elaborated form, this system was developed by the Italian and French schools of early instrumental writing and was later accepted by the baroque masters. Yet the whole topic of graces is far from being limited to certain styles and periods. There is hardly a phenomenon in music tied up more intrinsically with primeval art than the etiology of ornaments. In fact, this question is closely linked with the fascinating problem of the origin of music, the answer to which has been attempted by that eminent scholar of natural history, Darwin. He interpreted the singing of birds as the prime factor in natural selection. According to Darwin's theory, only the best singers among the males stood a chance of winning the favor of the females. Such a constant selection of "mastersingers" on the part of pretentious females led finally to the astonishing coloratura technique in bird songs that human beings admire so much. But this language of birds is nothing more than a superabundance of sounds that, if written in musical notation, would primarily be a multiplicity of graces.

Shifting from the realm of animals to that of men, the origin of human music has been explained along similar lines. First attempts of primitives to express themselves musically are likewise based upon the principles of tone variation. Here, too, self-creating forces are at work, developing motifs into a maze of ornamental patterns. Ages later, analogous methods of tone variation are prevalent in the music of the Orient. Even today they occur in the performances of the Arabs, Hindus, Persians, and Turks; they can also be heard in the oriental church song and in the Jewish synagogue all over the world. European music offers still another well-preserved and highly informative example of the same procedure—the music of the gypsies. Its essence consists in the above-mentioned principle of tone variation: a wealth of melisma, spreading over the melody, playing around it, hiding the tune in a multicolored variety of passages, shakes, portamenti, glissandi. Here, as in other cases cited, the ornament creates music by spinning forth its own motifs into scrolls and graces adorning the primitive melos.

This excursion into primeval music has emphasized an unmistakably serviceable character of the graces. To put it paradoxically: *ornaments are functional.* In other words, they are neither mere embellishments nor musical tapestry. What often is referred to as graces proves to be an integral part of the texture of the composition. We have already shown how ornaments functioned as prolongation of the short-lived instrumental tone in the era of the English virginalists. However, it is in the so-called rococo period, in the second half of the eighteenth century, that the graces most frequently display the purely decorative character of the notes with which they are associated. Just as ornaments have a beautifying purpose in the architecture, painting, and other arts of the rococo period, so they become adorning elements in music. Obviously, it would not be possible to eliminate such graceful elements without affecting the basic structure of the art work concerned, since they contribute so bountifully to the finesse and elegance of the style and its expression.

Any musicological investigation of that period leads automatically into a study of the details of the important eighteenth-century treatises; no previous time supplies richer documentary evidence. Germany, France, Italy, and England handed down their traditions through a medium modestly called "textbooks" by their scholarly authors. The information contained in these has become today a *sine qua non* for the performer who seeks a genuine approach to the music of the time.

A list of famous eighteenth-century treatises or textbooks follows; the order of the titles is chronological according to years of their publication.

François Couperin, *L'art de toucher le clavecin*, Paris, 1717

Pier Francesco Tosi, *Opinioni de' cantori antichi e moderni*, Bologna, 1723

Jean Philip Rameau, *Pièces de clavecin*, 1731

Johann Mattheson, *Der volkommene Capellmeister*, 1739

Friedrich Wilhelm Marpurg, *Die Kunst das Clavier zu spielen*, Berlin, 1750

Johann Joachim Quantz, *Versuch einer Anweisung die Flöte traversière zu spielen* (published also in a French version), Berlin, 1752

Philipp Emanuel Bach, *Versuch über die wahre Art das Clavier zu spielen* (two parts), Leipzig, 1753, 1762

Leopold Mozart, *Versuch einer gründlichen Violinschule*, Augsburg, 1756

Jean Jacques Rousseau, *Dictionnaire de musique*, 1767

Daniel Gottlob Türk, *Clavierschule oder Anweisung zum Clavierspielen*, 1789

This list is a digest focused on those figures whose creative influence may be followed into classical channels. We have already discussed the valuable comments of Muffat on the Parisian performers and Lully's orchestra. The student of historical interpretation must not overlook Dieupart and his *Select Lessons for the Harpsichord*. The textbooks by Geminiani and James Hook are important—to quote only at random a few names and works that any detailed investigation would have to include. Turning to the most renowned contributors, the Bach family, we find that several of its members play a part as writers on ornamentation. There is Philipp Emanuel's *Versuch*, and the lesser-known brother, Johann Christoph (the "Bückeburg Bach") with his *Musikalische Nebenstunden*. Johann Sebastian, the father, made a chart for his cherished son Wilhelm Friedemann, a very condensed but accurate index to his own ornamentation. This latter contribution is very helpful, especially since Johann Sebastian's grace execution and that of Philipp Emanuel do not coincide in certain details.

The father-son motif is further reflected in the preface of Leopold Mozart's *Gründliche Violinschule*, the first edition of which appeared in 1756, the year Wolfgang Amadeus was born. The precepts of this *Thorough Violin School* were also the principles for the son's training. And here the circle closes: Wolfgang Amadeus, in his mature years, became an ardent advocate of Philipp Emanuel Bach. He was in the best classical company, for, in his enthusiasm, Haydn called Bach's essay *die Schule aller Schulen* ("the school of schools"), and many habits in classical performance can be traced to this very source. And so we see centered around the inspired figure of Philipp Emanuel Bach an interplay of forces extending far beyond the limited sphere of importance which today's estimation accords him.

PHILIPP EMANUEL BACH ON "MANIEREN"

Bach's greatest son, with his *Versuch*, contributed to the musical world something of far more than academic and musicological importance. This volume, coming as it does directly from the workshop of the practical musician—the text illustrated with tables and masterly examples—offers us in fact a veritable encyclopedia of the interpretative problems of its period. The three editions of the essay appeared respectively in 1753, 1759, and 1797. They contain a realization not only of the style and interpretation of the two great baroque masters, Handel and Johann Sebastian Bach, but also of all preceding and contemporary instrumental styles as expressed in English, French, and Italian scores. Thus, the eclectic quality of the treatise becomes obvious and proves to be one of the great advantages of the *Versuch*.

For all these historical and practical reasons, it is convenient to use this treatise as a ground plan for our presentation of ornaments. In the following pages, the different types of graces will be taken up in accordance with Philipp Emanuel's nine chapters on *Manieren*. Naturally, we do not intend, within the scope of our presentation, to restate Bach's material and formulations in detail; it is aimed rather to present some of his more general points, stressing those of obvious meaning to the performer today. Our digest of ornaments, while retracing Bach's outline in its organization, will at the same time include comments on the subject of graces by Quantz and other authorities. The chapters given us by Philipp Emanuel Bach on *Manieren* are as follows:

I.   *Manieren* in General
II.   On Appoggiature
III.   On Shakes
IV.   The Turn
V.   Mordents
VI.   The *Anschlag*
VII.   The *Schleifer*
VIII. The *Schneller*
IX.   On the Ornamentation of the *Fermata*

GRACES: GERMAN, FRENCH, ITALIAN

In the opening of his essay, Philipp Emanuel explains the basic function of the graces. He indicates where ornaments are useful, as well as where they are indispensable: besides their main purpose of linking the notes, they also enliven them, and give them special weight and emphasis. Graces, we learn, help to bring out the meaning of the score, whether it be sad, happy, etc.—to point up whatever mood the music expresses. In addition, they enable the performer to display his talent and taste.

Bach's discourse offers a cross section of ornaments belonging to virtually all the different national schools of his time, in relation to instrumental as well as vocal performance. "I have endeavored to collect the *Manieren* of various nations," states Philipp Emanuel, "for nowadays the graces of the French do not gratify our taste in music, toward which the superb Italian style of singing has contributed so much. I have added a few new *Manieren*. I believe that the ideal way of playing the clavier and other instruments should combine the clarity and brilliancy of the French performance with the pleasant and soothing style of Italian singing. Germans are particularly equipped for such a task, provided they rid themselves of prejudices."

So speaks a genuine German master who realized that the music of his country had a specific mission in amalgamating the superior elements of the French and Italian schools. And we have, too, the striking statement of Johann Sebastian Bach, quoted by Philipp Emanuel in order to fortify his position: "One style may be better than another, yet each one offers something of specific value. No style can be so perfect that it would exclude improvement."

The Bachs, father and son, with the humility of the truly great, understood and affirmed that there was much to learn from foreign accomplishments. Recognizing and utilizing them, they opened the door of progress for their native art. In fact, the whole topic of graces is only one of the countless instances in history where the co-operation of different national styles, rather than national seclusion, has led to the finest artistic achievements.

APPOGGIATURE

Philipp Emanuel starts in the first of his chapters with a *Manier* that takes us right into today's workshop. The opening group is concerned with what German music calls *Vorschlag*, the Italian *appoggiatura*, and the French *port de voix*. Today, we must differentiate two types: first, what generally is called appoggiatura, coinciding with Bach's *Vorschlag*; second, suspension, for which the German *Vorhalt* is the synonym. Such a differentiation was superfluous in the eighteenth century. Every keyboard player executed the figured bass in the routine way. He took care of *Vorschlag* or *Vorhalt* according to the standard rules of counterpoint, as in the treatment of the dissonance (its preparation as a consonance, its suspension on the strong beat, and the following resolution to the lower tone).

Bach cautiously avoids confusion in his practical treatment of *Vorschlag* and *Vorhalt*, but in theory he uses the term *Vorschlag* for appoggiatura as well as for suspension. While his chapter on this ornament turns out to be a complete register of appoggiature, dwelling on numerous variable and ambiguous cases, the schoolmasterly Quantz leads the truth-seeking performer out of the labyrinth of intricate appoggiatura cases and simplifies the matter by showing, in a somewhat less scholarly but more instructive fashion, the principal ways of employing the appoggiatura, and how it occurs most frequently in general use.

Quantz specifically demonstrates what happens when the appoggiatura is to be taken from above, and, vice versa, when approached from below. If the preceding note is higher than the one before which the appoggiatura appears, we should take the appoggiatura from above:

But if the preceding note is lower than the following one, then, similarly, the appoggiatura must be taken from below:

In addition, the interpreter is admonished to discriminate between two types of appoggiatura: (1) *anschlagende Vorschläge*, those that start with the time of the main note, and (2) *durchgehende Vorschläge* (passing appoggiature), those that start before the time of the main note. Quantz goes out of his way to clarify the correct performance of these, and we are grateful for the care he has taken because, as his own example will show, the eighteenth-century execution exhibits by no means the reading one would expect today.

We are given additional information as to correct interpretation. There is alteration of rhythm as in previously discussed examples (Lully, Muffat). The dots must be sustained, held longer than the precise time value indicates. The notes where the slur starts (namely the second, fourth, and sixth) are pushed. Quantz warns us not to confuse this case with the execution following, in which the second, fourth, and sixth notes are dissonant against the bass on the down-beat. Such dissonances are to be rendered "boldly, vivaciously," whereas the true appoggiatura tones have a flattering, coaxing expression. They must never be played in the following manner:

Appoggiatura reading in general, asserts Quantz, should be adjusted to the French manner of playing. And he admonishes the performer not to violate "the taste of their inventors, who have received such general approval." Like the Bach family, so the music master of the Prussian king, Frederick II, here places objectivity of artistic judgment above the prejudices of national cliques.

What note receives the accent? Bach, as other authorities do, answers this question in favor of the appoggiatura. Leopold Mozart, however, feels that very short appoggiature should yield the accent to the principal note. Again, comments on Beethoven's playing corroborate the fact that he followed Bach's advice. Türk's *Clavierschule* suggests that the performer should, whenever possible, divide the principal note. Thus the appoggiatura would receive half of the total value (a practice frequently heard in the readings of the Classicists).

ECCLESIASTICAL PERFORMANCE

Manuscript and portrait of Palestrina and the Sistine Chapel

Graf, The Opera and Its Future in Ame

LULLY'S STAGE PRODUCTION

Above: *costumes in the* Ballet de la Nuit
Below: *scene from* Armide

FIRST PART OF BACH'S "ST. MATTHEW PASSION"

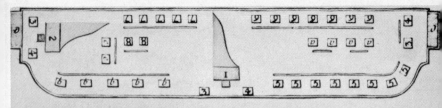

Renvois des Chiffres

1. Clavecin du Maître de Chapelle

2. Clavecin d'accompagnement

3. Violoncelles.

4. Contre - basses.

5. Premiers Violons

6. Second Violons, ayans le dos tourné vers de Théatre.

7. Hautbois, de même.

8. Flutes, de même.

a. Tailles, de même.

b. Bassons.

c. Cors de Chasse.

d. Une Tribune de Chaque côte pour les Tymballes et Trompettes.

DRESDEN OPERA ORCHESTRA, 1768 — *Rousseau,* Dictionnaire de musiq...

Groundplan of the theater orchestra, as arranged by the Dresden music director J. A. Hass...

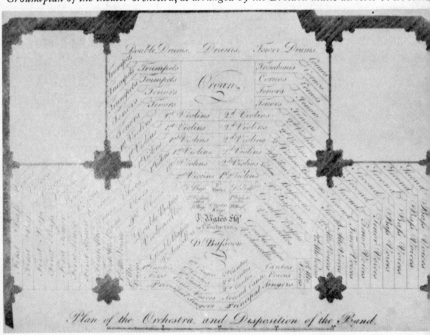

Burney, An Account of Musical Performan...

HANDEL'S "MESSIAH" IN WESTMINSTER ABBEY, 1784

Groundplan of vocal and instrumental forces

HAYDN CONDUCTS AN OPERA   *Courtesy V. E. Pollak*

The master at the piano directing in Esterház a performance of his opera
L'Incontro Improviso, 1775

Courtesy Metropolitan Museum, New York
FLUTE CONCERT OF FREDERICK THE GREAT
Maestro Quantz, at the piano, and his musicians waiting for the end of the King's cadenza

"Over this fugue, where the name BACH appears as contrasubject, the author passed away

BEETHOVEN: "APPASSIONATA"
Second movement of the sonata Opus 57

"THE MAGIC FLUTE": TAMINO'S ARIA

Mozart leaves the interpretation of the tenor part to the singer's imagination. The accompanying instruments, however, are firmly directed as to phrasing and dynamics.

MOZART: "AVE VERUM CORPUS"

Choral composition with string accompaniment and organ with figured bass. The manuscript, written in 1791, appears considerably more elaborated than earlier classical scripts.

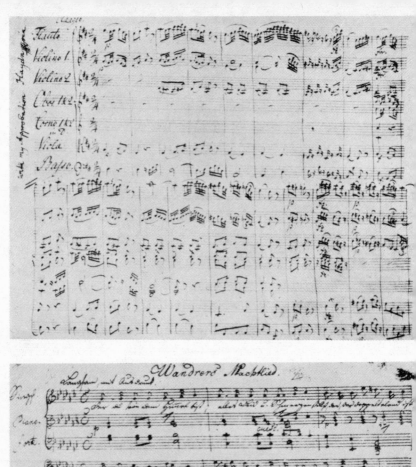

HAYDN'S "OXFORD SYMPHONY" AND "SCHUBERT'S
"WANDRERS NACHTLIED"

LIED PERFORMANCE

Schubert (pencil sketch by Moriz von Schwind) accompanying the baritone Vogl

ROMANTIC MONSTER PERFORMANCE

Caricature by Gustave Doré of Berlioz conducting a giant chorus

Chopin's Pleyel

Mozart's Reiseklavier

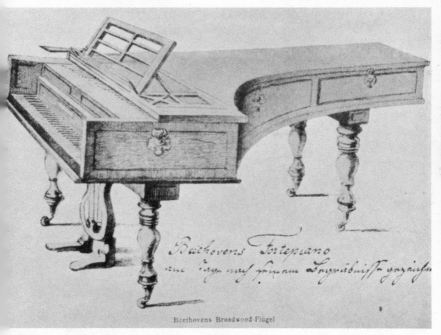

Beethovens Broadwood-Flügel

Beethoven's Broadwood

FAMOUS PIANOS

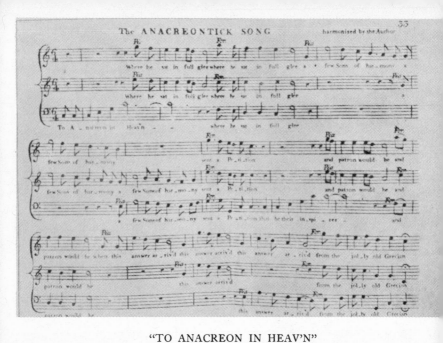

"TO ANACREON IN HEAV'N"
From John Stafford Smith's Book of Canzonets (1785)

ARTURO TOSCANINI AND EUGENE ORMANDY

When the principal note is dotted, the three units are divided in a way that gives only one third to the principal note and two thirds to the appoggiatura. However, the appoggiatura is entitled to the full value of the principal note, if the latter is followed by and tied to a shorter note.

The *Nachschlag* is disliked by Philipp Emanuel Bach, who calls it an "ugly afterbeat, much in fashion now and badly joined to the most melodious phrases."

SHAKES

Haydn, in two angry letters written to his Austrian publisher, Artaria, excoriated that gentleman for permitting the original signs in the manuscript to be interchanged at caprice of an engraver. In no uncertain terms Artaria was informed that the symbols of ornamentation in the composer's scores had specific and definite meaning. Haydn insisted that $t.$ was the sign for a shake, and that this must clearly be distinguished from $\mathcal{W}$, which stood for a short mordent. "Put my sign for the turn in its proper place," was his terse admonition. "The turn must stand over the dot, in case of dotted notes," he continued impatiently, "and leave ample space between the notes to make this plain."

While this composer-publisher correspondence throws some light on the question of the shake, and explains a few doubtful points in an authoritative way, it also brings up the question as to the extent to which other classic manuscripts, from Haydn to Schubert, may have been distorted through the easygoing ways of Viennese printers. But even if publishing conditions were ideal, if printers were to put every sign for an embellishment in its proper place, and readers were faultless in their comprehension of symbols indicating ornamentation, there would still remain the inevitable quandary over certain details regarding the performance of the shake—details concerning the tempo, how to start the grace, whether the closing *Nachschlag* is permissible, and others.

Philipp Emanuel Bach specifies four different types of shake, namely: (1) the shake proper; (2) the shake from below; (3) the shake from above; (4) the imperfect shake, half shake, transient shake, or pralltriller.

The most important of them, the ordinary shake, is designated by the sign ∿ , and starts with the diatonic second above, written without *Nachschlag:*

Johann Sebastian Bach, in his table of ornaments prepared for his eldest son, Wilhelm Friedemann, called the *Clavierbüchlein*, shows a *trillo* (shake) without a closing note, indicated by the sign ∿ .

The reason why modern performers contradict one another in their manner of starting the shake is readily explained: authorities themselves differ on this point. In contrast to Philipp Emanuel Bach (1753), Spohr (1833) states that every shake generally begins or ends with the principal note. If the shake is to start with the appoggiatura or with the lower note, it must be expressly written down. Noteworthy is Spohr's reference to Hummel's *Clavierschule* (1828) as having "first advanced this rule." Apparently the change occurred around 1800.

How fast or how slowly is the shake to be performed? Is there any rule? Does the flute render the shake as the violoncello does? Does the instrument render it like the voice? Again, do the soprano, alto, tenor, and bass execute a trill at the same speed? Once more, the methodical mind of Quantz systematizes performing habits of his time. There are also comments on the rendition of the shake according to national schools. We are informed that the very slow shake was habitual only in the French vocal performance. Quantz does not feel that this makes for a tasteful ornament; he considers the extremely slow shake just as bad as the rapid one with tremolo, called *chevroté, meckernd, Bockstriller,* a sound like the bleating of goats. (This particular trill lives on in Wagner's *Meistersinger,* in the pageant of the guilds, as a humorous sidelight on the old style.) Quantz reports the use of *chevroté* by some of the most celebrated virtuosos of his time. A special device of the Italians was the *Terzentriller,* in which, instead of the tone next to the main note, the third was used. Certain Italian violinists and oboists, we learn, indulged in this habit. An execution of shakes farther than a half or whole tone from the principal note seems strange today. Yet such grace rendition was a normal occurrence in the old performing practice.

As to the tempo of the shake, Quantz wants it played at an even, moderate speed, not too slow and not too fast. To avoid any possible ambiguity, Quantz used the four octaves of the harpsichord as a basis of tempo. For the one-line octave (third octave, two-foot octave), there are eight notes for one beat of the pulse (M.M. 80). For the two-line octave, there are also eight notes, but taken somewhat faster. For the small octave, there are again eight notes, but taken more slowly; and for the great octave, the shake must be executed considerably more slowly.

Quantz likewise establishes relationships for the human voice: the soprano singing the shake faster than the alto, the tenor faster than the bass, male voices more slowly than female voices, in the same balance and correlation. The instruments —violin, viola, violoncello, and contraviolon—assume analogous speeds. We see that instruments and voices correspond here very much as shown above in our discussion of the historical score (p. 65).

As to beginning and ending the shake, the *Vorschlag* must be taken at the same speed as the other notes of which the shake consists; and after the *Nachschlag* of the shake, before the final note, no *Vorschlag* should be taken.

THE TURN

The life-story of the turn is symbolic of the change from the originally ornamental to the purely functional grace. More so than any other ornament, the turn gradually developed from a mere embellishment into an expressive pattern highly characteristic of the building of romantic motifs, from rococo lightness and brilliancy to an emotional and heavy-hearted quality.

Philipp Emanuel Bach defines the turn as a simple *Manier* that makes a singing melody pleasant and brilliant. Again we see how the tempo affects the execution:

The principle is obvious: as the speed of the music increases, the value of the notes decreases, passing from sixty-fourths through thirty-seconds to sixteenths. Altogether, Philipp Emanuel specifies no less than thirty-seven different ways of performing the turn, reflecting the extremely varied application of this *Manier*. Out of this bedlam, three different patterns, as shown by Bach, can direct the performer of today:

The example is self-explanatory: turns vary according to their position, depending on whether the melody falls or ascends, and finally on whether the notes are neighboring tones in the scale.

Starting with Beethoven and with the departure of classical music from the purely ornamental style toward the romantic intensification of graces, the position of the turn is, in the great majority of examples, on the down-beat. This is corroborated by Schumann, who writes the turn out in this manner. The same is applicable to countless instances in Chopin's piano music. Confusion of terms, and the use of the turn with the so-called mordent, is responsible for the controversy over these ornaments for more than a hundred years. We have only to look into early nineteenth-century sources to find that the names of these two graces are interchangeable: thus Spohr refers to the double turn as *mordente*, starting with the upper note, in contrast to a version starting with the lower note.

The interpretation of the turn or mordent in later romantic scores shows the lengthening of its duration in such well-known examples as Wagner's *Rienzi* or *Tannhäuser*. Here the figure is executed in thirty-seconds, replacing the faster sixty-fourths rendering of Spohr. Doubt as to its execution in Wagner is eliminated by Liszt, who has helped us to read Wagner's turns by writing them out in his piano transcriptions of the operas.

Yet, strangely enough, even Wagner's closest associates could not settle the question of the proper playing of the turn. Liszt interprets the turn in *Tannhäuser*, in the passage at the entrance of the guests, as follows:

In contrast, Bülow made his orchestra play, in the *Rienzi* overture:

Thus, we see, the symbol ∼ was differently interpreted by leading exponents of the Wagner circle, the turn starting with either the lower or the upper note. No wonder Wagner took no chance in his later scores, and wrote the turns out instead of depending on the use of the sign ∼. In *Götter-dämmerung*, for instance, turns occur in different rhythmic meanings that, of course, could not be covered by one and the same symbol. The performer may feel safe in interpreting Wagner's turns from above in spite of the deviation of Bülow who, like his present-day emulators, was unhappy unless he could do things in a different way.

Baskets of beautiful expressive turns are integrated into the symphonic scores of Bruckner and Mahler. The latter, in his fanatic objectivity of script, never left any doubt for the performer as to the proper rendition.

MORDENTS

Philipp Emanuel Bach explains that the actual function of
the mordent is not only to connect notes, but also to increase
the sound and to add to its splendor. *Pincé* is the French term
for this grace, *Beisser* the German one. Technically, the mordent consists of one quick interchange of the main note with
its neighboring second below. Bach distinguishes between the
long and the short mordent, the long being played thus:

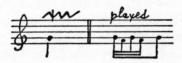

The short mordent is played:

In practice, the pralltriller is also confused with the mordent.
But Bach shows the difference and points out that they have
only one feature in common, namely, that they both slur into
a note from the neighboring second—the mordent *ascending*,
the pralltriller *descending*. For example:

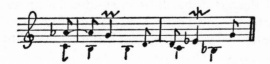

A special warning is given, at the end of Bach's comments on
the mordent, not to assemble too many *Manieren* following
one another. Thus it would be wrong to place a mordent immediately after a shake.

ANSCHLAG, SCHLEIFER, SCHNELLER, AND FERMATA

In 1833, Spohr writes that of all earlier ornaments only the
shake, the pralltriller, the mordent, and the appoggiatura have
been retained. However, he admits the existence of "others
without name." Because of their importance in old music, we
shall quote, from Bach's *Versuch* (chaps. vi to ix), some of
his observations on the performance of the *Anschlag*, *Schleifer*,
Schneller, and *fermata*.

Bach cites two cases of the *Anschlag*, especially marking the
dynamics:

to be played:

The grace starts piano and the main note forte. The idea is to
play the grace more weakly than the principal note.

As the name, *Schleifer* ("slide") indicates, the proper execution of this grace should make an idea smooth and fluent.
Two—or three—small notes, to be played before the main note,
constitute a "*Schleifer* without dot." If it consists of two notes,
the grace is represented by two tiny thirty-seconds:

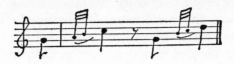

This two-note type must always be performed quickly. The other type, however, is not invariably rendered with rapid speed.

The *Schneller* is a short trill, a kind of inverted mordent. The smallest space is devoted to it in Philipp Emanuel Bach's review of graces. It occurs in contrary motion, as the highest tone of the grace must be *geschnellt*—produced with a stiff finger, rapidly:

It never occurs unless the passage is staccato.

Fermatas, according to Bach, may occur in three different ways, as a hold (*a*) upon the next to the last note, (*b*) upon the last note of the bass, (*c*) upon a rest after the bass note. A *fermata* (a stop, pause, hold) is indicated by a slur with a dot below it ⌒. Upon this mark, the performer holds the tone in accordance with the character of the music, asserts Bach. This statement is significant, eliminating the possibility that the *fermata* could be disregarded altogether in modern performance of old scores, as a "note to be dwelt upon longer than its value indicates." Bach makes it clear that the *fermata* must under no condition be ignored, contrary to the practice of a certain group of present-day interpreters.

In conclusion: The reader of this cross section through eighteenth-century ornamentation will have realized that the graces have been a chief object of transformation in the hands of composers and performers. Obviously, the conscientious modern interpreter of national styles will consult original sources for detailed direction, such as Couperin's *L'Art de toucher le clavecin,* in the case of French scores. For the playing of English music, Purcell's *Lessons for the Harpsichord or Spinett* should be investigated, and, naturally, all the treatises previously cited contain very important material. However, for the general orientation of the student, Philipp Emanuel's *Versuch* remains the best choice: its obvious closeness to Johann Sebastian's world, and its full indorsement by the Classicists, certainly place this treatise in the foreground of historical approach to all problems of ornamentation.

DANCE TYPES

Six years in the galleys for singing the saraband.—SPANISH ROYAL DECREE, 1583

The ideas of the various musical forms are not absolute: that which constitutes their form, their very content, has been changing constantly throughout the ages. Each period alters to some extent the design and shape of musical forms, and quite frequently even their original structure. Their names alone remain. Thus, what has been called a madrigal or a minuet in one century proves—upon closer stylistic scrutiny—to be dissimilar in idea and effect to a dance called by the self-same name in another age. While such a transformation of content can be observed in virtually any phase of musical history, this remarkable process of metamorphosis became the particular fate of a variety of forms centering around the conception of dance music, resulting in a flowing, never resting transmutation of types. No matter how strong the original components, or how colorful the national qualities—irresistibly, the power of stylistic assimilation affects them all. In any epoch they become exponents of the spirit and technique of the corresponding style period.

Thus, dance types conceived in early instrumental periods yield to the natural desire for technical change and artistic variety in the baroque, rococo, and classical epochs. New expression dispenses with the old patterns, tempos, steps. And yet, the very essence of older forms, with all their capacity for further development, can frequently be realized in spite of fresh influences. Fascinating indeed is the spectacle offered by the metamorphosis of the different dance types. Always strong enough to live to a ripe old age, they die only to rise again to new life, thanks to an intrinsic capacity for adjustment to prevailing musical conditions.

Madrigal and minuet, the two instances cited above, display conflicting meanings throughout history. There is the religious, the secular, the concert madrigal. In the *ars nova*, the madrigal represents the art song of the period, derived from troubadour poetry. In the Renaissance period of the sixteenth century, the madrigal is usually a composition in free part writing, influenced by the melodious music of the south. Again, German developments show considerable assimilation of the Italian models. For all these divergent types and forms in different times a single name is used—madrigal.

In dance music, likewise, ambiguity surrounds the meaning of different type names, and to a surprisingly intensified degree—surprising because, naturally, the dance music accompanied specific step patterns that were inevitably standardized, as in the case of the minuet. But as time went on, the music became divorced from its original purpose of dance accompani-

ment, appearing to be an end in itself. It is in this latter character, as independent instrumental composition, that dance
music enters on a phase in which its interpretation becomes
uncertain and creates problems for present-day performers.
In a beer garden nobody expects much concern about the reading of the polka. Nor does the average dance-band leader worry
very much about the phrasing of the tango. However, a minuet
in Bach's suites, or in Beethoven's symphonies, presents a number of perplexing questions to the pianist or conductor of today.

A simple experiment will quickly reveal the uncertainty surrounding interpretation of the minuet. Suppose we play recordings of miscellaneous minuets taken from any type of classical
music. A great variety of tempos, phrasings, and shapings of
the form will be apparent. Before long it will seem that there
are almost as many kinds of minuet readings as there are records
on the market. And as our experiment progresses, we become
resigned to the fact that even the comparison of so many readings offers no useful standard for the minuet. We shall try
another approach. This time we shall concentrate on a single
minuet of which several different recordings are available. Is
there any such thing as uniformity of the minuet idea? We
find that virtually every performer has his own, and conclude
that interpretation is determined by mere guesswork. What
are the reasons?

The position of the minuet within larger compositions is variable. It is found as a middle movement in cyclical forms—usually between the adagio and the finale. Occasionally it also appears as an opening or concluding movement. The designation
"minuet" is not always given for formal identification. There
are a considerable number of compositions bearing unmistakably
all the characteristics of the minuet, yet not expressly so called.
Instances occur in instrumental and vocal ensembles, sometimes
in arias of classical and preclassical scores. Facing such a di-

versity of purposes, it is a complex task to define the character of the minuet, even if we limit ourselves to a single style period. With so many changes of function, the form eludes generalization. Clearly, it is but a step from such a variety of uses to a variety of conceptions, and therefore of interpretations.

To be sure, there are certain minuets the proper reading of which is taken for granted. There is the old favorite from the first finale of Mozart's *Don Giovanni*, inevitably chosen for the child's earliest repertoire. Yet the case is more involved than one would gather from the self-assurance with which the little child goes to the piano and picks out the F major melody on the keyboard. In fact, Mozart's brilliant tone portrayal of the festival scene in the palace has become the classical prototype of polyrhythm, so significant in modern writing: the three-four time of the minuet is contrasted with two-four and three-eight time, resulting in a rhythmical permutation most audacious for 1787. All this is an ingenious musical juxtaposing of court and peasant dances; the trio of masked guests are disguised aristocrats, while the others are country folk. Clearly, Mozart refers here to the slower minuet type, of very moderate tempo, as danced at court since the days of Lully.

Thus far we have centered on the minuet to show the inescapable uncertainty as regards rendition. It goes without saying that similar ambiguity could be demonstrated as readily for any other of the dance types. On their long journeys through many countries, they have met with numerous adventures—some have traveled under assumed names, others have appeared in disguise. One and the same dance type may be heard as a meditative organ prelude in a church and as a seductive tune in the street. Small wonder that such variegated milieus as are displayed by the life-story of the dances have obscured the perspective for the modern performer.

THE FUNCTION OF THE DANCE

Whereas the interpreter can do without knowledge of the historical ramifications, he must have clearly in mind the function of the particular dance he is playing. The question is whether the music is an accompaniment for actual dancing or whether it is its own *raison d'être*. It is not sufficient for the performer to know merely the formal changes that have taken place, because purpose and place are the important factors determining interpretation.

This is true not only of dance music with its broad scope; almost every form in music has likewise been applied in divers ways. Even the other extreme, church music, definitely displays various purposes—that of fostering devotion and meditation, as well as that of supplying routine accompaniment for the service. In military music also the occasion decides the choice of instruments—one setup for the march in the street, another for the concertized program. The importance of classifying music according to the place of its presentation was early recognized. Monteverdi differentiated between music to be performed at court, in the theater, in the home; he distinguished chamber music and finally dance music.

But since the Renaissance, dance music has become almost too elastic a concept. It thrives everywhere—from royal palaces to dens of iniquity, from the bourgeois home to the outdoor entertainment of the masses. Unlimited by class boundaries as the dance primarily is, in its literal sense, another more fantastic outlook on musical forms seeks the dance even beyond the confines of its definition.

Among those who championed so universal a conception of the dance was Richard Wagner. However, the same master who dreamed of *Gestenmusik* ("music of the gesture") hesitated to employ wholeheartedly in his own music dramas the

more earthy qualities of the dance. It is well known that the
bacchanale in *Tannhäuser* originated as an attempt to appease
the Jockey Club and operagoers of Paris, who, in Wagner's
first production, felt cheated of their beloved ballet. Other
exceptions—the short *Ländler* of the apprentices in *Die Meistersinger*, and the siren scene of the flower girls tempting Parsi-
fal—do not offer that salutary loosening of tension so irresistibly employed in Latin opera. It has never made any difference
whether composers incorporated in their original ground plans
the rejuvenating forces of the dance, since the unwritten laws
and unshakable traditions of the producers of opera have later
incorporated a ballet into the show anyway. Before Don José
has a chance to kill Carmen, the audience is cheered up by a
big chorus and ballet scene. The tragedy of the abandoned
Gretchen, as Gounod feels it, lingers in the memory of the
audience with the serene pantomime finale. In Puccini's *Tosca*,
a torture scene and a gavotte are friendly neighbors.

All this, of course, is foreign to the spirit of Bayreuth. It
seems grotesque that certain thesis writers have been unable
to resist the temptation of hunting for the "ever present" dance
element in the music dramas, from the *Flying Dutchman* to the
Ring. Wagner himself detected the dance in absolute musical
forms. Beethoven's Seventh Symphony was to him the "apoth-
eosis of the dance." Picture this family scene, as recounted by
Cosima Wagner: Richard wildly dancing the finale of the
Seventh in his salon, as his father-in-law, Liszt, plays the score
on the piano!

Wagner's contention has the support of certain theorists.
Hugo Riemann sees the step of the minuet in the variations of
Beethoven's piano sonata Opus 26, and likewise in the andante
of the Fifth. If an interpreter inclines to such conceptions, they
are bound to color his performance. Naturally, it makes a considerable difference in the execution of Beethoven's triple beats

whether they be conceived as music of heavier accents or whether they convey brighter elements of the minuet, suggesting a more fluent tempo and smoother phrasing. Be this as it may, the detection of dance features in absolute forms is a purely subjective procedure, which paves the way for a practice that has recently become quite prevalent. Certain ballet groups have made choreographic interpretations of symphonic scores from the Classicists to Shostakovich. However, the absolute music of the classical masters is of such stature and character that it is bound to absorb the perceptive capacity of the attentive listener. Visual imagery, under such circumstances, can only detract. In the vast realm of music, there are innumerable instances where the composer himself has indicated the programmatic nature of his work—either explicitly in the score or in collateral writing. These are the works to which pictorial interpretation should be limited.

Of course there is no argument about the scenic significance of a suite made up of real dances. Originally designed in smaller units as an accompaniment for courtly ceremonies, this species later came to combine several movements of different characteristics. Composers soon discovered its ideal potentialities for independent instrumental use.

THE PRECLASSICAL SUITE

Out of the maelstrom of types, there finally emerged a limited number of dances that became the foundation of baroque suites such as the standard ones by Bach and Handel. In addition, a few national types were included in the framework.

Two principles contributed to the building up of the suite: (1) the grouping of homogeneous types; (2) the grouping of contrasting types. The baroque suite was founded particularly upon the latter. The music is characterized by unity of key and similarity of themes, but there is still a complete contrast of the individual dances. In the first instance, the reverse is true; that is, tonalities and motifs change, while the dance movements are alike. The merging of contrasting types led logically to the instrumental suite.

With the foregoing in mind, we turn to the wealth of beauty Johann Sebastian Bach has left us in his various suites. It is fascinating to observe how his genius, so immersed in the ecclesiastical, could fixate with the pen the worldly charm which his dances emanate. Bach—and this is important to remember —did not do a great deal to idealize the forms of the dance. His composition was true to the nature of the types, and used their native qualities. Therefore, the Bach suites must be performed with exuberance of melody and utmost liveliness of rhythm—in short, as real dances. Simultaneously, the chief characteristic of the general Bach style—the linear polyphony —must always be distinctly felt. Although the counterpoint in these suites is never of heavy caliber, its importance must always be made manifest.

It would be a mistake to assume in those keyboard compositions in which Bach alluded to other national types—as he did in the French and English suites—that the performer must brood on the French or English way of playing at the particular time. He may, as a matter of fact, dispense with any minute investigation into national styles, because Bach captured the musical essences of the respective countries in his own way. In performing a French suite of his, one is playing Bach predominantly. Whenever he adapted or arranged another style, it automatically became first and foremost Bach.

Returning to the general interpretative problems in relation to the dance types, we shall now examine each in accordance with its constantly fluctuating features. Naturally, the performer must be conversant with all the relevant changes, the more so because there are so few directions in the old scores. Curt Sachs, in his *World History of the Dance*, has provided us with a veritable encyclopedia on the subject. His exhaustive research has become the definitive guide in the countless vexing problems of the dance and its interpretation.

Sachs divides the periods of the dance, after the Middle Ages, into three principal eras: (1) the age of the galliard, from 1500 to 1650; (2) the age of the minuet, from 1650 to 1750; (3) the age of the waltz, from 1750 to 1900. We see that the first era of the dance with which we are concerned here dates back to a time as early as the discovery of America. It is not surprising, then, that some of the types have historical importance only. As we advance farther, we find an increasing number of dance types that have survived through centuries and finally reached the present.

When we turn the leaves of old dance scores, one name occurs again and again, with four variations in spelling, depending on whether the volume happens to be of Italian, Spanish, French, or English origin. The name is "galliard." The immense popularity of this dance is reflected not by music alone, but also by the literature of its time. Shakespeare liked to allude to the galliard, and Elizabeth the queen, at the age of fifty-six, went through several of these dances each morning as setting-up exercises. Little as the galliard may mean to the musician today, its importance was so universal in its own time that Sachs uses it to label the period from 1500 to 1650. Appearing first in Lombardy, it served as a regular afterdance for the pavane. Thus, light triple time brought relief from the preceding austere four-four time. While some correlative dances remain, the leading figure, the galliard, has vanished.

Of all the dance types developed before the nineteenth century, the minuet is most familiar to the interpreter today. This is because it became an integral part not only of the preclassical suite but of the classical sonata and symphony also. Thus it proved to be more elastic and adjustable than the other old dances that are now obsolete. As we shall later see in detail, the features of the minuet were assimilated to an astonishing degree by new formal conditions in changing centuries. Its tempo runs through the entire gamut of speeds, from extreme slowness to the greatest rapidity. It is precisely at this point that danger lurks for the interpreter. Not only in the ever changing minuet, but in all the other fluctuating dance forms, the first and principal question to be settled is: What is the correct tempo? Even if we pretend to have adequate answers, how can any precise indications for tempo (since they must be referred to a period before the invention of the metronome) be offered at all?

It can be done. It was the methodical mind of Quantz that solved this problem half a century before the advent of Maelzel's invention. In his *Versuch einer Anweisung die Flöte traversière zu spielen,* Quantz presents a method based on the human pulse. He assumed that there are eighty beats to the minute. This figure, in turn, is analogous to eighty time units on the metronome. Taking full advantage of Quantz's scheme, we easily translate his pulsations into the standard units of Maelzel's metronome. By mutual adjustment, any tempo can be stated precisely, eliminating ambiguity. (In a later chapter we shall deal with other historical instances of premetronomic fixations of tempo.)

The *Versuch* contains also a register of dances, the tempos of which are, as it were, mathematically specified. It would not be wise, however, to follow Quantz's suggestions blindly. The royal flute master, like certain famous interpreters today, had a slight preference for the virtuoso element in rendition. Therefore, employment of Quantz's figures now requires some caution, especially in relation to works of a time prior to his own. This must be kept in mind as we examine the dances discussed in the pages that follow.

DANCES FROM THE GALLIARD ERA

THE PAVANE

The pavane and its story do not lead us back to the Italian city of Padua, with which it has been linked through etymological speculations. Its true place of origin was Spain, where, at the royal court, it was used as a festal introductory dance. Still, more than any other type, it lent its measure to solemn, festive, and religious occasions, which provide the framework for pavane performance in the grand style.

However, the very slow four-four step underwent a gradual acceleration. This happened when the place of the pavane as the opening of the suite was taken by types such as the ceremonial but more energetic French overture and the still lighter and faster *allemande*. An appropriate rendition even of a modern design like Ravel's *Pavane pour une infante défunte*, written to assuage the grief of a friend, must be considerably slower than it usually is. The latest mangling of Ravel's music, with its tender humanity, into a swing tune, is a procedure against which no law yet protects the dignity of masterworks.

THE COURANTE

The courante goes through virtually chameleon-like changes in its evolution. At the opening of the sixteenth century, the courante was a pantomimic wooing dance. A century later, it is a slow court dance in three-two time. The conflicting descriptions of it must be interpreted according to characteristics that have constantly changed through the years. A cross section of rather confusing courante designations can be gleaned from the following: "swift corantos" (Shakespeare); "largo" (Bassani); "rather quickly" (Kuhnau); "pompously" (Quantz). The reason for the variety of modes is the fact that the old dance has practically nothing in common with later types called by the same name. As the Rococo lightened everything up, so the stately court courante gradually developed a moderate and eventually a fast tempo. This explains the seeming contradictions in the quoted descriptions. The slow courante, which Corelli's teacher, Bassani, marks "largo" in 1677, and which Handel probably heard in Italy, is not the same dance that Shakespeare's comment in *Henry V* describes as swift. It would be absurd to underestimate the immense value of great literature—from the Bible to Cervantes and Goethe—in musicological research. It is true that poets are not obliged to pass a final examination in the history of music or aesthetics, and their comments must often be taken with a grain of salt. But Shakespeare was a keen observer and a man of extreme musicianship. It would be foolish to discount his contribution even on so technical a question as the setting of tempo in a particular dance type.

Quantz groups the courante with two other dances, the *loure* and the *entrée*, thus revealing their close relationship: these three dances, he informs us, were performed pompously, with the bow detached after each quarter, whether dotted or not. The tempo is given as M.M. $\downarrow = 80$. The dancing masters of the early eighteenth century considered the more stately features fundamental in teaching; and in this connection the courante received the nickname of the "doctor dance." Depending on heavier or lighter accents, three-two (six-four) or three-four are the time signatures. The up-beat of an eighth, also augmented to three eighths, remains the initial characteristic.

THE SALTARELLO

The saltarello shows distinctly how one dance type borrows the characteristics of another to such a degree that its name appears to be but a pseudonym. There are four types, all called by the same name: the Italian version of the Spanish *alta danza*, the French *breban*, and the saltarello, which is described by an authority in 1455 as a triple rhythm with up-beat; in other words, it was then similar to the courante. In 1508 the *Intabolatura de lauto* presents a new model, starting on down-beats and ending on up-beats—what still is called saltarello has in reality turned into a galliard. In 1600 the situation changes again; the saltarello now follows the galliard and exhibits a different rhythm.

Sachs explains how, after the rigid separation of the court dance and the country dance, the saltarello became the dance which always followed the *basse danse*. The latter, we are informed

> has one characteristic which for a long time it shared with no other dance: in the fifteenth century it lacked any regular arrangement of steps, any repeating phrase of movement. These two dances (*saltarello* and *basse danse*) fused into an inseparable unit. Even in the Middle Ages we have this contrast of the two forms: dances which were stepped (*geschritten* or *getreten*) and dances which were leaped (*gesprungen*). The *istampita* and the *saltarello* have become one.

While this discussion may seem to turn on an abstraction irrelevant today, in reality it contains the kernel of a most timely and popular manner of performance. In jazz the daily bread and butter of the players comes from their ability to improvise and transpose from the written music. They may play the text once as printed, but when repeating they fill in a great deal, altering the original by a method which has been dubbed "faking." This habit had its inception in the medieval contrast of the two main forms of dancing—the stepped dance (*istampita*) and the leaped dance (saltarello). No sooner did the *istampita* and the saltarello become merged than it seemed superfluous to use a new tune for the afterdance. Instead, the latter consisted only of a variation, a rhythmical abbreviation of the main dance. Just as the medieval fiddler could dispense with the printed text of the afterdance, so the modern saxophonist fabricates his own version of the main tune. In the mensural notation of the Middle Ages, such transposition into a new rhythm was called *cum proportione*. Consequently in Germany *Proportz* became the name for the *Nachtanz* ("afterdance"). A late instance of a saltarello as a symphonic afterdance is found in the *Italian Symphony* of Mendelssohn.

THE SARABAND

The saraband surpassed all the other dance types in a lengthy chain of almost unbelievable transformations. Here we observe a metamorphosis so complete that its story borders on Ovidian fairy tales. Today one seems to take it for granted that the saraband should conjure up associations of dignity, even of piety. This is quite in keeping with the Spanish ancestry of the dance and its aristocratic poise, as reflected in old pictures. Again, such a view coincides with the limited information one can gather about the saraband from certain lexicons, where austerity of expression and slowness of tempo are stressed exclusively. But let the credulous one who relies wholly on such conceptions of the saraband beware, for a great shock is in store for him. "Woe to the dirty fellow who has brought this barbarism upon us," was the moralistic outcry (Giambattista Marino) in 1623, and the "barbarism" attacked was nothing else than the saraband.

Another critic, more musically inclined, flays the saraband as a dance in which "girls with castanets and men with tambourines exhibit indecency in a thousand positions and gestures." Even more, as early as 1583 the Spanish law stepped in and saraband dancing was no longer a private affair but a criminal offense! The penalty was 200 lashes. And in addition men were given six years in the galleys and girls were banished from the country for singing and dancing the saraband.

These quotations show why a single-track interpretation of the saraband will not suffice. Clearly the dance has been living a varied life, starting with an unbridled adolescence but attaining dignity in its prime. However, the saraband as we know it today is remote from the influences of its untamed youthful stage. And yet it is a mistake to suppress the early background as certain authors have done. They censor one of the most striking examples in history of the kaleidoscopic mutability of musical forms.

The saraband with which we are concerned is depicted by Mattheson as a dance of "grandezza" and severity. Quantz compares it with the courante, setting the tempo at three-four, M.M. $\downarrow$ = 80; he wants it performed in an "agreeable way." Quantz's tempo must be considered fast; after all, the saraband gradually assumed the place in the suite that the adagio occupies in the sonata and the symphony. In cyclical forms both saraband and adagio represent repose.

CHACONNE AND PASSACAGLIA

The dances known as the *chaconne* and the *passacaglia* are two forms virtually identical, although musicology and practice have been trying to draw fine distinctions between them. While both are characterized by a recurring *ostinato*, some historians have attempted to prove that the *chaconne* permits transposition of this *ostinato*. Choreographers, on the other hand, find in the *passacaglia* more studied, cautious movements. The idea of identity, or at least close relationship, can be traced far back. Mattheson speaks of the brother or sister of the *chaconne*, depending on whether the masculine *passagaglio* or the feminine *passacaille* is used.

As in the case of the saraband, the two *ostinato* forms have an early history one would hardly suspect from the severe character which is familiar to us today. Let us consider three *passacaglias* from three centuries: Bach's *Passacaglia* in C Minor; the finale of Brahms's Fourth Symphony; and one by a modern, the orchestral *Passacaglia*, Opus 1, of Anton Webern. Although these scores certainly belong to different worlds of expression, they have in common a primarily instrumental attitude and austere formalism. It was, perhaps, from eighteenth-century examples that Riemann jumped to the conclusion that the *ostinato* dances might never have been danced at all. Apparently he overlooked the many proofs, in both music and literature, that they actually were danced.

"Like quicksilver run the feet," says Cervantes. In *Don Quixote* he depicts the *chaconne* as a dance of immigrants from the West Indies. Its nature is wild and voluptuous; the tempo is rapid, and is kept so as the expression changes during the transition from sensuousness to restraint. With this in mind, it begins to dawn upon us how Quantz, as late as 1752, could give such rapid tempos for *chaconne* and *passacaglia*. Even considering Quantz's general tendency to faster timing, what he gives (*chaconne*, three-four, M.M. $\downarrow$ = 160; *passacaglia*, three-four, M.M. $\downarrow$ = 168) would be absurd if applied to the *ostinato* types of Bach. Naturally, every discourse on interpretation is bound to reflect what is in vogue at the particular time rather than the latest accomplishments that are prophetic of things to come. So Bach, even when using traditional forms, was ahead of the most conscientious contemporary comment. What Quantz said in 1752 is indicative of what had happened before his time. Today any account of contemporary interpretation is handicapped by the fact that performances of the significantly progressive works are extraordinary events, whereas the great majority of programs cover only the conventional.

THE GAVOTTE

The gavotte at this day is one of the few remaining symbols of the old style. In the popularity it has retained it ranks close to the minuet, which it habitually follows in the suite. The name is derived from the Gavots, natives of the French Alps. There is a court version also, and when it comes to sponsoring old dance forms Louis XIV seems ubiquitous. The gay four-four *alla breve* rhythm readily evokes a spirit of playfulness; kissing became part of the frolic, but this was later modified to an offering of flowers.

Quantz's tempo, M.M. $\downarrow$ = 120–132, is fast. Because of the steadiness and primitiveness of the rhythm and the pictorial quality of the steps, the gavotte easily lends itself to great ensembles, such as combinations of solos with chorus, orchestra, and dance groups on the stage. Thus serious and light opera have always used the gavotte as a reminiscence of happy bygone days. In contrast to such a conventional use, where either old tunes are quoted or new ones are just a modernized paraphrasing of the old, there is an up-to-date utilization of old dance forms in Schönberg's twelve-tone scores.

THE MUSETTE

The musette has been linked with the gavotte as forming its middle part (*trio alla musette*). Originally a dance in triple beat, of pastoral character—a kind of quiet courante—the musette provides an organ point for the melody of the trio, which has become the *b* in the *a-b-a* song form of other dances. Therefore its name, from the French *musette* ("bagpipe") denoting the drone of this instrument. Quantz wants the musette played "very flatteringly": three-four, MM. $\rfloor$ = 80, or, if notated in eighths, $\rfloor$ = 80. However, he admits that sometimes, according to the fantasy of the dancers, it is taken faster, so that only one beat of the pulse comes on each bar. This is a significant instance of contradiction between musical theory and dance practice. The theorist states what should be done, realizing at the same time how difficult it is to tie down the wilfulness of dancers to any standards.

DANCES FROM THE MINUET ERA

The minuet found its way to the royal court of Louis XIV from the countryside. Lully's stately minuets were danced in the ballroom at Versailles as well as on the stage in Paris. A piece of truly French origin, it derived its name from *menu* ("small"), which obviously has reference to the short steps of the dance. Lully's minuet, a blending of gracious gallantry and stately ceremony, has a very moderate tempo. His type is the most dignified minuet in history. We find it in orchestral suites as well as in instrumental works before 1700—always to be performed with distinguished slowness.

The eighteenth-century minuet is different from that of Lully. Its customary place, in the suites of Bach and Handel, is between saraband and *gigue*. Because of the slowness of the former and the rapidity of the latter, a happy medium must be sought in the minuet. Quite frequently Handel writes the minuet in three-eight time, giving it a lighter touch. Quantz suggests that each quarter be marked by a short and rather heavy bowing. His tempo was two quarters for one pulsation —translated to the modern metronome, three-four, MM, $\quarternote = 160$. This, of course, is exceedingly fast. Yet, grotesque as it seems, certain old sources go so far as to state that the minuet was taken twice as fast as an ordinary allegro. We turn to the consideration of rhythm for some light on this puzzling situation. As Sachs demonstrates, the music of the minuet was in three-four time, but the rhythm of the dance was in three-two. The right foot took the first two beats of the opening bar, the left foot the final beat of the first bar and the first beat of the second bar. Thus music and dance steps were in a very attractive contrast. Hence, dancing masters advised conductors to accent the first beat of the opening bar but not the first beat of the second bar, in order to avoid a pitfall for unrhythmical dancers.

This amounts to a veritable contradiction between dance and music—a counterrhythm, as it were. Now, it is conceivable that the unit of the minuet was the half, whereas the quarter represented only the step. The indication of speed ($\quarternote$) apparently referred only to the steps, while the true minuet time ($\halfnote$) was only half as fast, so indicating a tempo that could be considered in keeping with the conventional standard of the minuet. Here we are confronted with a most interesting case, displaying close connection between music and dance without pedantic coincidence beat for beat. Such a contrarhythmical idea, centering around the minuet, was obviously Mozart's inspiration for the scene in the *Don Giovanni* finale cited above.

We have already explained to what extent this minuet is of the stately type, and how it must be rendered accordingly. But Mozart also wrote many other types of minuet, rarely specifying the tempo. However, in the E-flat Major Symphony

(Köchel's catalogue, No. 543) he marks the third movement allegretto, which is as detailed an instruction as one could expect in premetronomic days. This tempo has become a model for other minuets where no special instructions are given, assuming that Mozart meant allegretto for all his minuets. Near the time of his premature death, Mozart composed the E-flat Major, the G Minor, and the *Jupiter* symphonies. Although these belong to the same creative period, the minuets in them are unlike in character. How antithetical are the C Major and the G Minor minuets—the first a piece of Olympian serenity, the other stormy music, almost a duel scene, the most tempestuous minuet in classical writing. Consequently no open formula for Mozart minuets, but only the music itself, can provide the proper enlightenment for the performance of the piece. In résumé, the Mozart interpreter must bear in mind, first, that the slower tempo applies where actual dancing was intended, as in *Don Giovanni*; second, that *tempo di minuetto* in cyclical forms is frequently but a recollection of the earlier dance minuet; and, third, that the expressive symphonic minuet of the later works must accord with the individuality of the particular symphony.

THE HAYDN MINUET

Haydn reconciled the symphonic idea with folklore. What Handel and Corelli accomplished for the concerto, Haydn did for the symphony: as Kretzschmar says, he made the spirit of the old suite at home in the milieu of the Italian symphony. And for those who failed to notice the new spirit in the old house, the minuet was added.

To attain this goal, Haydn took the original, the country minuet, from the very start; that is to say, he refrained from the stately, courtly type of Lully. The gaiety, the bucolic freshness, of the Haydn minuet are due to the earthy qualities of its rustic model, the old Austrian *Ländler;* it calls to mind Peter Brueghel's canvases in their most vivid and realistic portrayal of Dutch peasant life.

The tempo of the Haydn minuet shows better than anything else the change in spirit brought about in this dance type. Directions are accelerated from Mozart's *allegretto* to Haydn's *allegro ma non troppo,* and even to *presto.* The latter is demanded in the quartets Opera 76 and 77. In Opus 33, *scherzando* somehow describes the nature of the movement and, as we shall find, anticipates Beethoven's conception. However, the interpreter of the Haydn minuet must be careful not to go to the other extreme and indulge himself in speed. The prestos of Opera 76 and 77 are exceptions. Since in several of Haydn's sonatas the minuet takes the place of the slow movement, it must accordingly supply the moderate speed of the middle movement. *Tempo di minuetto* is a designation of numerous finales in smaller works of Haydn, as well as of Mozart.

Pohl, the conscientious biographer, asserts that Haydn's opus numbers have come down to us in strict chronological order. This is fortunate, because it reflects the development of the different forms throughout the composer's life. In the case of the minuet, the most important change, as the years go on, relates to the trio. The relationship between the keys of the minuet and those of the trio becomes more and more remote. While this was caused by a desire for increasing variety in form and harmony, the score gives no indication that variety in tempo also was intended. Many present-day performers feel that it is permissible, not to say obligatory, to change the tempo at the transition from the minuet to the trio: they slow down the tempo and resume speed at the repetition of the minuet.

Such a tempo change might, in rare instances, be properly motivated by instrumental and technical considerations. But this cannot be accepted as a general rule. Why should the interpreter try to outsmart Haydn by seeking additional diversity, when so masterly a mind has already taken care of the matter in its own way?

THE BEETHOVEN MINUET

The growing formal independence of the Haydn trio has marked a considerable step forward in development. For the next significant departure in the minuet, we turn to Beethoven. Two different types of minuets are clearly discernable in Beethoven's works: (1) the Haydn-Mozart type, (2) the scherzo type.

The first type is found in sonatas and chamber music, whereas only one of the nine symphonies displays this older form—namely, the Eighth. Appropriately, the tempo of this movement must be slower than that of the minuet in the First Symphony, which, although specifically called *menuetto*, bears only the name of the old form. In reality it belongs to the second form, the scherzo type, into which Beethoven transformed the older minuet, and which is generally acceded to be his great contribution to this dance form. Significantly enough, in his three piano trios Opus 1, Beethoven shows the use of both types. Of these trios, the first and second have the modern scherzo and the third the older minuet. Thus Beethoven, from the very start, reveals his revolutionary conversions of form. The Beethoven scherzo is indeed a great deviation from its model, the minuet. It adds to the Mozart-Haydn minuet something entirely new. The *a-b-a* form is enormously enlarged. The trio becomes an entity in itself. What often emerges from the Mozart minuet as playfulness, and from Haydn's as humor, reaches in Beethoven's scherzo a climax of almost superhuman exultation.

Altogether, there are sixty-three examples of the minuet or scherzo to be found in Beethoven's one hundred and thirty-five works. Seventeen belong to the first minuet type, and the remainder, forty-six, to the scherzo type. As in Haydn's or Mozart's scores, the minuet-scherzo is not invariably the third movement. It sometimes becomes a substitute for the second movement or for the finale. The piano sonata Opus 54 provides the only example of a minuet functioning as an introduction. As in the works of Haydn and Mozart, certain movements throughout Beethoven's works are clearly minuets, although they do not bear the designation.

The interpreter must first understand what type (minuet or scherzo) Beethoven intended, and must also recognize its function in the cyclical form. In a work like the piano sonata Opus 31, No. 3, where the minuet takes the place of the slow movement, the performer must display all the expressive and formal characteristics that are inseparable from the traditional type. In the Septet in E-flat Major, and later in the sonata Opus 49, No. 2, one and the same minuet type is used as finale (G major); but neither the piano sonata nor the chamber-music work belongs to the four-part cyclical type. The scherzo type is so characteristic in its features that, regardless of where it is placed or whether or not it is so named, it will unmistakably be recognized for what it is. Thus, the third movement of the First Symphony could never be mistaken for a minuet because of its fleeting but at the same time energetic quality.

Another problem in the performance of the minuet, scherzo, or trio is that of repetition. The foundation of the classical and especially of the preclassical minuet is the eight-bar period. Each period is repeated. To ignore such repetitions in playing the earliest minuets, such as Lully's, is incorrect. While the dotted double bar stands for an abridgment, sixteen bars are actually required for the melody. Omitting these repetitions amounts to an alteration of the form. In the performance of the classical minuet, there are certain established traditions. In the first reading, before the trio, repeats are used. After the trio they are omitted. However, in earlier times audiences were more tolerant of reiteration. How little sensitiveness there was, in general, toward recurrence of the same form, can be seen in old programs, with their constant accumulation of the same form types to a monotonous degree and at a length no audience in the world would endure today. When the classical composers did not intend repetition the second time, they expressly marked in the score, *da capo senza repetizione*.

In the Seventh Symphony, with its two trios, the question of repetitions is quite involved. It has become customary to observe all repetitions in the scherzo of the Seventh with the exception of that of the second trio, which has already been repeated. Of all Beethoven's trios, the one in the Seventh has been the subject of the most frequent and heated debates. The *assai meno presto* in this movement is marked $\mathca{J}. = 84$. Weingartner advocates a time about doubly as slow as that of the *scherzo* ($\mathca{J}. = 60$), fearing that otherwise the trio would "resemble a galop rather than the joyous and yet deeply-moving song which is here intended." What he does not mention is that the trio melody bears great resemblance to an old German wayfarer's song. Beethoven may have quoted this tune as he did other folk songs in various scores, assuming that the conductor would recognize the melody and play it accordingly in slower time, without specific instructions to do so. When Toscanini, the great living symbol of objective interpretation, last played the Seventh in Austria (where every other citizen is a self-appointed Beethoven expert), he caused great lamentation and excitement with his unerring fidelity to the original tempo markings.

RIGAUDON AND BOURRÉE

Among the old forms, the *rigaudon* and *bourrée* are another pair of dances still resembling each other today in their larger characteristics. However, more definite distinctions have been discovered than in the case of the *passacaglia-chaconne* parallel. "The *rigaudon* is of all the dances the most flimsy and shallow," asserts Mattheson. Naturally, the sailors whom he saw enjoying the *rigaudon* in the dance-halls of Hamburg would not like anything more sophisticated for their entertainment. Structurally, Mattheson considers the *rigaudon* a compound of the gavotte and the four-part *bourrée*. Such an admixture was often used by the Italians in the closing choruses of dramatic works. Quantz characterizes the *rigaudon* and *bourrée* as merry, sprightly dances performed with short and light bowing. His tempo is M.M. $\downarrow$ = 160. Like Mattheson, Quantz sees an analogy in character between the *rigaudon* and the gavotte, but the tempo of the gavotte is slightly slower (being given as M.M. $\downarrow$ = 120–132).

The *bourrée*, according to Rousseau, originated in the Auvergne. In its early rustic surroundings, it was performed to the accompaniment of bagpipes, in triple time, starting on the upbeat. The change from three-eight to four-eight was accomplished, for the most part, in the eighteenth century. In certain parts of the Languedoc, all dances in four-eight were called *bourrées*, and in other parts *rigaudons;* thus these terms became collective names for folk dances in southeastern France.

With the arrival of the *bourrée* at court and in the opera, the expression changed to what Mattheson in his *Perfect Conduc-*

tor calls "content and pleasant." It was cultivated in the French overture, and in old operas from Lully to Rameau and even later. The position of the *bourrée* in the suite is next to the last (between saraband and *gigue*). Bach writes his *bourrées* with two eighth-note up-beats, or with a quarter-note up-beat. However, the best-known example—that from the *Partita* in B Minor for violin alone—is frequently heard with a resolute expression, no hint of which is contained in the source material.

GIGUE

The *gigue* migrated from Elizabethan England to the neighboring royal court in Paris. Here it functioned as a contrast to the stately, ceremonial minuet of Louis XIV. Shakespeare's description in *Much Ado about Nothing* (Act II, scene 1), "hot and hasty, like a Scotch jig, and full as fantastical," leaves little unsaid about its quick and fiery character.

The eighteenth-century *gigues* confronting the interpreter of the present day are written with an overabundance of time signatures: three-eight, six-eight, also three-four and six-four. However, the majority of examples already show double rhythm; many are still hot and hasty. Because of these qualities, the *gigue* is used for the brisk and cheerful finale of the baroque suite. This "happy ending" function should be stressed in any performance of this type, as in the completion of the suites or *partitas* by Corelli, Bach, and Handel.

Since everything that Bach touched became contrapuntal, so, too, the *gigue* shows the marks of his polyphonic thinking. The movement being divided into two parts, he (and others) usually used the inversion of the theme for the construction of the second part. Both sections should be repeated in performance. It is clear that the tempo must not be excessively fast, since the fugal touch, which Bach employed so often in the *gigue*, must always be pronounced. Quantz's tempo is rapid —six-eight, M.M. ♩. = 80 (♩ = 160). "If the *gigue* is in six-eight," he says, "every measure is equivalent to one pulsation. The bowing is short and light." A comparison is made between the *gigue* and the *canarie*, both of which have the same tempo. According to Quantz, the *canarie* always consists of dotted notes and must be played with a short and sharp bowing, in contrast to the light bowing of the *gigue*.

ALLEMANDE

The *allemande* is sometimes said to be a token of the eternal struggle between France and Germany. Allegedly, after Louis XIV seized Alsace, this dance found its way to Paris. With the French antipathy toward Germany has always gone a secret admiration for German music. Thus, the rise of the *allemande* to immense popularity within a short time is not surprising, especially since the German connotation and likewise the original features were soon obscured and only the name remained. The German character of the dance is revealed by Mattheson when he calls it a serious dance of meticulous workmanship. It precedes the courante, which in turn is followed by the saraband and the *gigue*. This becomes the established sequence of dance types as reassembled in the suite. The up-beat of an eighth or a sixteenth in the *allemande* which is typical in the baroque examples, was apparently, about 1700, a *conditio sine qua non*. What in 1600 was a real dance of simple character and folk-tune rhythm, gradually developed into an idealized type.

Another *allemande*, which has nothing to do with the type just described, is a south-German form derived from the *deutscher Tanz*. This type is in three-four, resembling a waltz, but on the faster side, in contrast to the slower Austrian

Ländler. Related instances are found in the works of the Classicists, such as that designated *alla tedesca* ("in German style") in Haydn's Trio in E-flat Major.

THE WALTZ

There are a number of different accounts as to where and how the waltz may have originated before the last third of the eighteenth century. As early as 1670, we have a tune that is undeniably *Ländler*-like in character—*Ach du lieber Augustin*. People sang its refrain immortalizing an actual merry drunkard of a wandering Austrian musician, who, imbibing barrels of liquor, even acquired an immunity to the pestilence ravaging Vienna, and was saved from death in spite of his lying in one grave with others who had succumbed to the disease. Such a miraculous escape, of course, the Viennese attributed not only to the power of their wine, but also to their waltz. In *Ach du lieber Augustin*, and in all the tunes that followed later, the fundamentals of the Viennese dance are already clear: the very rhythmical three-four time, the bass note accentuated on the first beat, the two other quarters being somewhat limping and uneven.

One hundred years lie between *Ach du lieber Augustin* and another historic tune, which we may hear today in Mozart's opera *Don Giovanni*. It occurs in that delightful scene where a little band plays dinner music for the last meal of the demonic seducer. While Leporello, his valet, waits on him, they both try to identify the tunes that are being played in what appears as probably the earliest instance of a musical quiz in an opera. They recognize the music rather quickly. One tune is from *Figaro*, whereby Mozart humorously quotes himself. The other is a melody from Vicente Martín y Soler's opera *Una cosa rara*, performed in Vienna in 1776. It is a little waltz danced in the second act by the four leading characters, and was a sensational success, becoming one of the most popular hits of the time. Some historians consider it the model of the later waltz. It was in three-four taken in rather moderate tempo, being marked by the composer *andante con moto*.

In 1787, Mozart wrote from Prague:

> At six o'clock I went with the Count Canal to the so-called *Breiten,* a rustic ball, at which the beauties of Prague assembled. . . . I saw with wholehearted pleasure how these people jumped around with such sincere enjoyment to the music of my *Figaro,* which had been turned into all kinds of *contres* and *Teutsche.*

Mozart's tolerant enjoyment of the folk dance in Prague corroborates the idea that classical music was made to fit popular dance entertainment, just as popular dances were utilized in classical music. The *Teutsche* is another example of the interrelationship between high art and popular music. Herein lies a clue for the interpretation of the "German" dances and the *contredanses.* They must retain the genuine vigor and the rhythmic appeal of dance and folklore. In all these cases (whether it is the seventeenth-century *Ach du lieber Augustin* or the eighteenth-century *Cosa rara*), there are present the same constituents that make up the nineteenth-century waltz. All the tunes are eight-measure periods and minor subdivisions of phrases consisting of four bars, which again often fall into small two-bar motifs. The latter, as we can see, are the core around which the Vienna waltz is built, as in the case of *The Beautiful Blue Danube.*

However, the immediate predecessor of the waltz is the Austrian *Ländler,* an old peasant dance, which derived its name from the quaint and picturesque countryside on the western frontier of Lower Austria, called *Ländel.* It was danced in the *gemütlich* style of the old Austrians. When the *Ländler* occurs on the opera stage, as in Weber's *Freischütz*, it is appropriately danced and played in a stolid, good-humored, simple country fashion. The tempo is a very moderate one, never in whole bars, and with well-accented quarters. Indisputably it is in Schubert's *Deutsche Tänze* that there is a great similarity to the *Ländler*. In both cases, the tempo is the moderate triple beat. The melody, just as that of the *Ländler*, is related to Alpine folklore, to the tunes that are at home in the mountainous regions of the Austrian provinces of Tyrol and Styria. Even elements of the *Jodler* that we hear in the rock-perched cabins found their way into these dances, appearing as broken up-beats. We shall meet them again in the waltz of Johann Strauss.

Since Schubert's dances were inspired by the Austrian *Ländler* type, they must be given a rendition full of popular spirit and pointed rhythm, yet without any sharpness. There should be a distinct accent on the first beat and an emphasis upon the bass note. The same is true of all the music entitled "German dances" by Beethoven and Mozart. In Schubert's Opus 9, No. 16, there are two introductory bars of bass solo, probably the first appearance of this form. Today, such a start before the tune begins has become such a commonplace that any child would recognize a waltz by the opening "oom-ta-ta, oom-ta-ta" rhythm.

VIENNA TRADITION

In the era following the close of the classical period, Vienna's contributing role shifts to the genre of light and popular music. Two names appear and eventually encompass all of Europe with their tunes in triple time—those of Lanner and the elder Strauss. Historically, however, their work is but preparatory for the culminating development of the Vienna waltz in the hands of Johann Strauss the second. We have only to look at the titles of certain of the first Strauss and Lanner compositions to detect the historical tie-up: Lanner's Opus 1 bears the name *Viennese Ländler,* and his Opus 7 is called, like Weber's famous score, *Invitation to the Dance.* And this latter title is also that of Strauss's initial composition, *Aufforderung zum Tanz.*

Stylistically, all these works, regardless of their titles, are the same: here *Ländler* and waltz are identical. And often several dances are joined in a series with an introduction and coda, a form that Beethoven used in his *Ländlerische Tänze* and that for Johann Strauss the younger became the rule. However, soon a faster version of the *Ländler* emerged. And so the tempo of the reading depends on whether we play the very moderate *gemütlich* type consisting of three rather even quarters, ♩♩♩ | ♩♩♩ , danced in the old Vienna Biedermeier salon, or a more spirited form, ♫♩♫ | ♩♩♩ or ♩♩ | ♩♩ , the *Geschwindwalzer,* which, as the name indicates, was taken in a faster tempo than the first type. In either case, the chief characteristic of performance is the overemphasis of the first beat at the expense of the second. The third beat, the up-beat, is slightly retarded at the opening of the periods.

In spite of these fundamental facts surrounding the waltz, a veritable chaos exists today in the reading of it. Performances run wild, from one extreme to the other: anything can be heard, from slavish adherence to the letter, to the most grotesque vulgarizations of the refined old waltz. What is the reason for this bedlam? The Strauss score offers the interpreter, as in many other historic cases we have surveyed, only an approximation of the music. If there is need anywhere to speak of "music behind the notes," it is here. Caution and skepticism toward the danger of so-called tradition, as we urged it in previous instances, must in this case be converted into the reverse: namely, into search for true tradition. For in the Strauss score alone, not even the best interpreter could discover the rules of the game without familiarity with the tradition. Those irresistible, ear-catching tricks and the typical Viennese rubato are embodied in the unwritten tradition and not in the score script.

One principal feature unmistakably emerges from the Vienna performance: the true Strauss nuance has its definite function. Strauss played his rubato only at certain places, such as transitional points, where the rhythm or the key changes, or where the form is subdivided. In contrast to the more naïve forerunner, the *Ländler*, the Strauss waltz displays formal extension of the older waltz pattern. The periods are now stretched, different phrases are frequently bound together by welding the end of the preceding phrase to the beginning of the following. In such cases, the interpretation must closely follow the composer's design; that is to say, if metrical concentration is employed for greater rhythmic tension, it is superfluous for the performer to add his own rubato to what Strauss has already provided in his composition. Thus it goes without saying that the premise for a correct reading, in addition to a knowledge of tradition, must be a thorough understanding of the structure of the score. Herein the task of the waltz interpreter is not different from that of the Beethoven conductor.

Johann Strauss enriched the dance, introducing high standards of nineteenth-century performance into the ballroom of his era. Unique blending of tunes of the countryside with classical patterns, the technique of obscure introduction of the main themes coming as from behind a veil, are elements of a highly romantic conception showing how much the Waltz King was a man of progressive ambitions. Guido Adler has traced a number of such Strauss features to Bayreuth. And Wagner called Johann Strauss "the most musical brain of the century." Brahms, the unsurpassable formalist, defied doctor's orders and left his sick-bed to enjoy once more the playing of Strauss waltzes. "Unfortunately not by Johannes Brahms," he wrote underneath the theme of *The Beautiful Blue Danube*. If for no other reason than because of such supreme judgment, the interpreter of the "light" Strauss music must take his task very seriously. His performance must reflect the high ambitions of Strauss and also his admirable insight into how far the waltz could develop without leaving popular ground. It is with this in mind that the conductor may transpose the waltz suite of the ballroom into the sphere of absolute music.

AFFEKTENLEHRE

Musicological research into eighteenth-century theories of interpretation reveals a convincing correlation of facts. The material, naturally, is richer than that of the preceding centuries, the sources most competent, some of them coming to us from the pens of writers who were important composers as well. Various theories, concurring upon the fundamental approach to interpretation, center around the so-called *Affektenlehre*, the "doctrine of affections" (the German term *Affekt* is synonymous with "emotion," in the broader sense of the word).

This doctrine developed gradually into a musical aestheticism with far-reaching practical consequences—in fact, into a complete system of interpretation. Historically, the eighteenth century marks the culmination rather than the inception of this theory. As an aesthetic discipline of musical performance, the roots of the *Affektenlehre* were already imbedded in the antique Greek *ethos*. It occurred also in medieval music and served to guide performance in the Renaissance. All these preliminary thoughts and trends were finally resolved into the eighteenth-century doctrine, the influence of which continues to operate even today. Modern renditions of eighteenth-century music, aspiring to recall the spirit of that old time, cannot ignore substantially the ramifications of the *Affekten-lehre*. Today it must be remembered that its laws controlled the old interpretation and that every eighteenth-century performer was expected to obey its rules.

Reviewing first the general statements of various authorities, we learn that the musical expression of human emotions emerges as the final goal of interpretation. Philipp Emanuel Bach, whose theories are impressively supported by his compositions, explains: "Interpretation is nothing else but the capacity to make musical thoughts clear—according to their true content and affection—whether one sings or plays." And Quantz has this to say: "Musical interpretation can be compared with the interpretation of an orator. Orator and musician have in common the intention of mastering the hearts, of exciting or calming down the passions, of putting the listener now in this, now in that affection."

EMOTIONS: THE AIM OF PERFORMANCE

Prior to Quantz, J. D. Heinichen, in his treatise, *The Figured Bass in Composition* (1728), contends that "the purpose of music is to move the affections." Mattheson informs us, in his *Kern melodischer Wissenschaft*: "The true aim of melodies is nothing but such entertainment of the ear as to stir the emotions." And Meinrad Spies asserts in his *Affectus*: "To prove affections in human beings is the only goal of music."

We see that they all convey essentially the same idea: the purpose of the musical performance is to express the passions, to provoke affections, emotions. In the phraseology of the theorists, the music is either sad or lively, serious or tender, wild or gentle, indifferent or sensitive. It gives a picture of despair, comfort, peace, pleasure, joy, coldness, impatience. Reflecting, as they do, human nature and its psychic strata, the affections cannot occur as isolated emotions. They may intermingle and cross one another—like counterpoints, move into contrasting positions. No sooner has the musician done justice to one affection—to follow Philipp Emanuel's train of thought—than he provokes another: emotions are interchangeable. Unequivocally, Quantz demands that the performer recognize the affections expressed in a piece, always keeping his rendition in conformity with them. Thus, only interpretations based on an appropriate scrutiny of the affections, and their suitable musical application, are sanctioned.

The modern performer may wonder what guideposts his eighteenth-century colleague could watch in order to recognize properly the divers affections. How could he discover them in the various phases of performance, such as tempo, dynamics, and phrasing? Quantz considers first the intention and place of the performance—whether it is for a church service, for the theater, or chamber music; whether the occasion is festive or solemn, wedding or requiem. Every species has its definite laws of performance. Hence, the interpreter is told that church music demands more splendor and seriousness than that of the theater. It is more than evident that the ecclesiastical spirit calls for a more moderate characterization than the opera. Yet the problem is not as simple in practice as it sounds in theory. After all, we have been observing some cases in the history of interpretation where heaven and earth have, in musical performance at least, come very close to each other. Quantz knows that and discriminates: "If the ecclesiastical score contains fresh and bizarre thoughts—allegro and presto motifs—then they must be carefully disguised, must be tamed and made gentler." In a more general application, Quantz's instruction involves important consequences. For instance, it implies that the merry affections in the jubilant choruses of Bach's sacred cantatas should be differentiated in performance from similar exuberant movements in his secular music. According to this theory, even the ordinary allegro must be performed at a moderate speed in church—any suggestion of worldliness in tempo being banned from the sacred service.

As one would expect, the whole picture changes in the theater. On the stage the interpreter has virtually every freedom in tempo and expression. Quantz, with typical realism, goes to the extreme of encouraging singers to perform their intermezzi, during the *opera seria*, in a low and very vulgar *modus*. Since the musical thoughts associated with the intermezzi are commonplace, their execution must be drastic—neither gallant nor ornamental. Likewise in ballets, adjustment to the affections is necessary. The accompanist must pay attention to the individual temperament of the performers, to their movements and gestures. Never must the music be behind or ahead; it must be synchronized with the dance pattern. We see that even this early time supplies a precept that would settle the eternal conflict between dancers and their accompanists, with a direction to interpret in favor of the dancers. Heinichen gives examples showing the interrelation between these affections and the dances—for instance, in a "languishing *siciliano*." Sighing love is expressed in a sobbing C minor movement, and coquetry in a lovely three-eight beat with flattering *flauti unisoni*.

MAJOR AND MINOR

The determination of the true affections in instrumental pieces can come only from the examination of the texture and special directions, if any, of the score script. Primarily, one must pay attention to the keys. According to Quantz and others, the major key is an expression of the gay, the fresh, the serious, the profound; the minor, of the sad, the gentle, and the flattering. Keys are individually characterized: A minor, C minor, D-sharp minor, F minor, are especially for sad effects; others, major or minor, are for pleasant expression. Yet exceptions are possible. Mattheson follows such a specification of keys wholeheartedly: D minor is for quiet, agreeable, contented moods; G minor mixes seriousness with loveliness; F major expresses the world's most beautiful sentiments; D major may reflect sharp and stubborn but also delicate feeling if, for instance, softly playing trumpets and flutes are predominant; E major is for sad or desperate, suffering, penetrating effects.

Since, as is indicated by these examples, the performer cannot rely on the key alone, he must be carefully observant of intervals and phrasing. Close intervals that are slurred connote the flattering, sad, or gentle. Thus, a close relationship of affections, articulation, and keys becomes apparent. One helps another in determining the affection. *Staccatissimo* depicts a gay and audacious spirit. Philipp Emanuel Bach confirms the intention of gentleness in the adagio as expressed by slurs, and of vivaciousness as conveyed by staccato. Further characteristics by which to recognize the affections are provided by the dissonances. Quantz believes that consonances satisfy the soul, whereas dissonances excite unrest and anger. They are called the most important means of expressing affections, because without mixing beautiful sound with the ugly, there would be no musical method for provoking and satisfying the different emotions of the listener.

TIME SIGNATURES

Indications for determining the correct time are likewise furnished by the score script itself. Time signatures and notation automatically provide the necessary information for the tempo. That is to say, signs such as $\frac{2}{2}$, $\frac{3}{4}$, not only indicate the rhythmic disposition of the notes, but simultaneously are definite tempo connotations. Rousseau, Scheibe, and Mattheson concur in the opinion that each time signature has a fully developed character of its own. Mattheson has a special flair for six-eight; he calls it the "most beautiful measure in modern composition" (which recalls his similar attitude toward the key of F major).

The *Affektenlehre* developed a whole discipline for the purpose of achieving tempo diagnosis by external means. However, such determining of the tempo from notation was not new, and had been recognized before the eighteenth century. The main affection, according to Quantz, is to be found in such directions as *allegro, allegro non tanto, allegro assai, allegro di molto, allegro moderato, presto, allegretto, andante, andantino*. Each of these tempo indications demands a different interpretation. Each piece expresses different blendings—pathetic, flattering, gay, pompous, jocose affections so that, under changing conditions, the interpreter must constantly put himself into different moods.

Other theorists, like Petri or Marpurg, point to additional directions that, during the course of a composition, indicate change of affection: *doloroso, mesto, languido, lagrimoso, lugubre, pomposo, maestoso, affettuoso, amoroso, scherzando*. Such instructions are the surest signs of the underlying affection. Since the tempo must always reflect the emotional background, proper recognition also of the changing affection is the only dependable guide. As no passion completely equals another, the tempo cannot be precisely the same at all stages. It must be modified, slowing down for sad affections, and accelerating with energetic, happy motifs. Quantz considers an absolutely even tempo nonsensical. Leopold Mozart says: "Each tempo, slow or gay, has its gradations." D. G. Türk, in his *Clavierschule* ("Piano School"), published in 1789, devotes special attention to tempo modifications. In pieces expressing anger, fury, violence, Türk suggests, one may accelerate the most powerful parts and also the more agitated parts between those of gentle sentiment. Vice versa, parts toward the end of a piece marked *diminuendo, diluendo, smorzando*, may be played with hesitations. The introductions to main movements may also be retarded. Türk used diagrams to indicate these accelerations and retardations of the tempo; so did G. F. Wolf (in his basic work, *Instruction in Piano Playing*, 1784), putting the tempo rubato signs above or below the notes.

THE INTERPRETER'S EMOTIONS INDISPENSABLE

Taking into consideration the principles illustrated in all these examples of tempo, key, and harmony, we realize how the emotional capacity to reproduce all affections became the basic prerequisite in the musical interpreter. As Lohlein in his *Supervision in Violin Playing*, Sulzer in his *General Theory*, and others have concluded, it is only when the performer fully experiences the composer's feeling, that he is capable of arousing the corresponding emotion in those who listen to his performance.

A characteristic explanation, quoted from Junker's *Funda-*

mentals of Conducting, shows how the *Affektenlehre* actually functioned as interpretative practice. The example concerns the final chorus of Graun's *Death of Christ*. The composer had marked the parts accompanying the chorus, "Here we sinners lie grieving," to be played staccato. Junker proffers his assistance to the performer by informing him that these staccato pulsations must not be played precisely: they symbolize the heartbeats of the sinners stirred by emotion at the death of Christ. And those heavy hearts certainly did not beat with even pulsations. On the other hand, if the same staccato were written in the score of an opera, to illustrate the anguish of a condemned slave, it would have to be played strictly in time. The modern musician, reading about such a naïve and external interpretation, may smile at this blanket explanation of religious and theatrical staccato. (After all, it is likely that the poor slave's heart was pounding irregularly too!) Yet, the Junker-Graun example illustrates the interpretative routine of a whole epoch and, as it is a representative case, we must accept it at its face value.

It cannot be denied, however, that, on the long way from eighteenth-century ideology to certain types of modern interpretation, much harm has also come from banal attempts to use and develop the *Affektenlehre* indiscriminately. Many grotesque exaggerations of its features have occurred lately, producing a modern caricature of the old theory and playing into the hands of dilettante interpreters.

THE MANNHEIM SCHOOL

Capital cities in musical and political geography are quite different things. There are places of first importance in musical history that one would naturally not discover on an ordinary map. We have only to think of Cöthen and Esterház and the lasting fame those townships acquired through the activities of Bach and Haydn. In the eighteenth century, it was not London, Paris, Vienna, or Berlin that enjoyed the prestige of fostering the outstanding European orchestra, but the small city of Mannheim, in southwestern Germany, then under the jurisdiction of the Elector Palatine Karl Theodor.

In order to verify Mannheim's claim of having sponsored the most distinguished orchestral ensemble of the time, one has but to read some of the truly panegyrical descriptions by contemporary critics. We learn of a forte like thunder, a crescendo like a cataract, a diminuendo as gentle as a crystal brook rippling from afar, and piano that recalled the soft breath of early spring. "Nowhere in performance," we are assured by C. F. Schubart, author of the contemporary *Ideas toward an Aesthetic of Music*, "were light and shade better marked. Nowhere were the half and whole tints of the orchestral palette more clearly expressed." The extraordinary interpretations of the Mannheim orchestra were also recognized by Dr. Charles Burney, who, having made extended tours through Europe, described them in a scholarly report, *The Present State of Music in Germany*, calling the orchestra the best on the Continent, and characterizing its crescendo and diminuendo, piano and forte, as new colors—the colors in music having their shades as colors like red or blue have them in painting.

CONSERVATIVE AND PROGRESSIVE DYNAMICS

The parallel with painting is taken up by J. F. Reichardt:

> I must not speak of the masterly effects produced in the Mannheim orchestra by the swelling and diminution of a long note, or of several successive notes, which gives, if I may so

speak, to the whole coloring a darker or a lighter shade. This would be considered too great an innovation by Hasse and Graun.

This last statement (coming as it did from the Berlin *Kapell-meister*, who was himself a performer of authority and experience) indicates how the rival camps of interpreters were divided: Graun and Hasse were the exponents of the conservative school, decrying the dynamic innovations, while the Mannheim conductors, Stamitz and Cannabich, figured as champions of progress. Reichardt's statement rightfully gives credit to Niccolò Jommelli for the new device of dynamics. He recounts in particular how, the first time Jommelli made use of the crescendo, "the audience gradually rose from their seats. It was not until the following diminuendo that they realized they had almost ceased breathing."

From the enthusiastic statements by Schubart, Burney, Reichardt, and others, dynamics emerges as the most characteristic feature of the Mannheim performance, and, within this, the crescendo and decrescendo technique in particular. It is obviously because of these accounts that historians like Abert attribute the inception of the crescendo-decrescendo technique to Mannheim, while, in reality, it came into being much earlier. Its vocal counterpart is mentioned in a textbook of singing, *Rudimenta musices,* published in 1686, in which the author, Wolfgang Mylius, cautions the pupil: "You must not fall from forte to piano, but gradually let the voice crescendo and decrescendo." Hence, transitional crescendo was already known in the seventeenth century—other sources confirming it as a familiar feature of dynamics, as common as the echo principle, and accorded the same recognition. In 1752, Quantz explained how to perform the alternation of piano and forte with good judgment: in order to avoid violence in the transition from one dynamic extreme to the other, such changes should be made crescendo and decrescendo.

CRESCENDO IN ITALY AND GERMANY

At the beginning of the eighteenth century, crescendo and decrescendo were an Italian specialty, just as, at the century's end, they gave distinction to the Mannheim style. Scipione Maffei, in 1711, describes the manner of using crescendo in orchestral concerts at Rome. It was there that Niccolò Jommelli, the opera composer (called "the Italian Gluck") heard and admired the crescendo technique. When Jommelli was appointed court conductor in Württemberg, he imported the new device in dynamics from the south, and developed it into the most distinguishing characteristic of his orchestral performances. This is corroborated by Burney's remark that Jommelli caused a revolution of taste in Germany.

From Stuttgart to Mannheim was no great distance for a new musical device to travel, even in those days of the coach-and-four. Anticipating the interpretations of Stamitz and Cannabich by some years, Jommelli had displayed the misnamed "Mannheim device" in performances of his own operas: he had employed *crescendo il forte* in the score of his *Eumene*, and his playing ultimately developed a fine blending of contemporary German and Italian traits. However, for such eclecticism his compatriots had little appreciation. When Jommelli returned to his Neapolitan home, he was rejected as *troppo tedesco* ("too German").

Schubart acknowledged Jommelli's priority and realized that this great inaugurator was the first to indicate the musical coloring in the score. Of this he wrote:

Jommelli has gone so far as even to mark the finest shading for the player. It appears to me that musical shading is a recent innovation. About fifty or sixty years ago, the Italians wrote it for the first time below their compositions; previously, all pieces of music had been executed at the same intensity of tone, or left to the discretion of the player.

From this it becomes evident that the performer, before Jommelli and Mannheim, used his own discretion and judgment as to shading, in order to avoid a constant intensity of tone. The absence of specific directions up to that time is obvious. However, beginning with Jommelli, the choice of modulation to piano or forte, crescendo or decrescendo, no longer resided in the will of the performer, but had to be sought in the instructions of the composer himself. Thus, the historical fact emerges that, in relation to dynamics, the great change from improvisation to binding script occurred in Stuttgart and Mannheim, through the efforts of Jommelli, Stamitz, and Cannabich.

Even without benefit of a single document, we would realize today that all the unheard-of tricks of the Mannheim orchestral rendition could not have been the result of improvisation in performance. The Mannheim playing was, on the contrary, the consequence of careful rehearsal and elaboration of definite indications in the score script. Yet, notwithstanding the helpful new dynamic symbols which so aroused Schubart's astonishment, it is obvious that only excellent players could have performed with such brilliancy. We are told that Stamitz, and after him Cannabich, developed the Mannheimers into orchestras in which "were more soloists and composers than in any other in Europe." This reads like a present-day statement about one of our leading American orchestras. But it held true then as it does now, that superlative playing cannot be achieved solely by means of technical proficiency and knowledge of the instrument. It requires also that the performers be expert musicians, with a capacity for identifying themselves with the essence of the interpretation in the true spirit of the composer. However, in old Mannheim—just as today—one had to take the bitter with the sweet, for Junker asserts: "Even mediocre pieces may enchant through their rendition"—which is all too readily applicable to certain performances by prominent orchestras of our time.

JOMMELLI AND STAMITZ

The Jommelli-Mannheim dynamic scale, assuring a brilliant effect of light and shade by means of binding instructions, must be considered complete even if judged by our modern standards. It seems that decrescendo, the anticlimax, came into general use somewhat later than crescendo.

A rather difficult question arises as to the relationship of the Jommelli-Mannheim effects to other renditions of eighteenth-century music. Handel paid more attention to dynamic elaboration than Bach, who in turn cared more for phrasing than Handel. Schweitzer explains that the essential feature of the Bach performance is not shading but accentuation. He demands, for Bach, architectural dynamics in great plans, instead of the emotional dynamics employed since the end of the eighteenth century. He accuses certain interpreters of doing their best to make Bach unintelligible, "by confusing the great and small dynamic nuances into one."

Any performer scrupulously following the baroque script, with its paucity of hints as to shading, is obliged to do without the crescendo-decrescendo device. On the other hand, those who date this crescendo technique from Stamitz and Mannheim neglect the tone-poetic expression of the music of the

Renaissance, and that of the eighteenth century based on the theory of the affections. The difference between the earlier interpretations and those of Mannheim, as Rosamond Harding, G. Schünemann, and others show, is that an already recognized type of dynamic performance achieved a new tone-poetic effect and finally became a specialty, celebrated through the splendor of the Mannheim orchestral renditions. Beginning in the fifties (the decade that brought the life-work of Bach and Handel to an end), an already habitual form of expression acquired new meaning and emphasis. While the Jommelli device came from Italy to Germany, there is documentary proof that crescendo-decrescendo methods were likewise well known in France after 1750.

Everywhere in Europe, from about 1770, interpreters were enabled to work from the script and to adhere more objectively to the composer's intention. However, the performer must remember that the so-called Mannheim effects of Stamitz and his school concerned the dynamics, without necessarily involving simultaneous variation in tempo. This is mentioned because of the typical feature, in many modern readings of eighteenth-century music, of associating accelerando with crescendo, and ritardando with diminuendo. There is, of course, no indication for such a procedure in old scores or in the documents that corroborate them. The opposite might easily have been intended: in order to produce a broader tone, the volume was to be increased without any hastening in the case of crescendo, and decreased without any retarding for diminuendo. However, fusing definite features of tempo and dynamics—such as the habitual slowing down during a *morendo*—is doubtless a typical nineteenth-century practice.

From the many new portals of expression opened by the Mannheim school, the Classicists, as regards not only dynamics but also other concomitant devices (particularly of form and instrumentation), took the Mannheim road to further progress. Recognizing this influence, Burney showed himself to be a man of remarkable foresight when he wrote the observation following:

> It has long seemed to me as if the variety, taste, spirit, and new effects produced by contrast and the use of crescendo and diminuendo in these [Mannheim] symphonies, had been of more service to instrumental music in a few years than all the dull and servile imitations in the styles of Corelli, Geminiani, and Handel, had been in half a century.

PART TWO

CLASSICISM: THE SCRIPT BECOMES BINDING

IV. Phrasing and Dynamics

IMPROVISATION DISAPPEARS

WITH THE classical period as a turning point, the score script becomes increasingly binding. The relation between score and performance reflects a new interdependence. The written character of the work tends to exclude any license from the performance. What the composer wants is more and more frequently shown in detail. These facts can best be demonstrated by comparison of handwritten manuscripts of the masters.

MANUSCRIPTS OF HAYDN AND BEETHOVEN

We see how, in his *Oxford Symphony* (cf. picture facing p. 225), Haydn marks his wishes regarding tempo, phrasing, and tonal quality. Thus, the player of the first violin part knows which tones Haydn wanted slurred and which ones he wanted separated. The tempo is indicated (adagio) and the dynamic marks are not written as vague generalities, but individual signs are given for the respective instruments.

Similar observations can be made in any other of Haydn's works, no matter whether we refer to solo or chamber music, to an oratorio, or to an orchestral score. In Haydn's Symphony in D Major (*The Clock*), those who play the instruments in the "ticktock" accompaniment—from which the symphony derived its name—the bassoonists, second violinists, cellists, and double-bass players, are clearly instructed to play piano and staccato. Compared with the scores of the preceding period, the register of the composer's instructions is ample enough to insure a loyal performance. This increase in the number of signs is part of the method by which the classical composer communicated with his interpreter through the medium of notation.

If we examine, in addition to the works of Haydn, scripts by Mozart, Beethoven, or Schubert, we shall readily find out what their graphic pictures have in common. We shall see likewise in what ways they contrast with the scores of previous periods. The initial page of the *andante con moto* in Beethoven's *Sonata Appassionata* displays further markings, as for crescendo and decrescendo $<$ $>$. The Mannheim devices are written out in words: in the first measure, *piano dolce,* and later, *rinforzando.* This manuscript is a characteristic example of Beethoven's method of writing and correcting his scores— of replacing one part by pasting over another—and his complete disregard for external neatness. (Cf. facsimiles, facing pages 209, 224, and 225.)

If the reader turns to the manuscript of Schubert's *Wandrer's Nachtlied,* he again sees, as in the case of the Haydn, Mozart, and Beethoven manuscripts, how the initial tempo, tone volume, and articulation are prescribed by the composer's own hand. There is a minimum of such markings in certain baroque scores. We seldom find even a hint as to the principal tempo or intensity of tone. Bach, in *The Well-tempered Clavichord,* or in *The Art of the Fugue,* leaves everything to the performer's imagination. To be sure, it cannot be said that all preclassical scores entirely neglected such signs. There are sporadic instances of their existence even in times preceding

Bach. However, it was not until the script became binding that a profusion of symbols became a practical necessity.

END OF FIGURED BASS

The comparison of the classical score with its predecessor reveals a further departure: the *basso continuo* has vanished from the script. In the orchestral and vocal scores of preclassical times, we see the figured bass part as an inevitable characteristic of concerted rendition. Thus, the keyboard part was executed ad libitum, interpreted in an improvisatory way. But improvisation, as the art of making music extemporaneously, ceases to be a factor in classical interpretation. The figured bass is relegated to oratorio and church music (and occasionally, even there, we look in vain for the organ part of some of the classical Masses).

The classical manuscript emerges as an entity well defined in every part, whether written for vocal or for instrumental, for secular or religious performance. The classical score becomes a masterpiece of elaboration hitherto unknown in music. And the new attitude of the composer toward his interpreter, as symbolized in the manuscript, may be summarized in a dual formula: (1) the binding script, (2) the disappearance of the figured bass.

If interpretation as a subjective art could not become fully entrenched in music prior to the Renaissance and the awakening of individualized expression, then objective interpretation found its logical inception in the classical score. It is only since the latter part of the eighteenth century that sufficient clues have been made available, by the new classical script, to provide all the information necessary for a performance of work-fidelity. Of course, objectivity is an interpretative ideal that may be applied by modern performers to the baroque masterworks as well, in spite of their lack of instructions. And the classical score, notwithstanding its more detailed directions, still remains open to either the subjective or objective approach. However, our examples demonstrate how the elementary requisites for this objective type of performance become increasingly available around 1800, when more and finer lines on the canvas complete the picture projected by the classical score. These lines, in musical terminology, are the symbols of phrasing, dynamics, and tempo. In the following sections we shall take up their evolution and application.

BACKGROUND OF PHRASING

The minuet of Haydn's symphony *The Clock*, like its tick-tock movement (which we have discussed above), is carefully marked in details. Again, the player sees which notes are to be played staccato, and which ones slurred, while a third group of notes appear undesignated. In Haydn's original manuscript, however, only the second and the sixth measure of the minuet have the indication for a slur over the sixteenths, whereas most editions give the bowing throughout the whole minuet in the corresponding measures.

In such a case the editor in charge furnished the score with those markings which he deemed necessary for the interpretation, in spite of their absence in the original manuscript. Most likely Haydn intended an analogous execution of slurs even in the bars where he nonchalantly omitted them. In other classical manuscripts there are countless examples of the same type: what is taken for granted is not always marked. We must understand that the general tendency of scoring toward a binding script was still a novelty in Haydn's period. Naturally, it took some time for the new devices to penetrate into every feature of the manuscript. Especially the young discipline of phrasing, as we shall see, did not come into full application until the turn of the nineteenth century. It is necessary, however, to investigate its background in order to comprehend the use of phrasing prior to its actual incorporation into the classical script.

Phrasing is a feature common to both speech and music: it serves the same purpose in the language of words as in the language of tones. What may be called articulation in music is equivalent to diction in speech. Thus it is clear that phrasing occurs everywhere: in the tune of the torch singer and in the aria of Caruso; in the speech of the idiot and in that of Shakespeare. While phrasing is universal and ageless, in the sense that it has been exercised since Adam and Eve and the arch-beginnings of musical utterance, the applied discipline of phrasing in the performance of music is young. D. C. Türk, in his *Clavierschule* (1789), feels entitled to boast of priority in the employment of phrasing. We shall see that this is historically an exaggeration. Yet this important source, renowned as a basic work of its period, proves by comparison how little was known or done in a practical way about the factor of musical articulation in the field of teaching. It is in a somewhat humorous manner that Türk introduces his analogy between tone and word language, with the following illustration:

He lost his life not, only his property.

He lost his life, not only his property.

Obviously the wrong punctuation changes the meaning of the sentence to the point of distortion. Türk justifiably concludes that the same danger of wrong punctuation exists in music.

ARTICULATION AND PART ORGANIZATION

Today the term "phrasing" has a dual significance: (*a*) articulation, the diction of music—the distinct, clear execution of tones and motifs, as exemplified in terms like "legato" or "staccato"; (*b*) phrasing proper—the process of demarcation and organization of the structural parts, exemplified in larger bowings as a symbol of tones united in a group.

In order to realize fully that these factors do not cover the same ground, we have only to remember that not infrequently we hear a symphony played with brilliant articulation and yet with incorrect phrasing. In other words, only the technical demands are met, not the aesthetic. The ideal interpretation, however, demands both—correct articulation and correct phrasing.

Discrimination between the two types of signs for phrasing, indicating (*a*) articulation and (*b*) phrasing proper, is the first task of the conscientious performer. This, however, is more easily said than done. As mentioned before, in many scores little was provided to indicate the intended phrasing. It was rather the exception if some hints in this direction were furnished by the composer. Even the great classical masters sometimes were vague in designating their intentions. Haydn and Mozart did not write enough marks for phrasing to insure certainty of rendition. Beethoven, probably in the haste of creative excitement, sometimes promiscuously used bowing marks, which he otherwise employed with more discrimination to designate either legato or motifs joined to larger phrases.

This easily traps the performer: it may lead him to inaccurate phrasing when only articulation is meant. Thus, the interpreter's work must begin with the correct discrimination of these possibly confusing signs of phrasing.

The scarcity of phrasing marks is explained by the history of interpretation. Most of the great composers prior to the nineteenth century supervised their own performances and thus could enforce their wishes personally. In most cases, important instructions were given verbally by the composers to their singers and instrumentalists. Frescobaldi and Byrd were their own performers on the keyboard. Palestrina and Monteverdi, Bach and Handel, Haydn and Mozart supervised not only the renditions of their scores, but likewise all the rehearsals preceding the productions of their works. Last but not least, as a general characteristic of the old performing style, the interpretation of parts was left to the discretion of the players. In other words, the players were expected to render their parts according to their instinct and musical common sense, to phrase correctly without the help of signs and symbols.

BREATHING AND BOWING

While indication of phrasing by signs was the logical result of the trend toward a binding script, it cannot be considered an exclusive achievement of classical score writing. Proof of the existence of phrasing even in medieval performance can be found in documents such as the textbook *De modo bene cantandi*, 1474, written by Conrad von Zabern, who explains where the singer may take a breath. In Zabern's co-ordination of technical and expressive performance, this amounts to what we today call phrasing. Up to the eighteenth century, such prescriptions were usually given in reference to vocal rather than instrumental performance. But there is no reason to suppose that phrasing was not equally well employed in relation to the latter. If the opera director Hasse in Dresden discussed all details of execution with his concertmaster, a consideration of phrasing must have been included in these routine conferences. The concertmaster in turn transmitted the conductor's intentions to the players, a historical procedure which we shall explain in connection with the so-called double direction of this period.

The evolution from a score without prescribed phrasing to one with phrasing indications may be ascribed to Gluck, Jommelli, the Mannheim orchestra, and, of course, the Classicists —all representing the new school of interpretation by which improvisation was not tolerated. Logically, it was after performance was emancipated from cembalo direction, and when the score script became binding, that a permanent change came about. In Sulzer's encyclopedia, *General Theory of the Fine Arts,* the following explanation is provided:

> After the first note of each measure, the other strong beats should be less marked. The first note of a bar within a phrase must not be overaccentuated. Failure to heed this may spoil the whole performance. The caesuras are the commas of the song, which, as in speech, must be made manifest by a moment of relaxation. This is accomplished either by letting the last note of a phrase die away and firmly attacking the following one, or by diminishing the tone somewhat at the end of the phrase and increasing at the beginning of the next.

This account of the means by which correct phrasing was to be accomplished is dated from the year 1774. At that time Haydn and Mozart had already published numerous important works; Beethoven was a child of four. In 1834, Pierre Baillot (with Beethoven's friend Kreutzer, a leading exponent of the French violin school) states in *L'art du violon:*

Slight separations, such as rests of short duration, are not always indicated by the composer. The player must therefore provide them, when he sees that it is necessary, by letting the last note of the phrase die away. Indeed, in certain cases he must even let it end shortly before the completion of its normal duration.

Sixty years separate the precepts of Sulzer and Baillot, supplying a perfect frame for the period of Classicism. Even if we follow the hypothesis that musical theory is habitually behind its day and seldom truly representative of all the contemporary facts, the interval of time between the two documents assures a clear picture of phrasing habits about the year 1800.

Thus it becomes clear why the problem of correct articulation, and especially of bowing, is particularly acute in the modern approach to the instrumental music of the eighteenth century. While the music of the baroque period is much performed today, the bowing instructions in the scores are furnished by the editor, not the composer. Today there are many interpreters who, in a conscientious attempt to be objective, believe that the omission of bowings in the manuscript forces them to make the same omission in their playing. We have been shown, however, that the lack of bowing marks in the script was merely a matter of tradition in old score writing. Monotonous, unphrased execution of the preclassical works proves to have been as unbearable to the listeners of their era as it would be to the modern ear. Philipp Emanuel Bach is our principal witness, when he states that "insight into the character of the piece is necessary. The signs determining whether notes are to be slurred or to be played staccato are often missing." These signs were considered essential and the lack of them deplored. Similar ideas concerning the need of phrasing were expressed not only in eighteenth-century Germany, but also in France and in Italy. It suffices to quote Rousseau's *Dictionnaire de musique* (1775), which contributes the following on the topic "phrase":

> A singer who feels his phrases and their accent is a man of good taste. But one who renders only notes, keys, scales, and intervals, without comprehending the meaning of the phrases —even if he be precise otherwise—is nothing but a "note-gobbler" [*n'est qu'un Croque-sol*].

These sources clearly permit our concluding that phrasing as an indispensable feature of the old performance, and the actual introduction of signs of phrasing into the scripts, are historically two different matters. As the documents prove, centuries before a binding script had incorporated the marks of phrasing as a part of scoring, the practice of phrasing flourished in both vocal and instrumental performance. The modern interpreter must, therefore, not limit himself to the available signs. He must reconstruct the old score according to Bach's above-quoted precept of "insight into the character of music."

DYNAMICS

And God said: Let there be light!
And there was light.—GEN. 1:3

Light! Fortissimo! A C major chord in the most extended position, performed by a four-part chorus and full orchestra, symbolizes forever in music the glorious illumination over chaos. Haydn, in his oratorio *Creation,* found the universal expression for the moment when God created heaven and earth. As the fortissimo of *Creation* symbolizes light, so all dynamics in great music are derived from the natural expression of the human creature—from the way he expresses himself in actual life, in happiness, ecstasy, sadness, or deep mourning. It is this allusion to nature that, in musical expression, turns excite ment, anger, power, into fortissimo, and fear, grief, calm, joy, into pianissimo. Dynamics, in the music of all periods, proves that the musical instinct responds to the aural symbols of life itself.

Thus, the dynamic crescendo correlates with increasing intensity of psychic activity. Rage, enthusiasm, happiness, surprise, provoke noisier demonstrations than tenderness, gentleness, and the subtler degrees of inner experience. The powerful demands the greatest intensity in tone, which, as fortissimo, follows as a musical corollary. The finale of Beethoven's Fifth, the terrible "No!" with which the furies in Gluck's *Orfeo* deny entrance, are well-known illustrations; while the converse, in the use of pianissimo, can readily be shown in examples that made history, ranging from Monteverdi's *Lasciate mi morire* to the whispering *Je t'aime aussi* in Debussy's opera *Pelléas and Mélisande*.

These parallels with primary human and natural manifestations are indispensable for the modern performer's designation of the dynamics in the preclassical scores when all signs are omitted. They are useful also in relation to many classical works if, as in certain cases, only inadequate clues are available. In a manuscript like Schubert's *An die Musik*, the singer must infer the dynamics from the meaning of the words and the general musical setup. As our facsimile shows, only the accompaniment is marked "piano"; the singer's part shows no dynamic instruction. Clues of this kind are invaluable for a more elaborate dynamic expression in the older vocal music.

THE ECHO

Primeval man called loudly to the rocks—forte. Awestruck, he heard the answer—piano. For ages the echo, an elementary contrast of dynamics, has been a playfully used feature in musical performance of all styles.

In the eighteenth century, the forte-piano contrast was still an unwritten law of dynamic execution: all repeated phrases were habitually executed piano. Kretzschmar contends that in the symphony, suite, or sonata, wherever repetition of a motif occurs, either in entirety or in part, the repetition must be played piano as in the echo. The all-important question for the modern interpreter is: How was dynamics generally employed in preclassical times; where, besides in the echo, was piano used, where forte? The negligence of old composers in marking the dynamics has led certain performers to limit the more elaborate use of these devices. On the other hand, some interpreters assume that a variety of dynamic inflections was unquestionably intended by the masters, and therefore feel justified in superimposing dynamic nuances in their readings, for better or for worse. As far as preclassical instrumental music is concerned, the performer must remember that the movements of the suite originated from folk and court dances that have retained dynamic characteristics of their prototypes. Of course, the elaborated echo effect can be traced to the traditional repetition of the old dances. D. G. Türk, in his *Piano School*, expresses the opinion that every repeat of a period should be piano; inversely, if the period is rendered piano the first time, it should be forte in the repetition. Obviously, this contrast of dynamics in repetition lives on in eighteenth-century tradition; however, it is questionable whether the rule can be generally applied after 1800. Yet the tradition is still apparent as late as the middle of the nineteenth century. Czerny states that the *scherzo da capo* should be "played pianissimo, almost without expression." Taking this rather surprising statement at its face value, we learn that the rule most commonly observed was the sudden and complete change from strong forte to weak piano.

Of course, the handling of dynamics in repetition, although

a major factor in old forms, represents only one side of the problem. We are still in need of more broadly applicable rules for our modern performing practice. Some general information is provided by Philipp Emanuel Bach and Leopold Mozart, as well as by Sulzer and the ever reliable Quantz. Philipp Emanuel, in the second part of the *Versuch*, tells us that "in order to do justice to the music, one must constantly make use of the ear, because the necessary marks are not always found in the score." And Leopold Mozart, in his *Violin School*, states: "In performance one must try to find the affections and express them correctly, as the composer meant them to be employed. One must be able to alternate the weak with the strong, even when no instructions are given, and to put them in the right places." From Quantz's *Versuch* we learn that "it is by no means sufficient to observe forte and piano only where written. Every accompanist must know the art of employing these dynamics, even where they are not indicated." Sulzer, in his *General Theory of the Fine Arts*, offers information on this point: "The signs *f* and *p*, signifying the strong and the weak, do not suffice. Often they are supplied only to prevent gross errors. If they were really to be sufficient, it would be necessary to write them below every note."

The substance of all these assertions is that, even without any instruction, the interpreter must be able to alternate forte and piano in the right places, in accordance with the dynamic habits of the time. Bach, Mozart, and Quantz say the same in varying words. Again, all their statements coincide with Sulzer's theory, appearing at a time when Beethoven was already living. To embrace the entire era of Beethoven, we can turn to Czerny again, who, having had the benefit of Beethoven's teaching, says in his *Piano School:* "In old works, where dynamic signs are only occasionally marked, the performance depends on the taste and insight of the interpreter."

Thus we see how slavish adherence to the script in modern interpretations of old music, with its lack of dynamic instruction, is bound to result in misrepresentation to the point of distortion.

THREE CLASSES OF DISSONANCES

Further clues to dynamic distinction are provided by the harmony as such. Philipp Emanuel Bach points out that every tone foreign to the key can very well stand a *forte*, regardless of whether it occurs in dissonance or consonance. This is very convincing: the dissonance had been the enlivening element of all music since the era of medieval counterpoint. Quantz would not fail to be very systematic about these accentuated dissonances. He distinguishes clearly three classes of dissonances, to be played *mezzo forte*, *forte*, and *fortissimo*, respectively. He also explains that the theme of the composition calls for dynamic emphasis. Likewise, all other notes of importance (in a theme, in a contrapuntal passage, or in a harmonic structure) must be stressed by means of dynamics. The notes introducing the theme must be marked; the dissonance must be made stronger than its resolution.

Quantz also discusses the proper execution of a particular sign, often misunderstood in modern execution:

> If a *forte* is written below a long note and a *piano* immediately after, and this without change of the bow, then the note must be played very forcefully, with a little pressing of the bow, but must at once, without unnecessary motion, be decreased and transformed into a *smorzando*.

Quantz's explanation is confirmed, in almost identical words, by Leopold Mozart.

The problems of crescendo and decrescendo performance

have been discussed in the section on the Mannheim school above.

ACOUSTIC CONDITIONS

Scarcely any phase of interpretation is so at the mercy of the general acoustic conditions as is the dynamics. Needless to say, it makes a considerable difference whether an orchestral performance takes place in Carnegie Hall or in one of the Austrian salons where so many of the Haydn, Mozart, and even Beethoven symphonies were frequently presented. It is a generally known fact that our orchestras are larger than those of the days of the classical masters. However, the great composers did not, contrary to certain claims, necessarily eschew a major instrumental setup. In a letter to his father, April 11, 1781, Mozart wrote: "The other day I forgot to tell you that the symphony's performance was *magnifique* and very successful. There were forty violins, all the wood winds and brass doubled, ten violas, ten double basses, eight cellos, and six bassoons." For the performance of the Seventh and Eighth symphonies, February 27, 1814, Beethoven used eighteen first and eighteen second violins, fourteen violas, twelve cellos, and seven basses. And writing in 1817 about a trip to London, he asks his pupil Ries whether there was "double harmony." As we see, neither Mozart nor Beethoven was necessarily opposed to heavier orchestral settings. On the other hand, there is the incident when Beethoven refused to conduct an orchestra of sixty musicians in the Viennese *Musikvereinssaal,* insisting that the number should be reduced before he would agree to direct the concert. Obviously, the master's attitude changed according to specific circumstances, choice of the work, quality of the players, and the character of hall.

The need of adjusting dynamics to existing acoustic conditions was recognized long before the Classicists. Practitioners from Cavalieri (in the preface to his *Rappresentazione*) to Quantz (in his *Versuch*) acknowledged and dealt with this problem. That incorrigible realist, Quantz, goes into all conceivable details, taking into consideration whether there is tapestry or paper on the walls, how much reverberation there is, and whether the listeners are near or at a distance.

PERFORMANCE AND PROPORTION

The interpreter must give special consideration to the acoustic and dynamic analogies between the modern and the classical performance. In order to facilitate a correct historical conception of orchestral proportions, the following tables will provide a survey of orchestral setups in the second half of the eighteenth century. This period is of particular importance, as it marks the change from the *basso continuo* orchestra to the classical one. Let us first look at the ground plan of a preclassical orchestra, as it appears in Rousseau's *Dictionnaire de musique*.

DOUBLE DIRECTION

We observe two harpsichords in the plan. From the first one, in the middle, the musical director, the *maestro al cembalo* (the conductor at the piano), led the orchestra. In addition to this supervision from the cembalo, there was also the special direction by the first violinist. Occasionally, the concertmaster would interrupt his violin playing and conduct with his bow. Hasse's Dresden concertmaster, Pisendel, is mentioned as an expert in this method of violin direction, which continued in many variations into the nineteenth century.

Such double direction may seem strange as compared with modern ideas of conducting. Over the performance there presided, as it were, a chief executive who controlled stage and orchestra, singers and their accompaniment, from the first cembalo. The violin director was in charge of the instrumental body only, especially the strings. This was suggested by the fact that the scores of this period placed the melodic lead, if not in the singer's voice, in the violin section. We also see a second piano on the extreme left of the plan, where the *basso continuo* player performed his part, frequently improvised. The ground plan shows a corresponding arrangement of desks for a cellist and a double-bass player each, on the extreme left, also on the extreme right, and behind the conductor's cembalo. The combination of this arrangement and the five bassoons shows how strongly the bass line was emphasized—an important point to remember for the present-day interpreter.

We might easily count the number of the other players, but the proportion of this opera orchestra, as conducted by Hasse, was, of course, not the model for symphony orchestras in the second half of the eighteenth century. Therefore, we must also turn to other sources, such as the charts of Quantz. Dated from 1753, three years after Bach's death, these tables offer valuable information for the transitional period between the baroque and the classic practice. Quantz uses the number of violins as a standard measure, and from it orders appropriately the number of the other instruments.

As the number of violins increases, the number of violas and also of violoncellos remains small. However, such a proportion is only logical in this period. The viola was merely a part of the greater bass group in the score—along with the cello, the double bass, the bassoon, and the low register of the *continuo*. It was not until classical times that the viola, and likewise the

4 violins:	6 violins:	8 violins:	10 violins:	12 violins :
1 viola	1 viola	2 violas	2 violas	3 violas
1 cello	1 bassoon	2 flutes	2 flutes	4 flutes
1 double	1 cello	2 cellos	3 cellos	4 cellos
bass	1 double	2 oboes	2 oboes	4 oboes
1 cembalo	bass	2 double	2 double	2 double
	1 cembalo	basses	basses	basses
		2 bassoons	2 bassoons	3 bassoons
		1 cembalo	1 cembalo	2 cembalos

bassoon, became a more individual part of the score. For this reason, Quantz, and other preclassical masters did not consider it necessary to augment the number of violas in their performances. Referring to an orchestra in the opera theater (as shown in our ground plan of the Dresden orchestra), Quantz likewise demands two cembali (harpsichords). As in Rousseau's plan, the first harpsichord should always be placed in the middle, with the keyboard toward the audience. In this way, the conductor at the harpsichord faces his singers on the stage. Close to the first harpsichord, at the right, the concertmaster is supposed to sit, a little raised and forward because of his task as violin director.

The violin and viola players might form a kind of circle, so that they all are able to see and hear the concertmaster as well as the conductor. Very often only strings are to be found at the right of the first harpsichord, while the other side is occupied by the brass and wood-wind sections, surrounding the second harpsichord. The bassoons are usually placed close to the audience, at the left of the conductor; the oboes are at the wall of the stage. The French-horn players, if any, sit between the oboes and the second harpsichord, at right angles to the flutes. That everybody should easily see the conductor was always the decisive consideration. This arrangement, corroborating the

Rousseau plan in important features, lasted until the time of the Classicists. Even so progressive a composer as Philipp Emanuel Bach considered the setup with harpsichords to be indispensable. Although the harpsichord could hardly be heard in outdoor concerts, its presence, Bach insisted, was nevertheless necessary to provide harmonious effects.

From the middle to the third part of the eighteenth century, still further changes become apparent. National styles of performance are necessarily reflected in the various orchestral combinations. Emphasis on the melodic or the polyphonic elements, respectively, is expressed in figures for instrumental proportions. The following table of the instrumental distribution of historic orchestral groups in Austria, Italy, Germany, France, and England represents the most important musical centers of that time. The year given with the name of the city in which the orchestra was resident indicates when the quoted proportion between the different instruments was in use.

We see different countries displaying their individual tastes. What an amazing figure for violoncellos in the Paris opera house—three or four times the usual number, and so many double basses in the Scala theater in Milan! Certain accessory instruments were not commonly used by any orchestra of this period (as shown by the next to last column of the table). More progressive steps—such as the elaborate development of the wood-wind and brass sections, and the percussion group—came to be the achievement of the classical orchestra. (The classical arrangement, both in players and proportions, was bound to differ from the previous setup because of the disappearance of the figured bass.)

ORCHESTRA PROPORTIONS

According to Mozart, Elwart, Weber, Gassner, Schuenemann, Haas

	Violins	Violas	Celli	Double Bass	Flute	Oboes	Clarinets	Bassoons	French Horns	Trumpets	Trombones	Harpsichords Percussion Others	Source of Information
1777 Vienna	12 – 15	4	3	3	2	2 – 5	2	2	2	2		2	
1844	16 / 8+8	6	8	4	2	2	2	2	4	3	3	1	Gassner (1844)
Salzburg 1777	12 – 16	4	3	3	2	6		2	2				Leopold Mozart
Prague 1813	8 / 4+4	2	2	2	2	2	2	2	2 – 4	2	3	tympani harpsichord guitar	Weber
Dresden 1768	15	4	3	3	2	5		5	2	2		2 harpsichords percussion	
Mannheim 1756	20	4	4	4	2	2		2	4	2		organ percussion	
1810 Paris	24 / 12+12	8	12	6	2	4	2	4 – 5	4	4	3		Elwart
1828 (Habeneck)	31 / 15+16	8	12	8	4	3	4	4	4	2	4	tympani	
London (Haydn-Salomon concerts)	28 / 12+16	4	3	4									
Milan 1770	28	6	2	6	2	2	2	2	4	2			

HAYDN: ESTERHÁZ AND LONDON

The great step forward toward the disappearance of improvisation was made by Haydn when he gave up the use of the figured bass in his symphonies. Since this abandonment, the function of the *maestro al cembalo* as a symphony conductor has become a thing of the past. Thus, Haydn's later symphonies do not require the cembalo accompaniment: his so-called London symphonies and the major part of his Paris symphonies indicate the gradual disappearance of the *basso continuo* in this very period. It must be mentioned, however, that Haydn agreed to conduct in London from the cembalo in order to comply with the English tradition.

Since there is no definite indication from Haydn's own pen as to where and when to use the *basso continuo*, what guide may the interpreter follow in this matter? The cembalo is needed where the basses and violas play in octaves. As Kretzschmar shows, the character of the *concerto grosso* also makes the piano accompaniment indispensable: symphonies that, though complete in harmony, might have gaps between basses and upper voices, require a certain tiding over by means of the cembalo. On the other hand, in scores where viola and second violin are made independent, and the cello is separated from the double bass (as especially marked in the script), the predominance of the bass line comes to an end and the *basso continuo* is superfluous. Other instruments take care of the function of the keyboard instrument. However, in opera and church performances, there was still conducting from the *basso continuo*. That Haydn was also an opera conductor of great importance is sometimes overlooked in the light of his other interpretative accomplishments. His theater productions in Esterház were considered model performances. Maria Theresa, the empress, claimed that "one had to go to Esterház to hear opera well given."

An old picture shows Haydn conducting his opera, *L'incontro improviso*, in 1775. He directs the performance from the cembalo near the stage, in order to have the closest possible contact with the singers. This setup of the Esterház opera justifiably differs from that in the Dresden theater, which was considerably larger in size. The Haydn orchestra shows thirteen members of the violin family (one cannot tell from the picture who plays first violin, second violin, or viola), in addition to one cello and one double bass, one bassoon, and two other wood winds (probably flutes). It is noteworthy that the instruments of the bass line, namely cello, bassoon, and double basses, are again placed behind the cembalo. The sum total of players corresponds with that of the orchestra list of Haydn in Eisenstadt, when he was in charge of Count Esterházy's orchestra. He had nineteen players, including the concertmaster: five violins (first and second violins included), one viola, one cello, one double bass, two oboes, two bassoons, one clarinet, three horns, three trumpets.

HAYDN'S HUMOR

If ever one of the guiding spirits in musical history was labeled foolishly, it was Haydn. For generations, the profound builder of the classical style has been patted on the shoulder with the familiar "Papa." His scores—the quintessence of exploratory courage, of searching and creative adventure—are stamped and interpreted as the humorous products of the good old-fashioned time when the peruke-wearing "Papa" succeeded so well in entertaining his noble audiences with all kinds of musical fun. We are particularly concerned with such notions because they condition the interpretative attitude erroneously.

As to the term "Papa Haydn," infallibly used in certain

program notes, it was Mozart's privilege to call him so, though Haydn was inseparably and desperately tied up in a childless marriage with a woman whom he literally refers to as *bestia infernale*. It would be wise to leave the use of the appellation "Papa" to Mozart; twenty-four years younger, he admired Haydn as his master (preferring to play Haydn's works rather than his own) and loved him as a warm-hearted friend. For such a dual relationship, "Papa," in the good old Austrian way, was the appropriate tribute of familiarity and respect. However, "Papa" certainly has no place as a clue to Haydn interpretation today, in an attempt to produce an old-fashioned *gemütlich* atmosphere of music-making, whereas in reality Haydn's scores represent the spirit of progress, depth, and artistic courage. Their obvious humor, as a counterpart of a creative mind of immense depth and profundity, must not be deteriorated into an attempt to be funny at any price.

Probably the best-known of Haydn's symphonic "jokes" occurs in the andante of the G Major Symphony, written for London. Called the *Paukenschlag* ("timpani stroke") *Symphony*, as characterized by the dynamic play of the kettledrum, it received the appellation of *Surprise Symphony* in Anglo-Saxon countries. The idea is that a sudden fortissimo was supposed to stimulate and keep awake the somnolent, stiff audiences of British old ladies at London concerts. Be this as it may, we see in the script how the disposition of the music holds the dynamic surprise, the rhythm preparing for the event on the second beat of the sixteenth bar. Every second bar, excepting the eighth, corresponding to the sixteenth where the unexpected fortissimo occurs, has a *tenuto* on two. Thus, it is the task of the performer, instead of nullifying the fifteen bars into a meaningless pianissimo and then frightening the audience with the colossal fortissimo, to play the prior *staccato tenuto* change and reverse the accents with great care accordingly.

Haydn's music, which arouses the sense of the comic in us, works with musical means. The interpreter does not have to become a humorist or professional entertainer, but can obtain his effect musically by obedience to the score.

V. Tempo and
════ Metronome ════

INITIAL TEMPO

Tempo is the body of per-
formance.—BEETHOVEN

TEMPO feeling is a quality common to all human beings.
Yet, as the heartbeat varies in different persons, so the degree
of tempo feeling differs from one individual to another. The
sense of time varies with the age, the country, the race, the
century. Inevitably, there are remarkable variations in the degree of responsiveness to movement in music as between the
child and the old man, the lethargic Eskimo and the vivacious
Brazilian, between occidentals and orientals, between men of
mail-coach times and those of the air-mail era. Is it surprising,
then, that tempo, more so than dynamics or phrasing, is the
most difficult feature of musical performance to approach
through the intellect and the analytic method of interpretation?
The emotional response of audiences to tempo is determined
by the musical habits and conventions of the particular period.
Today, the military march in Beethoven's *Fidelio*, in spite of
its tempo instruction, *vivace*, might seem dull to an audience
in Spain, where the scene of the opera is laid. An old Viennese
waltz performed in the genuine slow *Ländler* tempo would
probably seem maudlin to a modern American tap dancer.

With such an uncertainty of reaction to tempo, the desire for
objectivity in setting the movement very early found expres-

sion in practical and mechanical devices. But neither the latest electric metronome nor Maelzel's good old model has proven adequate, since they provide only a mathematical basis for the correct rendering of tempo. If it is true that the tempo problem is one of intended effect, varying with the changing circumstances of performance, rather than one of arithmetical calculation, then it gives rise to this decisive question: What ultimate goal was the composer seeking with his tempo? At a rehearsal of *Tannhäuser*, Wagner complained to the conductor about his choice of tempi. The rejoinder was: "But what do you want? We play precisely the tempi indicated by your own metronome marks." Experiences of this kind prompted Wagner to forego the use of the metronome marks in his scores. He considered the lack of tempo indications in Bach to be the only logical procedure in the true musical sense.

However, one cannot think of our modern practice apart from Maelzel's little metrical machine—which we shall discuss where it belongs chronologically, in Beethoven's time. The life-work of Mozart and Haydn falls into a time before the invention of the metronome, and so the difficult task of determining the right tempo in classical and earlier scores can be based only on the musical material in the script, in conjunction with musicological facts. The tempo problem confronting the interpreter presents two aspects: (1) the initial tempo; (2) the later modification of the *tempo primo*.

WAS OLD MUSIC PLAYED MORE SLOWLY THAN MODERN?

Certain interpreters today think of the fundamental tempo in preclassical times as slower, more rigid and stately than the modern tempo. Widely accepted, this idea proves to be a prejudice based on the difficulty of comprehending the old notation.

The very sight of the old notes, such as the *brevis* □ and *semi-brevis* ○ , to a reader unaccustomed to old scores, suggests pro-traction—a slow atmosphere. The *semibrevis,* as the name im-plies, formerly only a subdivision, today occupies the whole measure and has thus become a false clue leading to prolonga-tion. In other words, notes that look long to the modern eye meant something quite different in their day: the *brevis* □ , the *semibrevis* ○ , and the minim ♩ are laden with connotations of slowness only in the minds of certain modern interpreters.

Time signatures also contribute to uncertainty regarding tempo in the performance of old music. For instance, the *alla breve* in our notation—since the disappearance of the old *longa* and *brevis*—has taken on a meaning of distinct emphasis on the liveliness of the tempo, indicating a beat of two, rather than of quarters, and thus signifying a speed double that of the or-dinary ₵. Performers do not always take into account the bar through the ₵, and play as if it were written ₵ The figure 2 is likewise sometimes used to indicate ₵. According to Quantz, each bar of an *allegro alla breve* should equal one pulsebeat, each ♩ receiving half a beat, corresponding to M.M. ♩ = 160.

Philipp Emanuel Bach states the necessity of fluent tempi: "I recognize the merit of speed in performance." He discredits "indolent hands that put us to sleep." Playing too rapidly, he asserts, can be corrected as fire can be lessened, whereas "a hy-pochondriac's listless fingers can never really improve." One cannot, however, isolate Bach's statements from the context and apply them indiscriminately to any situation. Naturally Bach knew the value of slow tempi also. His emphasis on speed represents a reaction against the traditional slowness of French music.

A method of employing the human pulse for setting tempi (anticipating Quantz's system) is mentioned as early as 1596, in Lodovico Zacconi's *Prattica di musica.* And Marin Mersenne, in his treatise *Harmonie universelle*, 1636, makes the time value of a minim equivalent to that of a heartbeat. Quantz's method is based on the supposition that the rate of pulsation of the human heart is eighty beats to the minute. The fallacy of treating music prior to his time as if grown infirm with age is convincingly demonstrated by Quantz, who made it possible even in premetronomic days to have definite standards for speed. Quantz's tempi, stressing, as do those of Philipp Emanuel Bach, the element of fluency in performance, completely dispel the illusion of slowness in preclassical music. We have already referred to Quantz's figures for quicker tempi in the section on dance types. However, in his impressive attempts to achieve objectivity by settling the tempo question, Quantz belongs to the classical era of interpretative thought. Even today, his table of tempi provides a most valuable source of information on the performance of music in his century.

QUANTZ'S TABLE
(Selections)

Simple time **C**

Allegro assai ($\frac{4}{4}$): each half-measure one
pulsebeat   M.M. ♩ = 80

Allegretto: each quarter one pulsebeat   M.M. ♩ = 80

Adagio cantabile: each eighth one pulsebeat   M.M. ♩ = 80

Adagio assai: each eighth two pulsebeats   M.M. ♪ = 40

Alla breve **₵**

Allegro—each measure one pulsebeat   M.M. ♩ = 160

Allegretto—each half measure one pulsebeat   M.M. ♩ = 80

Adagio cantabile—each quarter measure one
pulsebeat   M.M. ♩ = 80

Adagio assai—each quarter measure two
pulsebeats   M.M. ♩ = 40

Poco allegro, vivace, or *allegro* (as the mean
between *allegretto* and *allegro assai*)
$\frac{2}{4}$ or fast $\frac{6}{8}$ (*allegro*) each measure one
    pulsebeat   M.M. ♩ or ♩. = 80

The table is based on the pulsebeat, taken as 80. Quantz
himself admits that it is not possible to limit each piece precisely to the pulsations, and that his directions must be taken
only as an approximation. The explicit distinction between *alla
breve* and common time is important in its one-to-two ratio;
likewise the subdivision of adagio in the same proportion, the
adagio assai being twice as slow as the *adagio cantabile*. Within
this framework certain details are worthy of special discussion.

In allegro, three-four, which has only sixteenth- or eighth-
triplets, the first and third quarter of the first measure and the
second quarter of the second measure get one pulsebeat (three
pulsebeats on six quarters), M.M. ♩ = 160. The same is true
for nine-eight. In *adagio cantabile,* where the fundamental
voice is noted in eighths, one eighth receives one pulsebeat,
MM. ♩ = 80. However, if the movement is noted in quarters,
the song more arioso than sad, then each quarter equals one
pulsebeat, M.M. ♩ = 80. Here one must watch key and time
signature carefully. If *mesto, lento,* or *adagio assai* is prescribed,
then each quarter receives two pulsations, M.M. ♩ = 80.

With his differentiation of *adagio cantabile* and *adagio assai,*
Quantz himself raises the question: Is the quarter or the eighth
the unit of the beat? Very often (as in Haydn's very slow
adagios) the eighth represents the beat (more *adagio assai* than
adagio cantabile). However, the impression of slowness in
tempo can be offset by appropriate phrasing. Fast and slow, as
performing effects, are not necessarily a matter only of the
absolute timing: here, as in countless other instances, tempo
and phrasing work conjointly. A slower tempo is convincingly
enlivened through suitable phrasing. A fast tempo, in turn,

may convey an impression of subdued pace if the rhythmical units of the beat and their articulation properly counterbalance each other.

MOZART'S PRESTO

Like Quantz and Philipp Emanuel Bach, Mozart is associated with the principle of fluent tempi. Already renowned for his speed of execution, he played at Naples to an audience that, unable to account in any other way for his remarkable skill on the harpsichord, fancied that it arose from some magic power of the ring encircling one of the fingers of his left hand. Mozart compliantly removed the ring and recommenced his rendition. So far, so good, yet the same prestissimo performer was not always a friend of the express tempo, as he complains: "The eyes have no time to see, or the fingers to find the keys. It is much easier to play a passage quickly than slowly. In the swift passages you can miss notes without anyone's noticing it; but is it beautiful?"

Again, in a letter to his sister "Nannerl," with whom he shared so many four-hand performances on the piano, Wolfgang Amadeus writes an amusing satire on Clementi's playing. He derides the Roman's exaggerated speed directions, while assuring her that they were by no means taken literally when the composer of the *Gradus ad Parnassum* was acting as his own interpreter: "He is a *ciarlatano*," Mozart says, "like all Italians. He writes on a sonata 'presto,' 'prestissimo,' and 'alla breve,' and he plays it allegro in four time. I can swear to it, for I heard him myself."

Mozart's statements lend themselves to both points, showing on the one hand that he played rapidly, and on the other that he scoffed at rapidity. The danger of groping blindly in either direction on the tempo question is obvious. Generalizations such as "Mozart must be played fast," and "old music calls for rigidity," are sheer nonsense. History proves that Mozart was neither a presto nor a moderato performer, and shows that, as a true disciple of his father, he was educated and orientated in the precepts of tempo as embodied in the *Affektenlehre*, and performed accordingly. The modern interpreter of Mozart must seek his true tempo individually in every score.

TEMPO MODIFICATION

Thus far we have focused on tempo setting as it relates to the initial indication of the movement. However, the extent to which tempo modifications were involved in the interpretation of the eighteenth century is likewise a much debated issue. The phrase "tempo modification" as such has been in use since the time of Spohr and Wagner. Yet what the term implies was already known to writers and performers of the Renaissance, and has been employed ever since, as so clearly evinced in the doctrine of affections. Sources antedating the classical period never fail to make ample references to tempo modification, but stress vocal performance as its natural terrain.

The slowly growing art of instrumental playing, as long as it was confined to smaller dance forms, had little opportunity or need for time variation. As the dances became part of instrumental suites, the tempi of various dance types also decided the movement of the corresponding parts of the suite. However, after some of the older dances had become fully incorporated into the symphonic cycle, they were affected by the different nuances of specific instrumental rendition—such as the law of contrast, and other indispensable devices of interpretation. Hence Quantz's precept: "When a composition (especially a fast one) is repeated (for instance, an allegro of a concerto or a symphony), it must be somewhat quicker the second time, in order not to put the listener to sleep. With such tempo modification the whole performance acquires a new aspect: the hearer is refreshed, his attention revived." Such ideas are not in keeping with the modern outlook. On the contrary, it is almost a criterion of acceptable classical performance that the *tempo primo* be resumed at every recapitulation.

As the best solution of the problem of tempo modification, Philipp Emanuel Bach offers the golden mean between rigidity and freedom—symmetry. He insists that notes and pauses (*fermatas* and *cadenzas* excepted) be played strictly in accordance with the general movement. Otherwise the reading would become obscure. Yet he also concedes that one may commit the "most beautiful faults against measure with good intention." Such faults against the measure are nothing but another formulation of *tempo rubato*. And since variation of time played so important a part in musical performance, it appears necessary to discuss tempo modification in detail where it becomes a major problem for the interpreter, as in the case of Mozart, Beethoven, Chopin, and Wagner.

Mozart and Tempo Rubato

What the stolen time may be I can better show than tell.—Leopold Mozart

The letters of the masters frequently prove to be musicological documents of paramount importance. In addition to their biographical significance and potential contribution to aesthetics, they turn bright light on dark stylistic questions of past times. They guide research in discovering certain old secrets; they solve many a problem that otherwise would be hidden behind the notes of aged scores forever. Such is the case with the fascinating correspondence between Mozart and his father Leopold, the famous author of a violin method that was used all over Europe during the latter part of the eighteenth century.

This very correspondence is an indispensable documentary source for reconstructing the interpretative style of the period. Whereas the rich biographical material of the Mozart letters has been widely discussed and commented upon, the technical aspect of it deserves still greater attention. As we shall see, certain problems in performance are unmistakably explained through the study of this interchange of thoughts between Mozart the pedagogue and Mozart the composer.

In reading the Mozart correspondence, a certain term occurs—*gestohlenes Tempo,* in Father Leopold's German—the English translation of which is "stolen tempo." It is, however, in its Italian form, *tempo rubato,* that the term has become familiar to musicians. Everyone knows that this conception of rubato stands today for a specific technique of time variation, for a slight increase or decrease in the tempo of any passage. In other words, time is "stolen" where the values of the notes are augmented or diminished for the sake of expression.

WHERE TO PLAY RUBATO

What finally bears the name "rubato" has become one of the major characteristics in the performance of music of certain styles. For more specific information, let us first turn to a dictionary. Grove offers us the following:

> This license is allowable in the works of all the modern romantic masters, from Weber downward. . . . In the case of the older masters, it is entirely and unconditionally inadmissible. It may be doubted whether it [the *tempo rubato*] should be introduced in Beethoven, although many great interpreters of his music do not hesitate to use it.

Even in this short quotation from the dictionary, it becomes apparent that considerable uncertainty exists regarding the use of rubato. The author of the article in Grove seems positive in his assertion that rubato is possible with the Romanticists, but he feels that it is "unconditionally inadmissible" in the case of the older masters. An exception is made of Beethoven. It is always psychologically difficult to come to another conclusion than that of the most outstanding interpreters of the day. Apparently there was no conflict in the writer's mind regarding the other old masters, whose works evidently were given a rubato-less rendition.

And yet a great surprise is in store for us—for the simple reason that what is taken for granted by so many "great interpreters" happens to be in opposition to what the masters themselves have written about rubato. There is no better criterion. Why should interpreters rack their brains if the problem can be solved for them by the composers themselves? Solution is doubly offered—in the scores and in documents that furnish the information that the score may have omitted.

THE MOZART CORRESPONDENCE

On October 24, 1777, Mozart wrote to his father:

> He [the piano manufacturer Stein, from the city of Augsburg in southern Germany] is just crazy about Beeche [a piano virtuoso of that time]. Now, however, he [Stein] sees and hears . . . that I do not make any grimaces and still play *espressivo*, that I always accurately play in time. No one seems to understand the *tempo rubato* in an adagio, where the left hand does not know anything about it.

And just three months later, on January 29, 1778, Father Leopold's answer contained the following significant statement:

Reicher [another piano virtuoso] plays better cantabile. Both, however, have Beck's fault of retardation, in that they retard the whole orchestra with a wink of their eyes and with their movements, and later again continue in the previous tempo.

This Mozart correspondence reveals two important facts to posterity. First, it now becomes clear that Mozart himself played rubato—a discovery of great importance, since the majority of acclaimed performers strictly avoid the rubato as absurd in Mozart, which in turn is in keeping with the point of view of the dictionary on this very problem. Second, an insight is gained into the specific rubato technique of Mozart, according to his own description. The master himself discloses the secret —"the left hand does not know anything about it." This, as will become apparent later, is the foundation of any rubato playing. Moreover, if one substitutes melody for the right hand and accompaniment for the left hand, it becomes a general prescription for performing music rubato.

Leopold Mozart, strict pedagogue that he was, could not tolerate any sudden holding back of the reading to permit playing a passage more slowly, and then trying to make up for it later by arbitrary acceleration. What he wanted was a smoother balance between the parts.

Wolfgang Amadeus Mozart proved with his rubato technique that he was ahead of his time not only as a composer but also as an interpreter. The rubato, as he described it, emerged as a technique of performance that did not require any change in later styles. What later composers added was only a variation of the same idea. *Dass die linke Hand nichts darum weiss* ("so that the left hand does not know anything about it"), as Mozart puts it in the letter to his father, shows how it is the function of the left hand to provide an accompaniment in strict time. Appropriately, it is the task of the right hand to play an independent *espressivo*, carrying the melody somewhat like a singer. The tune must be performed cantabile, according to Leopold. "In a singing manner," a direction normally associated with a vocal rendition, appears now in the realm of instrumental execution, recalling the *bel canto* style in the Italian keyboard performance of the opening of the seventeenth century.

THE VOCAL BACKGROUND

The origin of the *tempo rubato* is a vocal one. Significantly, it is in a textbook on singing that we find it first mentioned. Its title is *Opinioni de' cantori antichi e moderni;* its author Pier Francesco Tosi; it was published in Italy in 1723. Tosi, speaking of rubato, naturally referred to singing. He showed how the tune—that is to say, its time—could be retarded or quickened at certain spots, the whole being left to the discretion of the singer. The purpose of his technique of "robbed" time was expression. Rubato was thus used where a particular phrase required special expressive emphasis. This was accomplished by diminishing or increasing the value of the notes—the bass, at the same time, maintaining its regular pace. After a certain phrase was rendered rubato, the performance would return to its regular rhythm, the melody and bass strictly corresponding with each other.

There is no reason to assume that Tosi, theorizing in his *Opinioni de' cantori*, invented first his set of rules, and that the obedient performers of his time only waited for the publication of the book to put rubato into musical practice. The opposite, of course, took place. Rubato must have been in the air, and Tosi captured it, tying it down to textbook rules. We know that the famous singer Pistocchi, a kind of Caruso in his time, displayed stylistic habits that were readily accepted and emulated by the whole generation. Certain of his mannerisms were seemingly identical with Tosi's rubato. And going back as far as the beginning of the seventeenth century, Peri, in the foreword to his newborn opera *Euridice,* comments on the nuances and free passages of the singer Signora Archilei, the details of which nobody could put into notation. We wonder what it was that baffled Peri, a composer imaginative enough to create, in the opera, an absolutely new form of musical expression. Obviously it was the same problem that even the greatest opera composer of later times, Mozart, could not approach by way of mere notation. It was simply the problem of rubato.

Returning to the *Opinioni de' cantori,* we are amazed at the coincidence between Tosi's vocal and Mozart's instrumental rubato. In both cases the same features appear: quasi-independence of the parts—melody and accompaniment—and, at the same time, correlation of the main beat, the whole being performed with such discretion that the listener could hardly determine how it was accomplished.

One might wonder how Mozart became so well acquainted with the Italian rubato method. His father doubtless initiated him into it. Besides, it was gathered naturally from the innumerable Italian influences to which Wolfgang, child prodigy, was exposed on his various trips to the south from his native Austria. His delicate ear quickly grasped the elements of *bel canto* as he listened to famous Italian singers; he also heard the performances in the Sistine Chapel during his visit to Rome in 1770. It has often been claimed that Mozart's music is a perfect blend of Italian and German elements, but the most convincing testimony should be felt to lie, if anywhere, in the admirable employment of originally vocal features in the instrumental texture of his scores.

All this, of course, must be realized in the Mozart performance of today. Yet nothing is more difficult than the execution of an expressive rubato without violating the strictness of the classical design. A genuine Mozart reading calls for emphasis of the vocal element—that is to say, the singing quality of the leading parts. One of the ways to this aesthetic end is the proper use of rubato—as Mozart himself suggested it. It is true, the example taken from the correspondence with his father refers to piano playing specifically. But one is entitled to transpose Mozart's prescription from the piano to any other instrument, or combination of instruments, even to the orchestra. Thus translating Mozart's piano formula into orchestral language, "right hand" means the leading parts (according to the instrumentation) and "left hand" becomes the sum of all those instruments that participate in the accompaniment.

There is still another important question unanswered, namely: Is it correct to employ Mozart's rubato technique in the performance of other works of his period?

LICENSE AND LIMITS

Fortunately we have other witnesses upon whose judgment we can depend, theorists as well as practical musicians. First-hand information is given by the composers themselves, among them Philipp Emanuel Bach. In the second volume of his *Versuch*, he writes:

> If the executant upon the clavier manages matters in such a way that one hand appears to play against time whilst the other hand strictly observes the beat, then *the right thing has been done*. In such a case the parts rarely move simultaneously, but they fit together all the same.

This certainly is an elucidating statement, and such a coincidence of viewpoints on the part of Mozart and Bach is more than we could have bargained for. Nothing could be more informative than Philipp Emanuel's instructions. Supported by the combined statements of the two masters, Mozart and Philipp Emanuel Bach, we are safe in assuming that the general principles of rubato playing in their time are clearly defined.

Research has proved the influence of Bach on Mozart, and when we find also a convergence of ideas in their performing styles, the picture becomes complete. Forty-two years separate the birth dates of Mozart and Philipp Emanuel. Children of different generations, both were typical interpretative exponents of their respective eras—one preparing, the other fulfilling, classical expression.

MELODIC CHARM

The contemporary verdict on Mozart's own performance is recorded in a few authoritative statements. Clementi, Dittersdorf, and Haydn all agree that melodic charm emerged as the main characteristic of Mozart's playing, in keeping with the style of his works. Clementi states: "Until then I had never heard anybody play with so much intelligence and charm. I was particularly surprised by an adagio and a number of his extemporized variations on a theme chosen by the emperor, which we were obliged to vary alternately, each accompanying the other." This charm emanated from the singing, expressive way in which Mozart handled the keyboard. Dittersdorf relates, in his autobiography, a conversation with Joseph II, on the question as to who was the most outstanding performer of the time. This composer, neglected today, close to the court and famous then, impressed on the emperor the incomparable artistry of Mozart. And "marvellous taste" is Dittersdorf's general characterization of Mozart's piano performance.

Haydn claimed, with tears, that Mozart's playing was "unforgettable, touching his heart, the staccato displaying the most brilliant charm." Mozart called Clementi a *Mechanicus*, describing thus in a word the superficial technicality of the Roman musician. Mozart's own ideal performance emerges as the opposite of such soulless virtuosity: he aimed for a lyric style of warmth and heartfelt expression.

The picture of Mozart as a performer is not complete without some light on his directing. His conducting is described as extraordinary, to the point of eccentricity. With fiery energy, he managed to "consolidate his orchestra so that it sounded like a single instrument." As a result of his journey to Mannheim, his style of orchestral performance was greatly influenced. Here, at the cradle of modern instrumental dynamics, Mozart heard, saw, and marveled at the execution of all those features which were considered the musical miracles of that time. It was in 1778 that Christian Cannabich, concertmaster and conductor of the Mannheim orchestra, invited the twenty-two-year-old Salzburg musician to stay with him, to attend rehearsals and concerts, and in this way to secure full information on the new artistic developments. Mozart's orchestral performances in later years, and likewise his opera conducting, integrated the Mannheim devices with his classical clarity.

The Story of the Metronome

METRICAL MEASUREMENT BEFORE 1800

The quest for an objective standard to determine tempo is as old as interpretation itself. While metronomic measurement is commonly associated with Maelzel's invention in Beethoven's day, important attempts along mechanical and mathematical lines had been made long before. As early as 1592,

Lodovico Zacconi, a Venetian monk of the Order of St. Augustine, published in his *Prattica di musica* a chapter on "Measure," in which he refers to the human pulse as the true basis for tempo in performance. The foundation of music, according to Zacconi, is the measure. Music manifests itself through a multiplicity of intervals; its units are similar to the human pulse. A similar comparison between musical units and the palpitation of the human heart occurs in Quantz. Reading his *Versuch*, we find some comment on the most important contribution prior to Maelzel's metronome—the *chronomètre* of Étienne Loulié. Quantz regarded this French invention somewhat skeptically as a "pig in a poke." He hesitates to recommend it: "This machine can hardly always be carried around by everyone." As the *chronomètre* had been forgotten, "it gives rise to doubt as to its efficiency or adequacy." Yet Loulié, in his *Éléments ou principes de musique dans un nouvel ordre*, published in 1696, made it quite clear that the practical purpose of the apparatus was to provide a means of assuring the right tempo in musical performance. The *chronomètre* consisted of a ruled perpendicular board, approximately 72 inches in height, with a right-angular projection at the top, from which a weighted string or cord serving as a pendulum was suspended. The pendulum could be adjusted to correspond to numbered holes in the upright, and by these numbers tempo was determined. Loulié's means of measuring time exactly emerges as the best seventeenth-century contribution.

Following Loulié's *chronomètre* was the *échomètre* of Joseph Sauveur (1701), likewise based on the principle of the pendulum, and used in conjunction with a metric scale. Only a few years later, Michel l'Affilard describes yet another pendulum for gauging tempo, in his *Principes très-faciles pour bien apprendre la musique* (1705). His work was designed for use in a convent, bearing the dedication *Aux dames religieuses*. The next venture derived from Louis-Leon Pajot (1732), who modestly gave the credit to Loulié, although he really accomplished an important advance by providing the metrical machine with a dial and pointer to indicate speed. *The Doctrine of Pendulums Applied to Musick* is illustrated with the following dialogue between master and scholar (quoted from *A New Musical Grammar*, by William Tans'ur, London, 1746):

> SCHOLAR. *Sir, of what Length must I make a Pendulum, in order to* beat *the true* Time *of the several* Notes *of* Musick; *as the* Semibreve, *the* Minim, *the* Crotchet, *etc.?*
>
> MASTER. I told you that *Four Pulses* of the *Pendulum* was the length of the *Semibreve, two* the *Minim, and four* the *Crotchet,* etc.

At the end the explanation is given:

> Now, I say, suppose a 30 Inch *Pendulum* should vibrate as the length of a *Crotchet,* then will one of 120 Inches be required to *beat one Minim;* and one of 7 Inches and a half to the *Time of one Quaver;* and 480 Inches to compleat the *Time* of one *Semibreve,* etc. Always observing, that a *Double length of Time,* requires a *Pendulum four times as long;* and a *half* of *Time* but *one fourth so long:* This being the true *Proportion* by which all *Pendulums* are regulated.

In 1795 Thomas Wright published *A Concerto for the Harpsichord or Piano Forte,* providing each movement with the numerical specification of the intended tempo. Explaining also how to determine the tempo by means of a pendulum, this system entailed the very first use of "metronome marks" in England. Thus, the efforts of Thomas Wright came closer than those of his predecessors to the modern objective of indicating the speed for every movement of the performance.

The nineteenth century is unquestionably Maelzel's, since

other inventions subsequent to 1800, such as Stöckel's chronometer (similar to a clock, both in principle and design), achieved no permanent success. However, Guthmann writes in 1806 about a chronometer that could be carried in the pocket like a watch. This device came very near meeting the requirements of executants. With a procedure comparable to that employed nowadays in *a cappella* performances—where the initial chord must be sounded discreetly on pitch pipes—the Guthmann watch was held to the ear and the tempo thereby communicated directly to the performer. One can see how such a contrivance might be quite attractive to interpreters today.

MAELZEL

Johann Nepomuk Maelzel, had he lived in our time, might have furthered musical performance with inventions even more ingenious than the metronome based on a combination of musical with mechanical fantasy. Maelzel's varied career, which ranged from piano teaching to serving as imperial court mechanician, ended en route to America, when he died shortly before reaching the New World of great inventions.

Beethoven and Salieri were among the first to evince appreciation of the metronome. The latter's approval was of even more importance to Maelzel than the prestige involved in Beethoven's word, since Salieri, as Austrian court conductor, was, by virtue of his various activities in opera and concert, Vienna's leading performer. In 1813, the *Allgemeine musikalische Zeitung* published the following article:

> As a token of the appreciation of this invention [the metronome] by local composers [in Vienna] as a means of protecting their works everywhere from all misrepresentations because of the wrong tempo, the *Hofkapellmeister* Salieri has, owing to his deep respect for the late masters Gluck. Handel, Haydn,

and Mozart, undertaken to mark their masterpieces in accordance with Maelzel's metronome, so that in the future their scores will be interpreted in the spirit of the composers, with which Herr Salieri is better acquainted than anybody else. He has already started . . . with Haydn's *Schöpfung* and *Jahreszeiten* and Gluck's *Iphigenie in Tauris*.

BEETHOVEN'S METRONOMIZATIONS

Beethoven's attitude toward both Maelzel and his metronome oscillated just as does the pendulum of that instrument, swinging from a lawsuit with the inventor, at one extreme, to immortalizing the little machine in the second movement of the Eighth Symphony, with its musical suggestion of the metronome's ticktock rhythm. However, Beethoven's real appraisal of the metrical machine was, by and large, not one of wholehearted approval. His own statements in this regard are of value not only for Beethoven interpretation, but also for the general outlook on the tempo problem and its relation to the metronome.

On the manuscript of his song *Nord oder Süd*, Beethoven wrote the notation, "100 according to Maelzel. But this must be applicable only to the first measures, *for feeling also has its tempo* and this cannot be entirely expressed in this figure."

We certainly could not expect more insight into Beethoven's point of view than the master himself has offered us in these few lines. He insists upon time rendition objectively in accordance with the metronome. Still, since mechanical designations cannot fully convey the tempo of feeling, the Maelzel figure must be adjusted after the initial bars. Although supported by Beethoven's own testimony, this necessity of varying the initial time is frequently disregarded by even the most sincere Beethoven interpreters in their determination to adhere objectively to the score.

However, the indispensability of the metronome was conceded by Beethoven again and again. On many occasions he considered the verbal tempo indications too vague, indefinite, and inadequate for supporting the interpreter. In a letter to Thomson he asks to be informed "wherever a song is marked andantino, whether it should be slower or faster than andante; for the signification of this word, like so many others in music, is so uncertain, that andantino sometimes approaches allegro, and is sometimes played like adagio."

It was in such a moment of concern about the ambiguity of instructions that Beethoven wrote to his friend Mosel:

> I am heartily rejoiced that you agree with me in the opinion touching the time designations that date back to the barbarous period in music; for what, for instance, can be more nonsensical than "allegro," which always means "merry," and how often are we so far from this conception that the piece says the very opposite of the designation. As regards these four chief speeds, which by no means have the correctness or truthfulness of the chief winds, we gladly allow that they be put aside. It is a different matter with the words used to designate the character of the composition—these we cannot give up, since *time is really more the body*, while these have reference to the spirit. So far as I am concerned, I have long thought of giving up the nonsensical designations "allegro," "adagio," "andante," "presto." Maelzel's metronome gives us the best opportunity to do this. I give you my word that I shall never use them again in my compositions.

Yet Beethoven's enthusiasm for the metronome did not last indefinitely. This is revealed by Schindler in reference to an edition of Beethoven's Ninth Symphony with metronome marks undertaken for the publisher Schott. Ries, in London, asked Beethoven for the metronomization of the symphony. But the copy somehow disappeared in Beethoven's Vienna apartment; thus the composer, disgruntled, was compelled to begin anew and designate all his tempi a second time. No sooner had he finished the task than the lost copy was found. Alas! The comparison of the two metronomizations showed a deviation of the tempo in every movement. Thereupon the master exclaimed angrily: "No metronome at all! Whoever has the right feeling, needs none; and whoever lacks it, has no use for one—he will run away with the whole orchestra anyhow."

This knowledge of Beethoven's mixed feelings toward Maelzel's instrument does not help his interpreter to solve the problem of metronomization in Beethoven's scores. After all, the instructions he gave when he had finally made up his mind are still binding: if the modern performer wants to be objective, he must obey them implicitly. However, certain contemporary documents have been used to indicate that, in general, Beethoven's markings designated too rapid tempi. It is argued that, if clarity and distinct execution are requisites of any successful performance, many of Beethoven's metronomizations are incompatible with such a goal. Nottebohm, the Beethoven scholar, says in his *Beethoveniana* in a chapter entitled "Metronomische Bezeichnungen": "The metronomization of some symphony movements, in particular, strikes us as too rapid." And he goes so far as to assert: "Concerning the very rapid marking of the last movement of the Fourth Symphony (*allegro ma non troppo*, $\quarternote = 80$), a mistake may be assumed." When Czerny edited Beethoven's piano works, he stated his loyal approach as follows: "We have endeavored, according to the best of our recollection, correctly to indicate the tempo, this most important part of a conception." But in spite of this pledge, he usually understates Beethoven's metronomizations by a few degrees.

No reasonable musician, in the final analysis, will venture to say that Beethoven was wrong. Attempts to explain the rapid tempi of his metronomizations have been based on the fact that Beethoven lacked the requisite patience and inner tranquillity for experimenting long enough with Maelzel's figures. It is true that, when Beethoven published the tempo markings for his first eight symphonies, in 1817, the metronome had been known to him only a very short time. On the other hand, Beethoven's works indicate a certain disregard for the mere mechanics of performance, which would help to explain his speed markings much more convincingly than the inference that he failed to "experiment with the metronome because of impatience." Obviously, Beethoven's attitude comes under the same head of aloofness from the material atmosphere in musical performance as his well-known retort to the violinist complaining about his trouble in playing a particular passage: "Do you believe I think of your fiddle when genius speaks to me?"

VI. Victory of Form

BEETHOVEN'S PIANO PLAYING

THERE WAS a project long in Beethoven's mind, one that would have been of priceless value had it ever been realized, namely, an edition of his works with instructions for correct reading, which were to specify (1) his poetic idea and its proper execution in interpretation; (2) a rearrangement of his pianoforte music then published for the new enlarged keyboard; (3) his personal instructions in reference to proper musical declamation. After 1823, the project expanded to include all his works, with an additional point of attention—the metronome markings. But of all these teeming ideas and their obvious tendency toward objectivity, none came to fruition. Therefore, if we want to trace the composer's ideas on his instrumental performance, we must turn to comments by his contemporaries, preferring those written by musicians who were expert performers themselves.

Beethoven as a pianist can be called a self-taught virtuoso if one ignores his childhood education in Bonn. He performed in public until he had to abandon concertizing because of his growing deafness. There were, however, occasional brief emergences in his later years, like the instance in 1814 when he appeared as pianist in the performance of his B Flat Trio, Opus 97.

LEGATO, PEDALING, AND DYNAMICS

As to Beethoven's general appearance at the piano, his pupil Czerny says:

> His attitude while playing was masterly in its quietness, noble and beautiful, without the least grimace, though he bent forward as his deafness grew upon him. He attached great importance, in his teaching, to correct position of the fingers—according to the school of Philipp Emanuel Bach, which he used in teaching me.

Specifically, in regard to phrasing, Czerny states that Beethoven was very anxious that his pupils should acquire a perfect legato, his own legato being, as may be imagined, wonderful.

Schindler, another of the few personal disciples of Beethoven, comments on his staccato. The signs used by the composer for his short notes were partly dots, partly short strokes, Schindler says; but this again is refuted by Krebs, who insists that Beethoven used dots (. . .) for ordinary staccato, and ⌢. . . . for *portando*. In other words, plain staccato dots are not merely incomplete strokes, as Schindler would have it. Even turning to the original manuscripts in order to detect Beethoven's authentic wishes, cannot fully solve these questions. Arthur Schnabel, in his edition of Beethoven sonatas, emphasizes the fact that Beethoven's original texts, especially those of his earlier works, lack explicit fingering and pedaling indications. Thus, the editor of the sonatas is forced to supplement the text to the best of his judgment. Our facsimile (facing page 209) shows this very lack in the variation theme of the *Appassionata*. It also shows Beethoven's haste of creative excitement: as previously remarked, there is a certain carelessness in Beethoven's writing, which, however, proves more valuable to mankind than the superlative pedantry of some other musical writers. At any rate, the state of some of Beethoven's manuscripts was responsible if his signs have been obscured or misinterpreted: often his copyist and printer could only guess at what was actually intended.

Relatively more care is given to dynamics. Kullak proves that the manuscripts of the earliest piano sonatas, written before the first Vienna trip, contained only one crescendo and never showed the compound sign $<>$. In spite of the proximity of the Rhenish town of Bonn to Mannheim, Beethoven could not as yet have absorbed, in his native city, the nuances of the Mannheim school that were just about to conquer Germany. However, the score scripts written after his study with Haydn pay considerable attention to a gradually growing dynamic scale. Schindler asserts that Beethoven especially accented suspensions on the second, more so than contemporary pianists. As to pedaling, Czerny's assurance that Beethoven employed much more of this than is actually indicated, either by his meager direction *con sordino* or by the asterisk (*), is of great importance. In the largo of the Concerto in C Minor, we are informed, Beethoven kept the pedal down for the length of the theme. This may suggest an offensive sound, but Beethoven's pedals were not ours, and on his much weaker instrument the effect produced differed from the pedaled tones of the modern grand piano.

RESTRAINED LIBERTY

A considerable controversy in relation to Beethoven interpretation is bound to center around the composer's tempo in general and his rubato in particular. Schindler states that Beethoven played "with few exceptions, free of all restraint in tempo: a *tempo rubato* in the most exact meaning of the term, as required by certain exceptional conditions, but without even the slightest trace of a caricature." However, he concedes that this manner of playing did not appear until the later years of his so-called third period. Such a reference to the three main creative periods of Beethoven's life (so generally accepted by his biographers) is transferred by Kullak to three analogous periods of Beethoven's interpretation.

Obviously, the changing outlook in creation was accompanied by a distinct evolution in Beethoven's performing style. There still remains this question: Did Beethoven, after he had matured and changed his character of writing and playing, also alter the way in which he originally played his earlier compositions? Ries, like others, asserts that "the master usually kept strict time." In other words, he did not completely forsake, during his third period, the earlier style in which freedom of meter played a lesser part. But, as the reference is apparently to works composed during that time, it remains a speculation, though a convincing one, that the older Beethoven changed his own interpretation of all his earlier piano works.

Czerny, in speaking of tempo, has this to say:

> Every composition must be played in the tempo prescribed by the composer and adhered to by the executant, notwithstanding, however, that in almost every line there are certain notes and passages where a little ritardando or accelerando is necessary, to beautify the reading and to augment the interest.

The essential point is a tempo modification of degrees, of restrained liberty in the interest of unity—in short, the application of rules that add up to the general conception of "classical."

The Beethoven interpreter must find his bearings between

the two extremes of rigid objectivity and unwarranted liberty. If the documents quoted are to be trusted, then he must reduce *tempo rubato* to its necessary minimum. But this condition being relative, no performer can feel secure unless he has more tangible material for his guidance. The complete schedule of the use of the ritardando in Czerny's *Clavierschule* is a welcome source of information.

Another question is, however, how much importance can be attached to the statements of Czerny. No doubt he had the privilege of Beethoven's personal teaching and friendship, which enabled him to hear the master repeatedly play his own works. In addition, he was a keen objective observer of all technicalities. The Beethoven scholar Nottebohm credits Czerny's comments with authenticity, referring to him as one of the few dependable witnesses on Beethoven's style. The preceptor of velocity was completely under the influence of Beethoven's teaching in his writings on interpretation.

Thus, as a possible means of orientation, Czerny's outline is one of the best available references for the performing style of the first half of the nineteenth century. It goes without saying that the intelligent student should not blindly apply these rules to his Beethoven performance, as a cook applies his recipe for a cake. Good judgment and discriminating taste must determine whether and when they are to be used. According to Czerny, a ritardando or rallentando is used:

1. At the return of the principal subject
2. When a phrase is to be separated from the melody
3. On long notes strongly accented
4. At the transition to a different time
5. After a pause
6. On the diminuendo of a quick, lively passage
7. Where the ornamental note cannot be played *a tempo giusto*

8. In a well-marked crescendo serving to introduce or to terminate an important passage
9. In passages where the composer or the performer gives free play to his fancy
10. When the composer marks the passage *espressivo*
11. At the end of a shake or cadence

CONTROLLED RUBATO

We can find nowhere in Beethoven a specifically pre-scribed rubato. As we shall see in a later section, the literal instruction, *tempo rubato,* was introduced by Chopin. Yet there are evidently passages where the aggregate of Beethoven's markings amounts to what the rubato instruction represents in later periods: a variation of time with gradual modification. For example, in the opening movement of Opus 111, the original instruction, *allegro con brio ed appassionato,* dissolves completely upon the very first appearance of the second theme. Here, *meno allegro* appears in the second half of the measure, followed by two measures marked *ritardando.* The next bar is marked *adagio,* while *tempo primo* is resumed with the eighth-note up-beat. Again, the repetition of the theme in the second part indicates a genuine *tempo rubato,* because at this point (after the corresponding *meno allegro* and *ritardando*) Beethoven demands that four measures be played *poi a poi più allegro.* Similar situations are to be found in many other of Beethoven's last works—at the end of Opus 90, and in Opera 101, 109, and 110. It is only in such places of agitated emotion, of intense expression, that we are obliged to perform with an appropriate amount of *tempo rubato.* Such slight and controlled rubato would coincide with the style of Beethoven's own rendition, as described by those who were privileged to hear him.

And so with the help of the contemporary documents, as well as through the revelations of Beethoven's own scores, we are finally in a position to resolve the dissonance that has held us in suspense since the beginning of our inquiry into the rubato problem. Now we know, contrary to certain opinions, that *tempo rubato* can be applied to Beethoven in certain passages. But it cannot be emphasized enough that this statement is not an invitation to indulge in the liberty of general rubato playing in Beethoven. Nothing could be more objectionable. From the documents, the principle of strict time emerges as indispensable, with an exception in the case of passages like those cited, where the poetic idea breaks from the regular bar lines and seeks freedom of expression.

The Poetic Idea

TRAGIC AND SERENE VANTAGE GROUNDS OF INTERPRETATION

For various reasons, with which all of his biographies are replete, the idea has become prevalent that for Beethoven form was but a vehicle for his so-called poetic idea. Taking a broad view of his foremost interpreters, one might easily build up a strong case in defending the poetic thesis, which in turn is based on certain statements of the composer, on romantic stories of his life, and on hypothetic anecdotes. Still more important are impressions of other great composers, such as Wagner and his poetic interpretation of the knock of Fate at the door (as described in our Introduction). Wagner calls the opening of Beethoven's quartet Opus 131, "the most heavy-hearted thing that has ever been said in tones." This explanation of the C-sharp Minor Fugue for Strings on the part of the composer of *Tristan und Isolde* is indeed very significant, although not everyone proves to have the same reaction. Some feel a meditative instead of a heavy-hearted mood.

We see again the uncertainty of external explanations if we consider the many versions given of the background of the Beethoven quartet Opus 135, *Der schwergefasste Entschluss.* The title, as given in German, connotes tragedy, whereas it most likely has a humorous implication. It may reflect a scene between Beethoven and his housekeeper over the weekly house money; or, in another mood, it may suggest the story centering around Herr Demscher, a wealthy Viennese sponsor of musicians. He had offended Beethoven by neglecting to attend a concert and was looking for some opportunity to regain the composer's friendship. It was suggested to Demscher that he contribute some fifty florins toward the subscription of the latest quartet.

"Muss es sein?" ("Must it be?") Demscher laughingly asked.

"Ja, es muss sein!" ("Yes, it must be!") was the uncompromising answer.

Anecdotes like these are amusing. If true, they are of biographical value, but they are never a real basis, never a dependable vantage point, for interpretation. Whether to portray the humor in the quartet Opus 135, or the tragedy in Opus 131, whether moonlight or passion be the background of a sonata, Napoleon or Fate the subject of a symphony, the performing artist must interpret the actual music regardless of the varied stories surrounding the compositions.

The finale of the *Eroica,* with or without the well-known Napoleon inference, presents to the performer the specific problem of a theme with variations, to be solved as a purely musical question without the help of the Little Corporal. After all, whether Beethoven thought of Bonaparte as a personification of flaming will (as he did when he first wrote the dedication on the often reproduced title-page of the *Eroica*), or whether, disillusioned, he had discovered the Corsican's imperialism and criminal megalomania (when he scratched out the dedication and replaced it with the words, *Per festeggiare il sovenire di un grand' Uomo*)—all this does not affect the reading of the music.

Turning once more to the Fifth—since its opening has recently acquired a new significance, the *"V* for victory" symbolism—one might speculate as to how much the new association will eventually affect the interpretation of the symphony. While the "knock of Fate at the door" has already changed the first five measures, will the *"V* for victory" symbolism involve a further interpretative alteration of the symphony's motto theme? It is today generally known that the rhythm of the motif corresponds to the formation of the letter *V* of the Morse code (. . . —). The metrical identity of the symphonic and the telegraphic notation has contributed a watchword in the cause of war. But time will pass and people in the third millennium may learn how the Fifth and the letter *V* stood for the final victory of the Allied Nations in the tumultuous bygone days of the twentieth century, as they will learn how the form of a fish was used as a secret symbol of Christianity in the first century. And posterity may possibly forget whether Beethoven, with the *Eroica*, rebelled against Bonaparte imperialism, or, with the Fifth, against the fascistic Axis (although Beethoven, as the greatest democrat in music, would no doubt gladly have dedicated all of his nine symphonies to the cause of freedom and liberation). Amateurish interpreters, in desperate need of anecdotes, will pounce upon the victory slogan story, skipping the bagatelle of a century or so between Hitlerian and Napoleonic wars, and probably indulge in a bleating fanfare compared with which the present *a piacere* ♪♫♩ will be but a poor joke.

Tragic or serene, the atmosphere and the mood of any of Beethoven's works are definitely and unmistakably expressed in the purely musical symbols of his script. Thus the interpreter will find Beethoven's humor embodied in harmonic jokes, merry rhythm, surprising cadences, and delightful changes of key. Likewise, the serenity of Beethoven's world and his poetic ideas must find their interpretative expression within the framework of the classical form.

FORM TRIUMPHANT

The fact that Beethoven worshiped form must be unmistakably revealed in the performance of his music. Even where the poetic idea suggested a sacrifice of form for the sake of dramatic content, Beethoven would not yield to such temptation. Fascinating proof of this is supplied in the story of the three *Leonore* overtures. It is well known how the composer experimented with these preludes to his only opera, in an attempt to find satisfactory dramatic expression within the limits of the sonata form. In the first overture, he limits himself to contrasting the leading figures, Florestan and Leonore, and concludes with the victorious Leonore theme. The second overture contains a slow introduction describing the misery of Florestan in prison. Afterward the two main themes are introduced. Then the development, growing more and more in excitement, rushes to the moment of greatest tension, when trumpet fanfare announces the arrival of the liberator. In this way, the whole drama is convincingly sketched. Beethoven completely abandons the recapitulation, and leads straight to the coda with Leonore's triumphant melody.

But hardly a year had passed when the composer, not fully satisfied, made up his mind to write a third version of the overture. The essential change was nothing but the restoration of the form he had sacrificed before for the sake of dramatic effect. He added the recapitulation and thus quieted his conscience—his sense of form. It is a clear issue: he abhorred slighting the form for the sake of the content. His works which followed—such as the *Coriolanus* overture, and the overture to Goethe's tragedy *Egmont*—display spiritual and technical balance between strict musical form and the poetic idea: form triumphant!

OBLIGATO ACCOMPANIMENT

Beethoven himself also points to the correct approach to his polyphonic texture. In 1796, he gave to his sonata, Opus 5, for violoncello, the title, *Pour le clavecin avec un violoncello obligé*. In a letter written in 1802, he boasts: "I was born with an obligato accompaniment." These quotations direct the interpreter to the realization of the main feature in Beethoven's contrapuntal style. He can best understand the meaning of Beethoven's word "obligato," usually applied to an instrumental part accompanying a vocal solo, by recalling how preclassical keyboard performers provided accessory parts for padding the voices, which were not treated melodically like the main parts. It was most unusual for the accompaniment to be elaborated, and in such cases it was called the "obligato accompaniment."

One generation before Beethoven, polyphony had reached a culmination in the baroque of Johann Sebastian Bach. This was followed by a reaction compensating for the former wealth of counterpoint by a stream of homophonous expression. The co-ordination of the polyphonic and the homophonic elements became one of Beethoven's main objectives. Doubtlessly, Beethoven acquired the fundamentals of his style through his instinctive and varied choice of teachers, whose schools of composition were so dissimilar. From his mature works, the blending of the two elements, polyphony and melody, emerges in unsurpassable perfection. A complete amalgamation had taken place. As early as his Opus 1, he shows how no part of the accompaniment can be taken out without destroying the whole texture. The accompanying voices are no longer subordinate, and thus broken chords, Alberti basses, and nonfunctional ornaments gradually disappear. Of course, there is still the setup of main and secondary voices, but the latter are called upon to perform more important tasks, all of which explains Beethoven's own term, obligato accompaniment.

The Beethoven interpreter must approach his problem armed, as it were, with the famous principle of Archimedes, who said: "Give me a place to stand, and I will move the earth." If this principle can be applied to the Beethoven rendition, the interpreter will certainly start with the search for the right tempo, and continue with a clear and definite conception of Beethoven's form. Into such a blueprint, he must integrate the other features of style, and he must be particularly conscious of the typical function of counterpoint in correspondence with Beethoven's ideal of obligato accompaniment. After the performer has made sure of the main tempo, he must proceed with proper regard for time modification in the previously declared sense. It is necessary that he always keep the individual shape of Beethoven's subject in mind. The composer's themes are all simple and clear-cut, even the lyric ones. As Romain Rolland points out, "Rousseau's *Return to Nature* is the watchword for Beethoven's artistic expression too."

The proper relation of the first and second themes will, in itself, lead to a well-defined framework held together by the tempo, which, in Beethoven's own words, appears as "the body of performance." The true realization of this trinity of tempo, form, and texture, will insure the correct execution of the whole movement. Naturally, in the Beethoven performance as anywhere, the main need is the inborn gift of interpretation—musical instinct and intuition—which can never be acquired by analytic methods. But, as Beethoven himself is the noblest example of tireless and continuous search for artistic truth, the talented interpreter must, for his part, use the utmost self-control in order to gain real insight into the works of the genius.

PART THREE

ROMANTICISM

VII. Classical
═══Romanticism═══

ROMANTICISM: AN ETERNAL FEATURE OF INTERPRETATION

GERMAN history traditionally dates the inception of the romantic movement from the deaths of Beethoven and Goethe. But Romanticism is an eternal factor in the performance of music. All epochs created romantic works, and no period has any special claim in regard to romantic interpretation. This becomes clear from the meaning of the term involved. If romanticism in musical performance stands for a more humanized way of playing—with subjective emphasis on the emotional, the fantastic, and the virtuoso element—then it cannot be confined to the style of nineteenth-century composers or interpreters. The performing style of the *ars nova*, the stressing of the poet's words in the Renaissance, as well as the fantasies of the Baroque, must be considered romantic. Even the Classicists played quite romantically under certain artistic conditions. In short, before its gradual development into the most important style-building principle of the postclassical era, Romanticism was operative as a latent force in the musical interpretation of former periods.

However, in the middle of the eighteenth century, a new musical style appeared, a style of highly emotional nature that embodied the seventeenth-century tendency toward an expressive music and the eighteenth-century interest in timbre.

Interpretation of this new style employed all possible timbres, not for the sixteenth-century function of polyphonic contrast and distinctness, but for the sake of emotional expressiveness. A new sensibility, a tender cantabile, emerged, first with the scores of Philipp Emanuel Bach, and later with those of Mozart. Yet another generation was to pass before these characteristics were absorbed by a new style of interpretation that dominated musical rendition throughout the nineteenth century.

THE CLASSICISTS ROMANTICIZED

Haydn conceives romantically that which is distinctly human in the life of man. Mozart discerns the superhuman, the marvelous, which emanates from the imagination. Beethoven's music engenders a haze of dismay, dread, sorrow, and expresses the timeless yearning which is the quintessence of romanticism. He may, therefore, be looked upon as a profoundly romantic composer.

These words were written by E. T. A. Hoffmann, composer-poet, writer of fantastic music and fiction, himself the hero of Offenbach's unique opera *Tales of Hoffmann*, and, again, the creator of the story that inspired Schumann's *Kreisleriana*. Hoffmann even places the three masters who symbolize the very core of Classicism—Haydn, Mozart, Beethoven—under the banner of Romanticism, showing the relativity of our modern classification. It is impossible to appreciate the importance of Hoffmann's view without realizing the fact that his fantastic being was a truly dominant power behind the musical scenes at the opening of the nineteenth century. Even the uncompromising Beethoven paid his respects to him. Whatever was thought, written, or interpreted in romantic circles in Germany during this period was influenced by Hoffmann's weird and brilliant fancy, which, in a rare blend of striking musical and poetic gifts, resulted in a most radical Romanticism.

With the Classicists romanticized, an era of growing individualism and interpretative subjectivity set in. Not the classic counterbalance of content and form, but the performer's individuality, gradually appears as the driving force of a personalized interpretation. Tradition and formalistic convention are overthrown. A definite turn from the objective to the subjective attitude takes place. The interpreter no longer "performs." He "reproduces" the art work. The very word "reproduction" evinces the fact that a specific process of re-creation is implied. Is not the employment of the interpreter's mental and emotional qualities imperative in the rendition of music that is but a manifestation of the most subjective experiences of life—music in which the composer has sublimated his dreams and visions? For even if such fantastic music could convey his hidden meaning solely through the note script, would it be sufficient for the performer to delineate the extravagance, buoyancy, and emotionalism of romantic works with objective reserve, to use a compass and ruler for his orientation in a utopian world? The classical score may lend itself to the tracing of its contours, so splendidly adapted for copying by the performer. But the romantic forms have already been relaxed for the sake of new expressive forces. With the Romanticist, the aim of the interpreter has ceased to be abstract, as in a fugue or a symmetrical sonata form. As the nineteenth century progresses, the romantic performance becomes more and more an appeal to the listener's imagination, to his subconscious, which is more exciting than the plea of a baroque interpreter for conscious intellectual understanding.

WORK-FIDELITY

In striking contrast to the attitude of wilfulness toward the score, there also prevails, during the nineteenth century, the contrasting thought of allegiance to the score. Despite the new enrichment through the romantic technique, the tendency to preserve the formalistic classical ground within the new music becomes manifest. Even in the theater, with the gradual separation of the music drama from the old type of opera, there appear reformative approaches in the production of dramatic scores, leading to perfect co-ordination of the scene and the music as performing forces. New designs for rehearsing, new heights of conscientiousness in the preparation of stage and orchestra, renunciation of even the smaller licenses indulged in by vocal luminaries, are the highroads to the unified art work of the future.

We shall now follow the different trends of the romantic century's interpretation as they appeared on the musical scene in vocal and instrumental performance. Our introductory outline follows, by and large, the chronology of schools. Characteristic of the romantic way, with its emphasis on human attributes, the first departure from classical interpretation did not occur in the more spectacular forms, such as the symphony, but in the intimacy of *Lied* performance.

LIED PERFORMANCE

The mode and manner in which Vogl sings and I accompany him, the way in which, during such moments, we seem to be one, is something quite novel and unheard-of for these people.—SCHUBERT

Nothing could be more romantic, more personal and human than the performance of the *Lied*. It is no accident that Schubert made his most pertinent contribution to interpretation in his approach to the new art song. When he elevated the piano accompanist to the status of an interpreter, with duties and rights equal to those of the singer, a great change came about; previously the accompanist could hardly have been considered an "interpreter" in song renditions. There had been just solo and accompaniment—only one interpreter proper, the singer. The pianist had functioned as a *continuo* player whose task it was slavishly to follow the voice and its whims. It was Schubert's achievement to create a new interpretative team, a unified ensemble woven out of the two, a performance in which both singer and pianist reproduced the song on terms of shared artistic responsibility. Naturally, such an innovation was made possible by the overthrow of the *basso continuo* regime, under which even Haydn and Mozart were satisfied with the use of largely homophonic accompaniments for their songs. Schubert, however, chose to interweave his motifs, to connect the phrases between the voice and the piano parts intimately. He entrusted the accompanist with the song's realistic hues, with motifs that colored and characterized, all together providing new and important material for interpretation.

POETRY SOUNDS AND MUSIC SPEAKS

The celebrated baritone Johann Michael Vogl (1768–1840) and Schubert became the first historical pair of *Lied* interpreters in this advanced sense. Both were fully aware of an artistic need to break with the past in song interpretation. Various statements prove such complete departure from the traditional style of song reading.

It is significant that Vogl was originally an interpreter of operas, acclaimed for his presentations of Gluck roles. His Orestes in *Iphigenie in Tauris* is mentioned as an extraordinary performance. Only an interpreter of Gluck's purified dramatic thought (not the routine opera singer with his virtuosic ambitions) could have found his bearings in the world of Schubert. Like that of so many other baritones of this dramatic genre, Vogl's force is best described in terms of declamatory and expressive qualities rather than sensuous beauty of voice and *bel canto* technique. It was Schubert's friend Schober, remembered as the poet of *An die Musik*, who brought the two together—the renowned opera singer and the modest, struggling, little-known composer—probably in 1817. Vogl immediately realized the necessity of a new approach for interpretation of this type of *Lied*, and wrote in his diary:

> Nothing else has so openly revealed the lack of a practical method of singing as Schubert's songs. How else could these veritably divine inspirations, these products of a musical second sight, have failed to create a tremendous impression throughout the musical world? How many would otherwise not have realized perhaps, for the first time, what is meant by speech: poetry in tones, words in harmony, thought garbed in music?

In the singer's words, a fine definition of the interpretative goal is here given. And the classical Austrian poet Grillparzer, Schubert's friend and witness of these performances, conjured up allegorically their spirit and style: "He bade poetry sound and music speak, not as mistress and maid, but as sisters, the two embracing above Schubert's head."

MELODIES INTERWOVEN

The piano received even stronger accent in song interpretation under Schumann. He continued where Schubert left off in liberating the keyboard instrument from the status of a mere accompanying factor—increasing its importance finally to such a degree that the center of gravity shifted from the singer to the pianist. And from the auxiliary position he occupied prior to 1800, the song accompanist advanced eventually to the foreground of *Lied* interpretation. It was only natural that Schumann, who underlined the fine traits of the text in his piano parts, should insist that the singer make a thorough study of the accompaniment also. A glance at the song *Der Nussbaum*, in which the melody is so completely interwoven between the voice and piano parts, shows the new distribution of thematic material, unknown in preromantic compositions. "The poetry must repose with the singer like a bride—freely, happily, and completely," reads Schumann's guiding advice.

We realize from all accounts that the *Lied* performance, although involving two artists, is amalgamated in one single conception. The pianist cannot be considered as an assistant artist by the singer. Clearly, the accompaniment must not, in exaggerated and misinterpreted modesty, retire to the harmonic background of its former *basso continuo* function. Although discretion remains a virtue of accompanying, in fact one of its chief premises, the proper balance must be found between dynamic covering of the solo, and an insignificant harmonic filling in, in songs where the piano has been treated as an independent part by the composer. The voices of the piano must be singing too, and must be given equal emphasis in the new art of romantic *Lied* performance.

BACK TO THE MANUSCRIPT

> *The original manuscript remains the authority to which we must refer.*—SCHUMANN

SCRIPT VERSUS PRINT

One of the most characteristic features in modern interpretation is the increasing tendency to turn to the original manuscripts of great composers as the dependable basis for proper rendition. Studying the composer's manuscript, rather than the printed edition, is the ideal way of approaching a master's score. The reason for such an attitude is obvious. In the course of time, certain errors of copying or editorial correction have changed the original to such a degree that the most determined objective interpreter can no longer find his bearings. Since normally the original is not available for study, a satisfactory substitute is a facsimile of the manuscript. The most progressive of our contemporary artists never miss an opportunity of securing photostatic reproductions of the texts of the works they play, if they possibly can. These copies frequently reveal that editors have ignored or misrepresented the composer's intentions, through either incredible carelessness or personal vanity.

Robert Schumann was, if not the inaugurator, then at least one of the earliest exponents of this back-to-the-manuscript movement in objective interpretation. In his essay on corrupted readings of masterworks, Schumann expresses a desire to remove all accidental or erroneous injuries to great historical scores. "The masters would smile," Schumann asserts, "at the reasons for some of the errors in performance." Nevertheless, while Schumann stresses the objective approach by insisting upon reference to the manuscript, he at the same time warns the interpreter against blind acceptance of every detail of the manuscript and against an exaggeration of the conception of objectivity.

To solve the seeming paradox, we must recall Beethoven's manuscripts, his haste and creative excitement, which caused divers and obvious errors in his original scores. Nevertheless, the manuscript must remain the "final authority," and Schumann uncompromisingly demands that "all artists and connoisseurs should compare the printed editions with the original scripts, whenever possible."

A case in point are examples taken from the works of Bach, Mozart, and Beethoven. In Bach's Toccata and Fugue for Organ in F Major, Schumann's unfailing contrapuntal sense discovers a number of wrong notes in the construction of the canon. Other mistakes in *The Art of the Fugue* can no more "be overlooked than a gap in a painting or a missing leaf in a book." Turning to Mozart's G Minor Symphony, Schumann doubts the scoring in the modulation from D-flat major to B-flat minor in the twenty-ninth measure. Mozart introduced into the score a passage more fully instrumentated than his first sketch. Later he seems to have forgotten to strike out the original notation, thus causing an ambiguity that Schumann's sharp eye detects. Obvious errors in copies of Beethoven's Fourth and Sixth symphonies are likewise brought to light. For instance, in the opening movement of the *Pastoral Symphony*, the copyist mistook simile marks (✐) for rests (✐). In consequence, a passage originally scored for violin and supposed to continue (on the ground of the simile direction) suddenly terminates, because of the mistaken rest sign.

These examples resolve the implied contradiction in Schumann's interpretative attitude: in any case, the performer is to adhere strictly to the original; yet he must also be on guard against the possible errors in the composer's own script.

FANTASY BEHIND BARS

To complete the picture of Schumann's interpretative ideology, we must turn to another aspect of his work, less technical and more psychological, touching one of the most complex problems in musical interpretation. In one of his fascinating letters, Schumann writes:

> The reason why many of my compositions are hard to understand is that they are bound up with my remote associations, and often very much so. Everything of importance in a lifetime takes hold of me, and I must express it in musical form.

Thus, the problem of Schumann interpretation is attributed —by the man who ought to know best—to the underlying associations of his musical fantasy. Again, Schumann asks his wife and closest adviser:

> I have arranged the *Nachtstücke*. What do you think of calling them: No. 1, "Funeral Procession"; No. 2, "Droll Company"; No. 3, "Nightly Carousal"; No. 4, "Round with Solo Voices"? While I was composing, I kept seeing funerals, coffins, and unhappy, despairing faces; and when I had finished and was trying to think of a title, the only one that occurred to me was "Funeral Fantasia." I was so much moved by the composition that the tears came into my eyes.

All of this proves Schumann's urge to poetic interpretation and gives a glimpse into his gropings for verbal hints. Now the question is: In playing a work like *Kreisleriana*, has the pianist the responsibility of imbuing his performance with his own acquaintance with the fantastic figures of Hoffmann's tales? Does the performer, in such a case, play "program music"? Schumann's answer is: Not at all! "A title," he states, "might aid appreciation by stimulating thought and fancy. It cannot help poor music and would not mar good music, but music which requires it is in a sorry state." These few words settle the problem: the composer himself makes it crystal-clear that in no way must the fantasy-provoking title of his piece be confused with an extraneous story of the music. To his own fanciful pictures he accords only subjective value, and he finally even reaches the point of considering titles for instrumental pieces nonsensical. And his attitude toward program music of other composers appears definitely antagonistic.

In the composer's own view, then, the Schumann interpreter must, first of all, grasp the character of his scores from the musical content—from the very structure of the score. Schumann grants that delving into the poetic background will stimulate the performer's thought and fancy. Yet he insists, in his writings on the subject, that it is the music that must always remain the primary concern of the interpreter. If we trace Schumann's ideology further, we see how he stamps himself as an aesthete of the *Affektenlehre*, with the following viewpoint on tempo:

> You know how I dislike quarreling about tempo, and how for me only the inner measure of the movement is conclusive. Thus, an allegro of one who is cold by nature always sounds lazier than a slow tempo by one of sanguine temperament. With the orchestra, however, the proportions are decisive. Stronger and denser masses are capable of bringing out the detail as well as the whole with more emphasis and importance; whereas, with smaller and finer units, one must compensate for the lack of resonance by pushing forward in the tempo.

These remarks about tempo could have come quite as readily from the pen of eighteenth-century theorists like Quantz, Schubart, or Mattheson. And Schumann's closeness to the *Affektenlehre* is irrefutably proven by his countless literary interpretations of music, such as that of Loewe's piano sonata, in which he sees "a green meadow and butterflies," or his vision, in Schubert's marches, of the "old Austrian veterans jogging along with ham and sausages on their bayonets."

Let us now summarize Schumann's statements for the guidance of his performer of today. Clearly, in rendering musical ideas of poetic or pictorial background, the interpreter must inquire into the sources of the fantasies. Yet in no wise must the fantasy-provoking heading of the piece be confused with an extraneous story of the music. Then again, Schumann's score script, being more detailed than that of his predecessors, sets down specifically what he wants conveyed in tones. Even so, no amount of verbal indications, which from now on join specific musical directions, can cover the whole ground, and it is here that room is left for the personal contribution of the performer. The true Schumann interpreter, portraying the author's world of dreams and fantasies on an instrument, does more than simply outline the score. He first makes the hidden poetic idea of the work his own, then he retraces the musical structure of the score in utmost loyalty.

RETURN TO THE PAST

BACH RENAISSANCE

After the death of Bach in 1750, performers were completely ignorant of the spiritual wealth bestowed on mankind by a forgotten organist in a Leipzig church. From a survey of representative programs between 1750 and 1829, it would be difficult to guess that such works as the B Minor Mass, the Passions, and the cantatas had ever been written.

It was left to Mendelssohn to accomplish the greatest interpretative task of his time: the nineteenth-century revival of the St. Matthew Passion. The story of this task coincides with Mendelssohn's boyhood, when, by one of the fortunate accidents in the history of musical performance, he became the pupil of Karl Friedrich Zelter, composer, conductor, and musical arbiter to Goethe. While supervising young Mendelssohn's counterpoint and composition, Zelter made him also a member of his famous Berlin *Singakademie*. Here, since the boy's voice had not yet changed, he joined the altos. The apprentice became acquainted with the great choral scores, gaining the particular type of inside experience that comes only through personal participation in the work of a performing ensemble. Soon he was to be appointed piano accompanist for Zelter's rehearsals, where he had to learn to accommodate his remarkable pianistic facilities to the firm beat of a pedantic conductor.

Zelter had acquired the manuscript of the St. Matthew Passion from the estate of a cheesemonger—an amazing tale, considered authentic by certain biographers, who also assert that Zelter was actuated by his mania for collecting manuscripts rather than by any real interest in the music of the Baroque. Be this as it may, no sooner had Mendelssohn had an opportunity of seeing the Bach manuscript than he was overwhelmed with the beauty of the score. Though at first Zelter refused him permission to copy it, Mendelssohn found ways and means to secure the parts and made up his mind to perform the Passion. His first attempt was with a small group of sixteen voices, about the size of the original Bach choir at the St. Thomas Church (p. 80).

The year 1829 marked the very first formal performance of the great work. With his interpretation, Mendelssohn, at the age of only twenty years, not only displayed technical insight into Bach's musical world; he restored the Passion along strictly historical lines, with a loyalty to the original rarely practiced in this time of rapidly increasing interpretative freedom. The general reaction following this performance proved that Mendelssohn had accomplished more than a sporadic rendition. Soon a revival of Bach throughout Germany was in evidence. The B Minor Mass likewise was given a performance when the Berlin opera director, Spontini, produced the second half, joining it in a program with Beethoven's *Missa solemnis*. Publishers, foreseeing an approaching demand, were encouraged to edit all of Bach's scores.

In 1835 Mendelssohn took over the directorship of the Gewandhaus in Leipzig, where, with the help of men like the concertmaster Ferdinand David, he developed Germany's most important school of interpretation in his time. Its ideal was that of conserving classical tradition and reforming the contemporary taste, which was threatening to run riot in the wild arbitrariness of various romantic trends.

The Mendelssohn school remained a symbol for objective music-making much admired by great musicians everywhere in Europe. Mendelssohn himself emerged as a reformer of taste, standing for marvelous clarity and unity in performance, for graceful melody, euphony, and classical brilliancy—a champion of interpretative tradition. His was a classical style of perfect symmetry, proportion, and elegance. He favored movement and fluent tempo and was violently opposed to dragging and slowness. Wagner's romantic differentiation between two contrasting types of allegro made no sense to him (cf. p. 281).

FLUENT TEMPI

Thus it was a disagreement about tempo that caused the frequently cited controversy between the two composers, the issue of which Wagner himself states in his essay *On Conducting*. Together they attended a performance of Beethoven's Eighth Symphony. Reissiger conducted, and took the third movement, *tempo di minuetto*, quickly—in *Ländler* tempo rather than that of the stately old minuet. Wagner was incensed, and still more so when Mendelssohn smiled appreciatively and said, "That is all right. Bravo!"

This was too much for Wagner. "I thought I was looking," he said, "into an abyss of superficiality—into complete emptiness."

The incident exemplifies the clash between the two conceptions: Mendelssohn's interpretation, based on classical principles, fluent, elastic, elegant; and the highly romantic, declamatory, so-called "neo-German" performance, of which Liszt was the inaugurator and Wagner the most important exponent. The neo-German style, as we shall see in more detail when reading Liszt's and Wagner's doctrines on interpretation, principally favored broad, singing melody, rhapsodic liberty, all of which was in contrast to formal, compact, "classical" treatment. Mendelssohn's desire not only for rhythmical regularity, but also for fluency in tempo, was general. "Never sing a song so that one falls asleep, Madame, not even a lullaby," he jocularly admonished a singer. His tendency to movement is reaffirmed by Hans von Bülow, who asserts that, in piano teaching, Mendelssohn liked to issue orders such as "Forward!" or "Get started!" or "Fire away!"

As a piano performer too, Mendelssohn, in strict keeping with his objective principles, was faithful to the classical scripts of the great masters, whose works he frequently played. His style is well characterized by C. K. Salaman's comment on his interpretation of Beethoven: "A more reverential, sympathetic, and conservative reading of the old master's text was never heard." Notwithstanding this traditional attitude, not all his individual traits could be excluded: "His touch was exquisitely delicate, and the fairy fancies of his *Midsummer Night's Dream* music seemed ever to haunt him in his playing, lending it a magic charm"—a fine example of inescapable subjectivity within the desired limits of objectivity.

THE PARISIAN PIANO SCHOOL

Though Mendelssohn in his own tone world enchantingly portrayed the romantic themes of fairy dreams and nature, he was completely aloof from the tone painting of external program music, as represented by the Parisian pianistic school of Herz and Kalkbrenner. This is shown in his letter to Zelter, in 1832, in which romantic mannerisms of the Paris pianists are treated with derision:

> Kalkbrenner has gone completely romantic. He is playing his dream, some sort of new piano concert, where he makes his conversion to Romanticism quite evident. He says, first, that it starts with indefinite dreams. Later comes despair, after that a confession of love, and finally a military march. No sooner did Henry Herz hear of this than he likewise quickly composed a romantic piano piece, and he, too, gives some kind of explanation. First, there is a dialogue between a shepherd and a shepherdess, then a thunderstorm, later a prayer with evening bells, and a military march at the end. You may not believe all this; but it is just as I say.

As this letter to his teacher shows, it is in a derogatory sense that Mendelssohn uses the term "Romanticism." He resembles Schumann in the vigorous denunciation of programs for music, notwithstanding the use of titles of romantic flavor for certain compositions. The attitude of both is that of "romantic Classicism," contradicting to some extent the habitual classification of the two masters as typical exponents of "Romanticism."

The interpretation of works like Mendelssohn's *Songs without Words* should be guided by the composer's unmistakable position: one must grasp the true style of these unpretentious

musical poems and their soulful character as fully opposed to
the superficial products of the celebrated Paris pianists, who
made salons and concert halls resound with their pseudo-
romantic sentimentality. Unfortunately, the facility of execution of the *Songs without Words* has long been the technical
premise—and their misunderstood poetic connotation the vehicle—of sentimentalization in the hands of piano-playing dilet-
tantes. The superiority of the Mendelssohn style was eventually acknowledged, even in Paris, outside the sphere of
influence in Germany. The Gewandhaus style—pure, graceful,
formal—had started to compete most successfully with the
virtuoso style—specious, dashing, sentimental. Finally Mendelssohn's piano compositions gained immense popularity with
the French. And Berlioz remarked that during examinations
at the Conservatoire the pianoforte started playing the G Minor Concerto of its own accord at the approach of the pupil,
the hammers jumping about even after the instrument had
been demolished and thrown out the window.

PURISM OF INTERPRETATION

Indefatigably, Mendelssohn was fighting for his interpretative ideals on two fronts, at home and abroad. From the
same, never changing standpoint of objectivity, he bitterly
criticized performances outside his personal domain, in the
churches and the theater. With disgust he commented upon
a Munich performance of Beethoven's *Fidelio*, in regard to
arrangement and cutting, calling Germany a "crazy country,
which can produce great creators but is a complete failure in
the art of interpretation." Despite the superior equipment of
the German orchestras and theaters, there were no real performers on the stage. Celebrated but capricious singers ought
to be repudiated. Those were to be favored who were less

known but willing to subordinate themselves faithfully and without virtuosic ambition to the ensemble idea of the classic opera. An opportunity to acquire a more detailed account of Mendelssohn's interpretative beliefs is provided by his *Reisebriefe*, written to his teacher Zelter, and to the beloved sister Fanny and other members of his family. Among them is a description of the holy services in Rome, striking in technical details, a complete master's thesis on ecclesiastical performance.

In spite of the bitter attacks to which he was subjected in his later years on the part of the neo-German group, and which he had later to share with Brahms, Mendelssohn had the gratifying distinction of being called the "leading light of musical Germany" by Schumann, who so generously also said: "I look up to Mendelssohn as a high mountain; he is a god."

Schumann's eulogy is only the logical result of a common interpretative ideal. The Liszt-Wagner ideology remained forever in opposition. To them, Mendelssohn and his followers were the "members of a musical temperance union"; their classicism was nothing "but a fear of expression."

Today, we can afford to look at the bygone struggle with historical detachment. As the grandson of the philosopher Moses Mendelssohn (who, by seeking to prove the immortality of the soul in his dialogue *Phädon*, gained the title of "the German Socrates") the musician Felix Mendelssohn stood for absolute purism. In spite of his romantic subject matter, he worshiped classical form and its interpretative principles.

ROMANCE AND BALANCE

An aeolian harp, . . . a violet.—
SCHUMANN ON CHOPIN'S PLAYING

The popularity of a style is not necessarily an advantage in resolving the problem of its authenticity. While no romanticist is more performed than Chopin, none is so widely exposed to misunderstanding and misrepresentation. And like that of Mendelssohn, the style of Chopin has suffered in performance through sentimentalization by amateurs as well as through aggrandizement by virtuosi.

Documentary descriptions of Chopin's playing suggest a picture of his own performance that is like a vivid portrait; its colors are technical and aesthetic statements on the part of the best contemporary musicians of his time. Historically seen, the problem of Chopin interpretation is rooted, first of all, in the question of the instrument; since his death, performing conditions have altered. Certain sources indicate that Chopin himself did not enjoy using the grand piano for his miniatures modeled on French taste, nor even for the outbursts of his Slavonic temper in the greater forms. He preferred small pianos, in significant contrast to Beethoven's choice of a Broadwood for its expressive power. What Chopin sought was the subdued quality and tonal charm of the smaller instrument, thus sacrificing greater volume even in works that might have been more appropriately performed on the grand. Though the square pianos of Chopin's time were already larger, they still had the wooden framework; it was this particular construction of the earlier pianos that permitted a blending of tone colors not easy to achieve with modern metal body construction.

The modern instrument can reproduce faithfully only certain tonal effects of Chopin's square piano. To realize the acoustic conditions under which he played, one must remember that his chosen place for performing was, not unlike Schubert's, an intimate circle of friends—an *entente cordiale* in the drawing-room rather than the public concert hall. Berlioz stresses the necessity of hearing him at "close range, in the salon rather than the theater," asserting that Chopin's playing had no point of resemblance to that of any other virtuoso of his acquaintance.

In today's large halls, performers must depend upon the augmented resonance of the modern concert grand to fill the wide space, and with the changing acoustic setup, the chamber style of performance must undergo proportionate alterations. On the way from the private home to the large hall, Chopin's tenderness, the melancholic gentleness of his touch, are bound to be drastically adjusted to augmented effects—like a small picture projected on a larger screen. We see, then, how Chopin's originals were but the result of his accurate and delicate judgment, eventually becoming aggrandized during a time that was only too favorably disposed to grandeur and power in interpretation. From documents, it emerges as an axiom that Chopin's own playing was of superlative delicacy, reaching so high a degree of restraint that contemporaries looked for an explanation in the notorious ill-health of the composer. Yet, whether Chopin's tubercular condition or his retiring psychic nature serves as a rationalization of his own performances, is immaterial. In delineating the true Chopin style, not physiological causes, but musical facts of unambiguous significance are related by musicians who were themselves not only masterly composers but also pianists, and so in the most favorable position to judge and describe what they heard.

THE WELL-DEFINED PHRASE

Before starting the roll call of these witnesses, we quote Chopin himself, with the following significant statement from one of his letters: "I could not have learned to play the piano in Germany. There people complain that I perform too softly, too delicately. They are accustomed to the piano pounding of their own musicians."

Nevertheless, the finest German artists understood Chopin's style very well. Thus, Mendelssohn praises him as a "thorough musician, who, in contrast to the half virtuosos and half classics of the time, has his perfect and well-defined phrase." Schumann calls for abandonment of emphasized virtuosity in Chopin interpretation, even for pieces like the Second Scherzo: "It must not be treated in bravura fashion, since that would destroy its delicate ethereal twilight effect; it lingers in memory like the scent of violets or a poem of Byron's." He further accentuates the fully poetic element when he says:

> The études are beautiful interpretations. You think of a solitary star fulfilling its destiny through the dark and lonesome hours; or of an aeolian harp, over which the artist's hands wander in ever varying mood, above whose deeper notes is heard an ever audible melodious voice—so he plays. The loveliest is in A (No. 25), a poem rather than a study; the softest notes are audible; it is a wave of harmonies to the distant ether, in which melody and voices mingle.

CHOPIN'S RUBATO

Turning now from the poetic to the technical, we find the *tempo rubato* question again appearing in the foreground of contemporary comment. We left this problem of time variation in connection with Mozart, after having gained insight into the rubato technique of the eighteenth century. With the progress of time, a marked change also in this particular feature of keyboard execution is generally assumed. Such a difference in rubato is taken for granted in the way the majority of pianists today read the music of the eighteenth and nineteenth centuries. If Mozart and Chopin readings are to be compared from the standpoint of rubato, the prevailing opinion is that if there is any time to be "stolen" at all in Mozart, it could never amount to the lavish use of rubato considered indispensable for the rendition of Chopin. How often are modern performances of his music plain rubato orgies, to which criticism seems to have become resigned!

A poll of performers would show that, with reference to the rubato question, one is little concerned with the classical and preclassical periods. It is the romantic music that is regarded as the natural show vehicle of rubato. And in this, first among all, the works of Chopin, according to dictionaries and other authorities, exemplify most completely the phenomenon of time variation. If anyone should dare to play Chopin without considerable doses of rubato, certain critics would be very much annoyed and firmly demand the use of it. We shall see, however, in what respects the too widely accepted rubato hypothesis, in present-day Chopin interpretation, differs from the one we are about to reconstruct from documentary sources.

Chopin was an ardent admirer of beauty in singing. The Polish composer's style was strongly affected by the vocal element of the Latin music atmosphere in which he found his home for the decisive phase of his life. This partly explains Chopin's absorption of the rubato style into the intensely personal lyricism of his piano compositions. The sensitive, declamatory, individual attitude implicit in the rubato offered a perfect solution of his problem—to exploit the piano for profoundly human, nervous, and expressive designs.

It was this very rubato playing that struck Liszt as the most fascinating technical feature of Chopin's performance. Here is what Liszt says—and also where he errs: "He [Chopin] was the first to introduce in his compositions that manner which stamps his virtuosity in a specific way and which he called *tempo rubato*—time stolen without any rule, flexible, yielding, and yearning."

This is a statement remarkable in more ways than one. Apparently Liszt was unaware of the classical rubato, and refers to Chopin's technique as an innovation. Obviously he was unacquainted with the correspondence between Mozart and his father, as quoted above. It seems, however, that Chopin was the first to introduce the term rubato as a direction written in the manuscript—namely, in the Mazurka in F-sharp Minor, Opus 6, No. 1. It must have been this novelty of directing the player's attention to time variation that led Liszt into the error of confusing the first rubato ever expressly demanded, with the first one ever executed.

Another observer of Chopin's time variation is Ignaz Moscheles, who explains Chopin's rubato as a specified means of gliding over harsh modulations in a fairy-like way with delicate fingers. Thus, rubato was applied in a purely functional way, so unlike the abuse of it by many modern executants with whom it degenerates from slight variation into a disregard of time—a vulgarized license of meter and confusion of rhythm smuggled into the Chopin performance in the guise of so-called tradition. It is this amateurish, incompetent use of rubato that has partly caused Chopin interpretation to deteriorate into a playground of sentimentalism and musical degradation.

In opposition to all the license and extravagances that performers today indulge in, we discover that Chopin regarded the rubato as by no means a departure from metrical accuracy, but as a sensitive adjustment of time values, a delicate elasticity and flexibility of pace. "The left hand," Chopin explained to his pupil von Lenz, "is the conductor. It must not waver or lose ground. Do with the right hand what you will and can." However, we must remember that the elder Mozart asserted that he would rather show than tell in words what the "stolen time" was like. The comparing of the left hand to a conductor might be confusing to a student who would assume that reckless independence of melody and accompaniment was advocated. He must realize that Chopin had to resort to an extreme formulation to make his point. In teaching, Chopin illustrated on the piano the meaning of his rule, which, verbalized and without a musical example, may lend itself to an exaggerated conclusion.

Recalling the points of view on stolen time expressed by Tosi, Mozart, and Philipp Emanuel Bach, their general idea of rubato is seen to be analogous to that of Chopin: the imperturbability of the beat in the accompaniment is stressed, while the melody must steal the time as it can. Other pupils of Chopin supplement von Lenz's quotation by testifying that their master "required adherence to the strictest rhythm." "Chopin hated," it is asserted, "all lingering and dragging, *misplaced* rubatos, and exaggerated ritardandos." Chorley, commenting in the *Athenaeum* upon one of Chopin's recitals in London, says that "he used rubato, but still subject to a *presiding sentiment of measure.*" And once more the already familiar formula reappears in the comment of Karasovski, first biographer of Chopin: "The bass went in quiet regular time, while the right hand moved about it with perfect freedom." Two factors of Chopin's playing emerge: balance and the controlling element. These features are instanced wherever we find contemporary accounts of his performing.

It is quite fascinating to observe how the foremost dance type of his native Poland, the mazurka, gave Chopin the rhythmical intimation of *tempo rubato*. The three beats of the mazurka, in a true Polish performance, were slightly uneven, not unlike the beats of the Vienna waltz, and yet somehow retained their triangular quality. Thus Chopin's fantasy was inspired by the faint irregularity of the mazurka, which still seems compatible with the fundamental character of triple time. How its rhythmical problem was actually solved by

Chopin's own performance is described by Sir Charles Hallé, who in his naïveté seriously reproached Chopin for playing certain mazurkas in four-four instead of the required three-four time. It is related how that "incorrigible Victorian, having counted punctiliously against the master's performance, offered to prove his charge, and Chopin, amused, confessed the crime at once, but insisted humorously that it was quite in the national character." Finally, Paderewski has explained the secret of the mazurka, which gives it "that peculiar accent on the third beat, resulting sometimes in three-four plus one-sixteen": such a performance involves a slight caesura before the third beat, which gives the effect of a prolongation of the second beat.

Returning from such detail to the general line of the Chopin performance, the modern interpreter will always have to remember Chopin's specific dislike of exaggeration. "Je vous prie de vous asseoir," he would sarcastically invite any pupil who indulged in arbitrary excursions from the score. So great was his aversion to melodramatic display that it interfered even with his appreciation of Liszt as a performer. Thus, after hearing Liszt interpret a Beethoven sonata, Chopin complained: "Must one always speak so declamatorily?" While he criticized the reading of his greatest pianistic contemporary for stylistic reasons, Chopin found the performance of a precise drillmaster enjoyable; referring to J. B. Cramer, he says: "Though he plays beautifully and correctly, he does not give way to passion like other young men."

It would appear from the evidence at hand that some of the so-called exponents of Chopin interpretation would do well to consult the opinions of the composer. Concertgoers have become accustomed to hearing Chopin in the grand manner. Chopin himself obviously desired his works played otherwise. The issue is clear. Chopin, willing to give a refined pedant

credit for emotional control, but merciless toward mere elo-
quence and rhythmical extravagance in a supervirtuoso, was
himself a rubato player of exquisite balance.

Balance! This is the very quality that differentiates the genuine Chopin interpretation from the spurious one.

VIII. Power and
Virtuosity

BERLIOZ

*Crescendo . . . like an im-
mense fire that eventually
sets the whole sky aflame.*

THE QUINTESSENCE of French romantic interpre-
tation is personified in Hector Berlioz, French in his blending
of tradition and revolt, romantic in his powerful, fantastic, and
ecstatic manifestations. All these traits are completely absorbed
in Berlioz' interpretative ideology as we know it from his
scores and also from his prolific writings, including essays,
critiques, an autobiography, and treatises. Comparable to Wagner in the wide scope of his activities as an interpreter, both
practical and theoretical, Berlioz managed in his most adven-
turous and varied career—from starving chorister to composer,
conductor, musicologist, critic, and finally librarian of the Paris
Conservatoire—to make the most important contribution on
orchestral performance that emerged in the Latin countries
during the nineteenth century: *Le grand traité d'instrumentation et d'orchestration* appeared first in 1844, yet its influence
is still felt today. Richard Strauss re-edited and augmented a
German edition in 1904, a work on orchestration that is one of
the most comprehensive of its kind. In addition to its classification of instruments, it brought to the fore the aesthetico-

interpretative problem of orchestral performance. *Le grand traité* also contains a significant epilogue on the theory of conducting. Here, as in his autobiography and essays, the author offers penetrating insight into an interpretative world of noble aims and grandiose display. The latter aspect overshadows the memory of Berlioz as a profound and loyal guardian of old masterworks. One knows him for his insatiable desire for the colossal in performance, for massive ensembles with galaxies of executants such as nobody before had dared to propose and very few since have ventured to emulate.

DREAM ORCHESTRA

Only the following list of the actual figures and suggested proportions of instrumental groups gives an adequate picture of the enormous aggregation that Berlioz hoped to raise and present in a hall to be especially constructed for his utopian dream of power in performance.

IDEAL ORCHESTRA OF BERLIOZ

120	violins (4 divisions)	2	little flutes
40	violas (10 able to play *viola d'amour*)	2	little flutes in D flat
45	violoncelli	6	oboes
		6	English horns
18	double basses (tuned G-D-A)	5	saxophones
		4	quint bassoons
15	other basses (4 strings each: E-A-D-G)	12	bassoons
		4	little clarinets in E flat
4	octobasses	8	clarinets in B flat or A
6	flutes	3	bass clarinets
4	flutes in E flat	16	French horns

8	trumpets	8	timpani
6	cornets	6	small drums
4	alto trombones	3	large drums
6	tenor trombones	4	pairs of cymbals
2	bass trombones	6	triangles
1	ophicleide in C	6	glockenspiel
2	ophicleides in B	12	old cymbals
2	bass tubas	2	large bells
30	harps	2	tam-tams
30	pianofortes	4	half-moons
1	organ		

This orchestra, totaling 465 instrumentalists (according to Berlioz, who discounts some duplications), was to be supplemented by a chorus of lesser size that would have brought the total of performers to 825. Evidently Berlioz felt that a chorus somewhat inferior numerically would blend best with his titanic orchestra. With such a setup he re-emphasized certain baroque tendencies, whereas today the view prevails that, irrespective of its size, the chorus should outnumber the orchestra.

With his aggregate of performers approaching one thousand, Berlioz envisioned a grandiose organization within the framework of which smaller vocal and orchestral units would take care of the more delicate and subtle parts of the composition. Berlioz dreamed of

a million combinations possible with this gigantic group, in richness of harmony, variety of sounds, multitude of contrasts, comparable to nothing yet achieved in any art.

And the composer of the *Symphonie fantastique* longed for the fantastic everywhere, producing excitement like

a hurricane in the tropics or the explosive roar of a volcano. There would be the mysterious rustle of primeval forests, the lamentations, the triumphant, mournful song of soulful, loving, and emotional nations. The silence would make one tremble by its solemnity. The crescendo would cause even an unresponsive nature to shiver. It would grow like an immense fire that eventually sets the whole sky aflame.

This sums up well enough Berlioz' dreams of orchestral performance, and shows how grandeur and power appear as interpretative forces. The dreams were never fully realized, however. Representative of what Berlioz did accomplish with colossal ensembles was the rendition of his *Requiem* on the occasion of the funeral of General Damremont, in the Dome des Invalides in 1837. Four extra brass bands augmented the orchestra, and there were no less than sixteen timpanists—which shocked the Parisians, who were not accustomed to such volume of percussion. In the *Tuba mirum* these four extra orchestras were situated separately, apart from the major ensemble, at the four distant corners—north, south, east, west—while of the brass only the French horns kept their place in the main orchestra. Ingeniously, this ground plan of main and subordinate instrumental bodies anticipated the setup of modern performances of the scores of Mahler and others in the colossal symphonic style.

LIFELONG CAMPAIGN AGAINST ARBITRARINESS

From this highly romantic augmentation of the performing apparatus, an analogous exaggeration of interpretation by no means followed. On the contrary, the rationalistic mind of Berlioz had a well-defined and uncompromising attitude toward the interpreter's task. In spite of the obvious emphasis on the composer's subjective experience, there is, in his expressed views, an insistence on objectivity in interpretation. It is strictly demanded that the interpreter regard himself as nothing more than the loyal medium of the composer. Metronome marks must be relentlessly obeyed; neglecting them amounts to dishonesty. Alterations and editorial corrections of masterworks are considered a veritable crime. Thus, Berlioz was enraged by the highly arbitrary revision of Beethoven by François Joseph Fétis, characterizing the latter's attitude as that of "a professor drunk with his own vanity." (This important and typical instance of the problem of editing and correcting will be taken up in a later section.)

Printed editions of masterworks were not the sole target of Berlioz' wholesale attacks on subjectivity in interpretation. He directed a lifelong campaign against arbitrary performing habits, a fight against license everywhere—in concerts, in opera— not limiting his purge to music, but eventually extending it to the stage and literature. The public also was assailed for its tolerance of the profanation and spoliation of masterworks by the veriest nobodies.

With such an uncompromising attitude on interpretative problems, it is only logical that Berlioz should take the strictest stand on the rubato question. And so he was bound to reject Wagner's style of rendition: "Wagner conducts in a free style, the way Klindworth plays the piano . . . such a style is like dancing on a slack rope . . . *sempre tempo rubato.*" And we may simultaneously look at the obverse of the picture—Wagner's resentment of the Berlioz manner of interpretation: "I have been indifferently edified by the manner in which Berlioz conducted the Mozart symphony (G minor)," and, in a letter to Liszt, "I heard him conduct some classical works, and was amazed to find a conductor who was so energetic in the interpretation of his own compositions sinking into the commonest rut of the vulgar time-beater."

SINGERS, ORCHESTRA PLAYERS, CONDUCTOR

The consistency of Beriloz' work-fidelity is further corroborated by his attitude toward vocal interpretation. Here, in the thousand-year-old realm of arbitrary performance, Berlioz goes to another extreme, making a unique demand: the singing teacher, he insists, must be a composer himself as a prerequisite of his ability to coach students in solfeggio. Only if the *maître du chant* knows how to write a score himself, can he really guide his disciples in the true meaning of another musician's works. A composer would not show his pupils how to scorn rhythm and measure with stupid arrogance, as most singing teachers do, but would guide them on the true way to interpretation of the authentic character of a song or a role. As to the traditional habit of improvised ornamentation, a singer who indulges in coloratura ad libitum is a historical absurdity.

No personal freedom is conceded to the individual orchestra player. Although his vanity may be hurt by being held like a child on a strap, it is only the conductor's conception that matters. The success of the rendition depends on whether all the orchestra members are willing and capable of accepting and reproducing a unified interpretation in their concerted work. Consequently, the conductor must stand in supreme authority. He must have those indefinable qualities without which the invisible tie between him and the performers cannot exist, without which it is impossible for him to transmit his spiritual experiences through the medium of a baton. The orchestra must be aware that the conductor himself feels, understands, is touched. Otherwise his feelings are not carried over to those whom he directs. The conductor's inner fire arouses their warmth, their enthusiasm. On the other hand, if he is indifferent, cold, he paralyzes everything around him like floating icebergs in a polar sea.

THE INTERPRETATIVE DUALITY

A remark that once more points up the complexity of Berlioz' position occurs in the epilogue of his *Traité*, where he says: "The interpreter must glow, feel, touch"—and thus, naturally, be replete with qualities intrinsically emotional, i.e., subjective. Yet the intellectual trend of his interpretative aims, his approach to the score, must remain objective, loyal to the composer's own interpretation.

In line with this aim of objectivity are also those innovations Berlioz suggested for the Paris Conservatoire—among them, a class for rhythm in which both singers and instrumentalists should be taught. No doubt Berlioz would have been pleased with the Dalcroze classes in our schools, where, after at least a century, some of his suggestions have been put into practice. However, his favorite idea, an academic chair of musicology, which he considered indispensable to guard the traditions of the past, has so far been realized only by relatively few advanced colleges in this country.

All the foregoing points show that if, in the beginning, we called the interpreter Berlioz a typical French romanticist expressing power and fantastic emotionalism, we must enlarge this picture by emphasizing the other equally important trend of his interpretation—rigid objectivity, purity. Such duality, it is sure, makes for a strange yet fascinating combination. However, we shall once more in the history of the nineteenth century encounter an instance of style amalgamation in which extremes meet in a powerful intellectual creation—the case of Wagner.

VIRTUOSITY

Ognun' suoi il segreti.—PAGANINI

Génie oblige.—LISZT

From the large and resplendent roster of romantic instrumentalists, two exciting figures have certainly survived the
mortality of interpretative musicianship—Franz Liszt and
Nicolò Paganini. The memory of their performances lives on.
Independently of the attitude of posterity to their achievements as composers, their performances still symbolize the
triumph of the human mind over the hand, presenting unsur-
passed examples of supervirtuosity, of the demoniacal in interpretation. The phenomena of their styles—each a miracle of
verve and audacity—appeared identical to their contemporaries.
That is why the twenty-year-old Liszt, at his Paris debut, received the appellation "the Paganini of the piano." At that
time Paganini, "wizard of the violin," was fifty, and at the
height of his career. But reports on Liszt's and Paganini's
renditions eventually became so similar that, reading them
today, one would hardly be able to differentiate these comments were it not for the specific technicalities associated with
the piano and the violin.

"He develops the capacity of his instrument to the utmost.
Triumphantly, his technique overcomes all difficulties. He is
the past, the present, and the future of the instrument." While
this panegyric could have been applied to either, it happens
to be a description of Liszt's playing. Another such statement
refers not to technical bravura, but to the inner quality of the
virtuosic performance: "In the adagio the artist seemed as if
transformed by magic; no trace remained of the preceding
tours de force. A soulful singer in legato style and of tender
simplicity, he drew forth celestial tones that came from the
heart and penetrated the heart." Again, either might have

been the subject of this enthusiastic quotation about the lofty legato—the pianist or the violinist. It is, however, a comment on Paganini.

But we do not always read of blind adoration. Adverse judgment also occurs, as for instance: "His passion knows no limits. He often wounds one's sense of the beautiful by destroying the melody. He arouses fright and astonishment." Such damning with faint praise might have been deserved by the arbitrary Paganini; yet it was Liszt who provoked this criticism, coming as it did from Clara Wieck, the female musical arbiter of their time.

The comparison between the two supervirtuosos, Paganini and Liszt, could be extended in many other directions. Both were willing and superbly equipped to supply the musical entertainment paid for by the spoiled and superficial *haute volée* in European capitals. These audiences expected a mixture between the concert hall and the circus. The profound had to be smuggled into the players' tours de force. It is for this reason that we read in their programs, full of the wildest gallops and escapades, the names of Haydn and Beethoven.

However, the original Haydn was not exciting enough for the sorcerer Paganini; therefore he decorated the classical music with what the nineteenth-century audience cheered as the "loveliest embellishments and graces." He himself said: "I have my individual method; to it I adapt my composition. Were I to play other works, I should have to adapt them to suit myself." From this rather arrogant attitude, we see that it was the satisfaction of the decorative taste of the virtuoso Paganini that mattered—not Haydn's thought or form.

G STRING ALONE

However, historically seen, Paganini and Liszt each made a major contribution to the development of instrumental performance, and they deserve equal credit for evoking the specific instrumental interest of audiences whose interest hitherto had been satisfied only by vocal pirouettes. The colorful and fantastic background of each personality completely fulfilled the popular conception of what a great artist should be. In appearance both were long-maned archtypes of the romantic musician: the handsome Liszt, idol of young girls' dreams; the ugly Paganini, demonic, like a figure out of Hoffmann. Their life-stories read like exciting romances, with princesses for heroines of plots that would make modern movie thrillers seem tame by comparison.

No doubt a murder story and musical interpretation make for a strange combination, but the Paganini legend has even this to offer. Thus, the wizard's mania for playing on one string alone was explained by a wild tale that had Nicolò in the role of a prisoner condemned to death. While waiting in a murderer's cell he was, however, permitted a customary last wish, and the boon he asked was to be allowed to keep his violin. Yet this was granted only on condition that there be but one string attached to the fiddle. The executioner would not run the risk of letting the virtuoso hang himself, *anticipado,* by knotting the violin strings together. And so poor Nicolò began to play on the one available string alone—holding his guardians spellbound. *Si non è vero è ben trovato:* if this story is not true, another one, still quite romantic, explains in Paganini's own terms his uncanny dexterity in performing on a single string.

The demonic *maestro* relates how, at Lucca, he composed and presented a novelty called *Love Scene,* for the special benefit of a certain lady in the audience with whom he was infatuated. In order not to attract general attention to his *affaire de coeur,* he addressed his lady in this discreet fashion— saying it in music, in the form of a dialogue between two lovers played on the E and G strings, the other two strings having been removed. No wonder such a musical compliment was well received by the lady for whom it was intended. The royal family attended the performance, and the princess was very eager to find out whether a virtuoso who could perform such feats on two strings might even be able to play on one alone. How could a Paganini refuse such a challenge? He accepted and shortly thereafter performed his sonata *Napoleon*, for the G string alone, written in honor of the emperor (who since the *Eroica* days was used to more meaningful dedications). At any rate, the incident in Lucca, love and princesses, were, according to Paganini, the source of the fascination that the G string held for him. He finally gained such mastery of this single string, encompassing three and a half octaves (with harmonics), that this type of performance was pronounced one of the wonders of the musical world.

THE RIDDLE OF PERFECTION

While the stories of a violinist in a death cell or in the more cheerful milieu of court ladies are quite entertaining, more useful attempts are needed to bring technical order to the accounts of Paganini's performance. The student of his technique will find ample material in the essay by Edgar Istel published in the *Musical Quarterly* for January, 1930, where fiction and facts are weighed according to their obvious worth. Credit for the best contemporary account of Paganini must probably be given to K. W. Guhr, a strict Frankfort conductor and a competent violin player, who was for many years haunted by the obsession of solving the riddle of Paganini's technique. In 1831 he published an essay, "On Paganini's Art of Playing the Violin." Very conscientious and typically German in his systematic approach to Paganini's fanciful tricks, Guhr catego-

rized the Paganini method into the following six points: (1)
a unique manner of tuning the instrument; (2) a specific system
of bowing; (3) an unusual skill in introducing left-hand pizzicato with bowed tones; (4) a profusion of natural and artificial
harmonics; (5) an uncanny skill in playing on the G string
alone; (6) a contrapuntal performance in which he simulated
the effect of a number of other instruments.

Reviewing these points, we are assured that in all these
respects Paganini's playing differed from that of any other
violinist.

His staccato was hardly comparable to what we usually
characterize by that term. He would throw the bow upon the
string, skipping through the scale with the most remarkable
lightness and rapidity. Another feature was the rhythmical
marking of the weak beats in a presto. For the pizzicato he
sometimes used special strings. Since the two lower strings—
the D and G—because of their thickness could not produce a
crisp and light effect, he used very thin ones instead. As in
the case of the piano performance of Liszt, actually to reproduce all of Paganini's technical achievements would require
the very same playing conditions in every particular. With
the instrument (fully equipped with four strings, or perhaps
with only two, or even one) in his left hand, Paganini would
hold his bowing arm close to his body, while the left shoulder
leaned conspicuously forward. In such a position, his method
of bowing was entirely individual, following no system previously known. Moreover, this bowing was often in direct opposition to the established rules of any school, with indulgence in
a reversal of the rules concerning up and down bowings. "With
what power did the master endow his long-drawn-out bow, and
in the adagio how did he breathe his tones, as it were, over the
instrument," remarks Guhr. Again, power is emphasized as
an important interpretative quality.

Yet Guhr, with all his delvings and following of the faintest clues, resembles the scholar Faust, who

> With ardent labor studied through,
> And there he stood, with all his lore,
> Poor fool, no wiser than before.

Such a contention cannot be denied, as Paganini, after reading Guhr's book, did not concede that the author's labor had solved his riddle. Refusing to divulge his secrets, Paganini would only stubbornly persist in his maxim, *O gnun' suoi il segreti* ("Everyone has his secrets").

Significant of the general preoccupation of the cultured world with the Paganini enigma is the fact that, in the year of Guhr's book, Goethe called Zelter's attention to an article, *Notice physiologique sur Paganini,* by an Italian physician:

> A remarkable article about Paganini is by a physician who knew and treated him for several years; he most ingeniously sets forth how the musical talent of this remarkable man was urged, directed, even finally conditioned by the formation of his body and the proportions of his limbs, to achieve the incredible, nay, the impossible. This he traces back, *pour nous autres,* to the conclusion that the organism, in its various aspects, engenders the singular manifestations of living beings. And here I will record one of the most pregnant sayings bequeathed us by our forefathers: "The animals are instructed by their organs." If we consider how much of the animal remains in man, and that he possesses the faculty to instruct his organs, we shall willingly return again and again to these reflections.

But whatever the explanation—mental, physical, musical— the phenomena presented by the great violinist who showed such superhuman perfection remain among the greatest feats in the history of musical performance.

GÉNIE OBLIGE

Paganini's motto, "Everyone has his secrets," shows his lack of magnanimity, and it is obviously here that the basic difference between Liszt and Paganini lies, as regards not only their characters but also the psychic basis of their music-making. Paganini, with all his phenomenal technique, remained in Liszt's thoughts "a monstrous ego, who could never be anything but a sad and solitary god." Count de Pourtalès, Liszt's biographer, believes that Liszt perceived that all greatness that does not communicate its sorrow fails to deliver itself. He also adds that Liszt knew that the world would never hear another Paganini. As Liszt sought to formulate these thoughts surrounding the process of giving one's self in performing music, he found this phrase which became his motto: *Génie oblige*.

It was only a few years before the death of Paganini that Liszt reached the zenith of his pianistic career. He continued as a traveling virtuoso for only a few years afterward. There were already signs of his growing interest in conducting. It is not possible to consider Liszt the conductor in the same light as Liszt the pianist. As regards his status as an instrumentalist, not even one of the greatest pianists of the era, Thalberg, proved comparable as a rival to him. In conducting, Liszt was no virtuoso at all. Moreover, he lacked the conventional technique considered prerequisite for adequate control of an orchestra in Germany. While his piano playing grew into the titanic and powerful, his conducting style developed into programmatic and poetic interpretation. Both tendencies can be traced to the artistic influence of Liszt's French apprenticeship and background, particularly to the influence of Berlioz. Liszt, under the spell of Berlioz' power, unquestionably inaugurated the later dynamism of the concert grand, dividing his pianistic genius between the interpretation of Beethoven and Paganini-like tours de force. The latter type of sound orgy is illustrated by a comment in which the satirist Saphir compares Liszt's pianistic power with that of a victorious field marshal:

> The conquered pianos lie scattered around him, broken strings float like trophies, wounded instruments flee in all directions, the audience look at one another, dumb with surprise, as after a sudden storm in a serene sky. And he, the Prometheus, who with each note has forged a being, his head bent, smiles strangely before this crowd that applauds him madly.

FREEDOM OF METER

But Liszt as a conductor was no Promethean conqueror. Fully realizing the more spiritual aims and the high purpose of an interpreter's task, he sponsored the best and really new music of his time—that of Wagner, Berlioz, Smetana, Cornelius, Raff—and forgot the fireworks and fury of his earlier pianistic career. There was less improvisation in his conducting than in his piano performance. A blending of loyalty to the work with free expression was his choice. Two sources are particularly informative as to his tenets as a conductor: the preface to his symphonic poems, and an often quoted letter written in 1853 to Richard Pohl, after Liszt had conducted at the music festival in Karlsruhe, provoking storms of protest as well as ardent admiration. In the preface to his scores, dated 1856, he says: "It is necessary to handle the measure in these works with insight into the effect of colors, rhythm, and expression. It is not enough to beat down the life-nerve of a beautiful symphonic performance."

In relation to his oratorio, *The Legend of the Holy Elizabeth*, the conductor of the work is asked not to mark the regular accents, as the composer considered the habitual "beating" a senseless practice and wished to forbid it in his own works. Music is a sequence of tones, desiring and embracing one another, which must not be enslaved by measure-slapping. Liszt explains that he wanted to eliminate the mechanical, measured "up and down" playing so customary in certain performances. Only a presentation in phrases without bars, with emphasis on the important thematic accents, with a finish of melodic and rhythmic nuances, is acknowledged as true interpretation. After the riot in Karlsruhe, Liszt defended himself in an open letter: "The works of Beethoven's last period demand progress in the style of execution. Thus, the true task of the conductor is not to function as a windmill, but to appear superfluous. The bond between the director and the directed musicians is only entangled by mere time-beating."

THE LETTER KILLS THE SPIRIT

The new method led to a slower and more rhapsodical interpretation of the scores of Beethoven as well as those of other composers. Justice must be done to the rights of a free declamation, in music as in poetry. Therefore, the mechanical maintenance of the regular beats—one, two, three, four, and again one, two, three, four—works in direct opposition to musical sense and expression. Historically seen, Liszt's method is but a renaissance of the Renaissance: the ideals of that period of reawakening are taken up anew. Free declamation, independence of meter, and superiority of the melos over the bars characterize the Liszt ideology, as they did that of the Renaissance interpreter. Liszt transposed the vocal features of the Renaissance first to his piano performance and later to the orchestra.

His criticism of notation corroborates already known points:

Notation, in spite of painstaking conscientiousness, can never fully suffice; although I have been trying by way of precise sketches to clarify my intentions, I do not mean to conceal the fact that certain features—and among them the most important ones—cannot be put down in writing. Thoroughgoing effects can be achieved only through sympathetic, lofty reproduction by the conductor as well as by the other performers.

Other traits of Liszt's interpretative thinking reflect the French influence of his apprentice years. Essential French qualities are: his poetic-programmatic points of view, the *idée fixe*, and the desire for impressionistic lights and shades in the romantic performance. Consequently, the neo-German school, owing to the ideology of its guiding spirit, Liszt, is built upon a French foundation.

The leitmotif of this German school is the belief that the letter kills the spirit of interpretation—a dogma that sprang from Liszt's association with Richard Wagner. In our analysis of the Bayreuth style, this angle of subjective performance will be more fully discussed. The French Romanticism of Berlioz and the German school of Liszt and Wagner lead, in respect to this problem of "literal" reading of the score text, into opposing roads.

=IX. Corrections=

MASTERWORKS REVISED

> *Detestable idiot! You have committed the most enormous of crimes—an assault on genius. Curses on you! Despair and die!*—BERLIOZ TO THE ARRANGERS

THE INTERPRETER'S corrective treatment of a work covers a multitude of deviations, from minor changes of the composer's score to subjective extremes in the rendition. The performer who, for practical or aesthetic considerations, prefers not to deal with the work in prototype, resorts to an arrangement. As the terms "arrangement," "revision," etc., in themselves imply, such versions differ from the "original" and may even lead to the exact opposite of what the composer wanted. Clearly, the performer of any arrangement, whether made by himself or by another musician, is from the very start of his approach to the score on subjective terrain. Even a strictly loyal reading of an arrangement is bound to be subjective, since it always reflects the tonal fantasy of the arranger rather than the original conception of the composer. Throughout history, the corrective attitude toward interpretation has always exercised its most favorable activities, as well as its worst abuses, in the opera. Certain arrangers feel inhibited by the formal environment of instrumental music. But the action on the opera stage offers many pretexts for tampering with the original under the plea of theatrical effects.

The mania for "correcting" masterworks was already in full swing at the beginning of the romantic era. A long period of arbitrariness was slowly waning, while the contemporary classical lawfulness, as represented by the binding script, had yet to become entrenched. Even in classical rendition, certain parts of the score were treated freely—for example, the vocal parts in opera, or all cadenzas in instrumental works. But the romantic interpreter preferred to view the classical work, in its totality, from a freer aspect, reflecting the artistic creeds of the time in which he lived. The task of showing any master's work in extravagant disguise, behind a veil of fantastic make-up, appealed immensely to the romantic interpretative fantasy. Its aim was to serve the exploration of the new and fanciful, rather than the lawfulness of the old.

With new emphasis on free interpretation, there appeared also a golden opportunity to revert to preclassical liberties in performance. One would take from the masterwork what seemed appealing, and just change or leave out whatever was "objectionable." On the other hand, the roster of "arrangements" includes all types of scores and comprises some masterly accomplishments. Among the musicians who devoted themselves to the arranger's task were some of the greatest. Realizing the impossibility of fitting everything to the same last, Berlioz, the archenemy of arrangers, felt compelled to introduce a dual classification. And so he distinguishes between "corrections from above" and "corrections from below," depending on whether the arrangement represents the craftsmanship of a genuine master or that of one who only thinks himself to be a master.

CORRECTIONS FROM ABOVE

Splendid instances of arrangements "from above" are found long before the romantic period. No less a master than Johann Sebastian Bach adapted the works of other composers. An illuminating example is his arrangement of a Vivaldi concerto, which we shall have occasion to contrast in a later section with the modern orchestra arrangements based on Bach's own works (p. 316). While Bach wrote such arrangements for his own enjoyment, Mozart, in the final years of his short life, made an excursion into the realm of arrangement for a practical motive. Van Swieten, a music-loving nobleman, intended to give a series of performances of some oratorios by Handel, in the Vienna court library. Mozart was appointed conductor of the enterprise, after the death of J. Starzer, who had already arranged the score of *Judas Maccabæus* for these concerts.

The main problem confronting Mozart was to dispense with the figured bass, and to incorporate the parts intended for organ or harpsichord into the newly arranged score. He preserved Handel's voice and string parts faithfully, employed a second violin and viola part to fill in the *basso continuo*, and also altered the instrumentation of the wind instruments. Flutes and oboes are treated in a more classical, individualistic manner than in the baroque scoring of Handel.

Mozart made this adaptation for a special purpose. Deviations from Handel were inevitable, if the figured bass was to be incorporated into the orchestra. Still, Mozart's attitude can be considered amazingly objective, since the "historical" approach in the performance of preclassical works was, at this time, by no means an acknowledged procedure. However, a few voices, in behalf of genuine historical readings, protested. As a result, Mozart, in his role as interpreter, was severely criticized by musicians like Reichardt. Sarcastically the latter reminded Mozart that it was not fair to do away with the figured bass of the Handel oratorio: would Mozart have liked it, if Handel had furnished an opera by Mozart with a heavy organ part?

CORRECTIONS FROM BELOW

An egregious example of corrections "from below" concerned none other than Beethoven. The censor who knew better than the composer was Fétis, who indulged in a Beethoven edition of incredible modifications and annotations (cf. p. 247). This Paris professor had written a *Traité du contrepoint et de la fugue* that had become a basic textbook at the Conservatoire, an *Histoire générale de la musique,* and a *Biographie universelle des musiciens* (in eight volumes), which, in spite of its deplorable limitations, is still a valuable work of reference today. Masterworks had to fit the theory emanating from these bulky tomes; otherwise Monsieur Fétis made crude adjustments, very much like those which befell the victims' feet in the story of the Procrustean bed. The Fétis corrections of Beethoven are instanced as an exemplary case in Berlioz' *Memoirs,* where much space is devoted to the incident. Berlioz himself appears to have had a part in it, so we take up his own explanation.

The publisher Troupenas had given Berlioz the scores of Beethoven's symphonies to edit, a task of which Fétis had first been in charge. Berlioz found the Fétis revision full of the most insolent changes and annotations. Whatever in Beethoven's music did not please Monsieur Fétis, he was quick to revise. In the andante of the Fifth Symphony, opposite the long-held E flat of the clarinet over the sixth chord D flat, F, B flat, Fétis made the following astonishing comment in the margin: "This E flat is meant to be an F; impossible that Beethoven should have committed such a blunder!" Correcting Beethoven, Fétis put an F in the place of the characteristic E flat, thus ruining Beethoven's suspension, which is not resolved until after the F has passed through E natural, producing an ascending chromatic progression, and a crescendo of striking effect. And Berlioz asks, wild with anger: "What?

They are making a French edition of the greatest works ever produced by human genius. And all because the publisher has commissioned a professor drunk with his own vanity, monumental works are injured, and Beethoven must stand for *corrections* like an average pupil in a harmony class."

THE QUESTION OF REPEATS

It was the changing of notes that brought about the Fétis-Berlioz quarrel. However, with alteration of tones "only," the long sequence of corrections begins, eventually involving everything changeable in the composition—notes, rhythm, instrumentation, and form. After demonstrating Fétis' subversive activities against Beethoven's symphonies, Berlioz also points out the next victim of the arrangers' frenzy—the form itself. The conductor Habeneck habitually suppressed repetitions, in spite of obvious *da capo*'s and dotted double bars. His interpretative purpose was to avoid repeating parts with which the listener was already familiar. Suggested by the romantic device of relaxing the form rather than stressing symmetry, performers of that time had already begun to eliminate the classical repeats—an expedient of very frequent occurrence in today's renditions, yet a crime in the light of Berlioz' objective standards. It is difficult to conceive that anyone could, with impunity, omit the opening double-bass theme in the scherzo of Beethoven's Fifth as Habeneck did—the same *chef d'orchestre* for whose Beethoven readings Wagner showed so much admiration. While the foregoing examples are taken from musical life in Paris, this propensity for correcting the works of others was not limited geographically to France, or chronologically to the opening part of the romantic era. On the contrary, toward the middle of the century arrangements were being made everywhere on a wholesale basis.

PIANO TRANSCRIPTIONS, ORCHESTRATIONS

No type of music escaped the arranger's pen. The principle? Not to have a principle, since many compositions seemed purposely transmuted into something that never could have entered the minds of their creators. Subtle piano miniatures, of course, would now appear in colossal orchestral arrangements. And, vice versa, what was written for concerted instruments, for voices, for opera, was transcribed for piano, perhaps also for trombone, and, if practicable, for piccolo. A high level of skill in transcription was attained by Liszt, unquestionably the outstanding instrumental arranger of the century. He played most brilliantly on his concert grand—Beethoven symphonies, Schubert songs, Verdi operas, works of any style. Arranging, as he did, much vocal music, he made the piano sing by reinforcing cantabile middle voices, the thumbs becoming the tenors, the discant sparkling in soprano coloratura fashion. Liszt boasted that he could make the piano reproduce any effect whatsoever.

Mendelssohn's objectivism furnished an effectual antidote for such transcriber's pride, in a single pertinent challenge: "Let me hear the first measures of Mozart's G Minor Symphony, with the broken triads in the violas, played on the piano so that they will sound as they do in the orchestra, and I will believe in your business of transcription."

Liszt enjoyed also arraying piano pieces with the full splendor of his romantic orchestra. This led to results typical of the trend of his time, such as his dilation of Schubert's piano solo *Wanderer Fantasy* into a bombastic symphonic poem, transcribed for piano and orchestra with astonishing disregard for style.

COVENT GARDEN

November 29TH, 1827

WILL BE PERFORMED

A New Grand Opera

CALLED

The

SERAGLIO

❊❊

The Music arranged and adapted from

MOZART'S

CELEBRATED *Opera*

WITH ADDITIONAL AIRS, Etc.

Composed by

MR. KRAMER

COVENT GARDEN.

October, 13, 1818.

A Comic Opera in

TWO ACTS,

called,

THE BARBER OF SEVILLE.

Founded on the Opera of that Name.

In which will be Introduced part
of ROSSINI'S & PAESIELLO'S
celebrated Muſick from
Il Barbiere de Siviglia.

The OVERTURE and NEW MUSICK
composed & the Whole Adapted to the
ENGLISH STAGE,

BY

MR. BISHOP.

The above-quoted announcements of Covent Garden, in 1818 and 1827, show what passed under the title of opera performance in those days. The absurdities are so patent that little further comment is required. However, as already mentioned, opera productions, more than any other genre of musical performance, have always lent themselves to the excesses of arrangers. It is the combination of music with the theater that opens wide the stage door for the entrance of changes under the false passes of "dramatic effect" and "appeal to the public." Thus, in the opinion of the Covent Garden manager in 1827, the craft of Herr Kramer was necessary to make Mozart's music presentable. And Mr. Bishop's master hand was required to provide a substitute for a piece that otherwise gave no promise of success—the overture to *The Barber of Seville*!

Yet, even Rossini's overture to *The Barber of Seville* belongs, in reality, to another of his opera scores. The original overture, based on popular Spanish dances, depicting musically the milieu of Seville, had been lost. The composer, in a great hurry to meet the deadline of the *première* in 1816, had to write the score in the unbelievable time of three weeks (no wonder he had no time to shave, and had grown a beard when he finished *The Barber*). Thus Rossini could not worry too long about the question of how little of his original music and how much of previous compositions would be used in the performance. As to the overture, it presumably found its way from the opera *Aureliano* via *Elisabetta* to its function as a curtain raiser for the comedy of *The Barber*. However it may have happened that the world today enjoys this most delightful music under the title of overture to *The Barber of Seville*—historically speaking, the master score is but a substitute. At any rate, the *première* was a failure, like the first performances of some other great operas, such as *Fidelio* or *Carmen*. That is why the score was remodeled for the London stage, the above-quoted arrangement marking a low ebb in opera production.

Berlioz' *Memoirs*, which would serve well as a Baedeker to guide us through the underworld of nineteenth-century opera presentations, tell of the success of Mozart's *Magic Flute* in the Paris opera under a new name, *Les mystères d'Isis*. A German composer was delegated to help patch up the music, concerning which Berlioz writes:

> He tacked a few bars to the end of the overture (the overture to *The Magic Flute*!), converted the soprano part of a chorus into a bass aria, made up a song out of the slaves' chorus, etc. Not satisfied with *The Magic Flute*, this evil-doer next pounced upon *Titus* and *Don Giovanni*. *The Mysteries of Isis* was played in that form, and printed and published with the name of that idiot Lachnith actually with Mozart's on the title-page.

This general state of affairs on the opera stage is nothing new. After all, it was the wilfulness and priggishness of the performers that necessitated the substantial reforms of Lully and Gluck in the seventeenth and eighteenth centuries, respectively. If during the Renaissance it was first the singer who, along with the composer, was given the credit for the creation of an opera, it was now the arranger who, knowing everything better than Mozart or Rossini, reaped the reward—at least the royalties that would have kept Mozart from a pauper's grave.

Referring to abuse of Weber's *Freischütz*, Berlioz breaks into a tormentuous *j'accuse*:

> This masterpiece of poetry, originality, and passion serves merely as a curtain raiser to the most miserable ballets, and has to be deformed to make room for them. And how they interpret what is left of it! What singers! What a conductor! What sleepy indolence in the tempo! What disunity in the whole! What an insipid, stupid, revolting interpretation! You vulgar

salesman! Till the curse of a new Christ shall chase you from the temple, be sure that everyone in Europe who has genuine feeling for art loathes you!

DEFENSE OF THE PURE SPIRIT

This fight of courageous convictions and indomitable temper came to a climax with Berlioz' struggle for the purification of the interpretation of Gluck. He personally revived *Orfeo* in 1859, using a contralto in the leading role instead of assigning a tenor to this part, as had been done in other French and German versions. The pure spirit and style of Gluck was Berlioz' obsession in the general disillusionment of his later years. And so the aging Berlioz would attend the opera as self-appointed guardian of genuine Gluck rendition, an imposing-pathetic listener to performances of which other *maestri* were in charge. He would not permit the "smallest license," since in his conviction there was no such thing as a "minor liberty."

Very characteristic of Berlioz in his active defense of the pure spirit is an instance concerning a correction of Gluck's *Armide*, when it was performed in the Paris opera under Meyerbeer. In order to make more striking a passage for the second violins, written by Gluck on the low D, Meyerbeer had it played on the open D and the D on the fourth string in unison. Consequently, these instruments seemed to have been doubled in number (as a most effective resonance was produced by the two strings). At first, Berlioz acceded to the correction and even complimented Meyerbeer on his happy and theatrical idea. However, he changed his mind and reproached himself, deploring his own and Meyerbeer's error: "Gluck knew the effect of two strings in unison as well as Meyerbeer. If he did not want them, nobody is entitled to employ them. But Meyerbeer has introduced other effects . . . that are incredible blunders and must be forcefully exposed."

Another great composer-conductor of the same era who altered Gluck was Spontini. One example of his corrections was the addition of certain wind instruments in *Iphigénie en Tauride*. But forgetting that he himself had succumbed to this fad of changing originals, Spontini cried out to Berlioz: "Is it not dreadful! Will they also orchestrate me after I am dead?"

X. Opera

Toward the Music Drama

SCORES TAILOR-MADE
FOR SINGERS

BY THE MIDDLE of the seventeenth century, the auspiciously inaugurated opera had already deteriorated to a musical theater production designed for singers and their undiscriminating audiences. The procedure was to find not the true interpreter for a given opera, but an opera for specific interpreters. Composers were commissioned to write scores for specific virtuosi, keeping in mind the type of voice, register, and personality. Interpretation consisted of singing alone. The singers did not act. Performers of secondary parts and the chorus were invisible. The old Venetian dramatic recitative, with its genuine reflection of the poetic meaning, yielded to a superficial recitativo treatment of the words for external declamatory effect or for continuity. In the *recitativo secco*, the orchestra being silent, the virtuoso singer poured forth his runs and trills without the slightest consideration for the action. Most of his ornamentations were improvised, according to his mood and taste. Embellishments that today would appear grotesque made the opera performance the hotbed of arbitrariness in interpretation. The score as written by the composer and the production as given by the executants in the evening's performance were two very different matters.

Lully violently opposed these operas made to the singer's order like a tailored suit. And the tyrannical *maître* of the court of Louis XIV did away with the fanciful ornamentation of even the favorite prima donnas. They, too, had to sing his recitative strictly in time. In Lully's arias, ornaments were reduced to a minimum, Italian cadenzas being entirely eliminated. But after Lully put down his enormous baton for the last time, all the vicious habits that he so vigorously fought rapidly crept back to the French opera stage.

One of the most typical features of opera production was, and still is, the considerable diversity between the printed version and the actual production of the work. This discrepancy can be seen not only in general and customary features (such as cuts, transpositions, dramatic rearrangements, with which opera readings are replete anywhere in the world) but in the all-important and permanent factor on the stage—improvisation. It is difficult completely to eliminate extempore in a musical performance associated with dramatic action. Furthermore, in the comic opera, the improvised humor plays a traditional part, and will continue to do so as long as the highlights of the old *opera buffa* delight audiences. When Gluck appeared on the Parisian scene about a hundred years after Lully, it was really a herculean task to rid the musical theater of all these practices, which had been playing havoc with the dignity of the musical drama. Gluck's ideals of *opera seria* were soon involved in the "quarrel of the buffoons," when Piccini, the exponent of the comic opera, was misled into a campaign of intrigues against the new style.

GLUCK'S REFORMS

Muses, not sirens, to sing in honor of gods.—WIELAND

The best authority on the interpretative goal of the new music tragedy is Gluck himself. To understand his reforms, we turn to the famous preface to his score of *Alceste*, which explains how he endeavored to eradicate arbitrary interpretation and to restore the composer's original thought, and in which he writes:

> I was determined to abolish all those faults that had stolen into Italian opera through the unwarranted pride of singers and the foolish acquiescence of composers, that had made it tiresome and ludicrous instead of the greatest and most impressive spectacle of modern times. I sought to restore music to its proper place—that of enhancing poetry by bringing out the sentiment and appeal of the situations without interfering with the action or impeding it with superfluous ornament. I believed that music bore a relation to poetry very much like that of harmonious coloring and pleasing light and shade to an accurate drawing, which gives life to the figures without changing their outlines. In consequence, I have been careful never to interrupt a singer in the heat of a dialogue in order to introduce a tedious ritornelle, or to stop him in the middle of a piece either for the purpose of displaying the flexibility of his voice on some favorite vowel, or that the orchestra might give him time to take breath before a long sustained note.

The whole musicodramatic theory of the Florentine opera is summed up in these tenets, while the interpretative style of Richard Wagner is clearly anticipated. Abuse of the drama for the sake of pure music is banned; a well-defined separation of the singer's performance in opera, as against the real music drama, is accomplished. Even the performance of the overture takes on great importance, as preparing the audience for the character of the drama they are about to hear; the prelude ceases to be a mere curtain raiser giving the hearers time to get settled in their seats. On the stage, from the opening scene to the finale of the opera, and in the orchestra pit as well, every performer is strictly bound to interpret according to his part. Consequently, the instrument of improvisation, the harpsichord, had to disappear from an orchestra now directed by a binding score script. Instead, new and variegated colors were added to or introduced into the orchestra, by the instrumentality of trombones and clarinets. As only the continuity of the dramatic action mattered, there was little disparity between the recitative and the aria, in order not to interrupt the movement and animation of the scene. The Italian galaxy of ornamental bravura and brilliancy either disappeared, or at least was fully subordinated to dramatic clarity.

Gluck eliminated the *recitativo secco* and provided instead a very expressive accompaniment for the vocal parts. But the superior goal of unity in poetry and music was achieved by reforms other than those concerned with vocal performance and a shake-up in the orchestra. The specifically dramatic aspects— the acting of the singers, their costumes, the stage production, and the *décor* of the opera performance—gained greatly in importance. Not in vain did Gluck live for years in the Vienna of superbly performed dance pantomimes, and in Paris with its great French *tragédie classique* and masterly actors. All his experiences and observations of a real dramatic art gave impulse to a new interpretative approach. While the musical aspect of the performance as such was only part of his concern, precise arrangements with the stage engineer, the ballet master, and the costumer transformed the Gluck opera production into a unified whole.

Contemporary opinion credited Gluck with a transformation of opera performance from a ludicrous exhibition to the most dignified type of spectacle, restoring the power of the word as the vital and creative impulse in musical declamation: "A music without solfeggio, singing without gurgling, a serious *Singspiel* without *castrati*, a poem without bombast—a fourfold wonderwork." The "Sophocles of music," as Gluck is significantly called, once again "commanded the muses, and not the sirens, to sing in honor of gods and heroes."

Emerging as one of the lasting reforms in Gluck's life-work is the victory of objective opera interpretation, culminating in the integrity of the musicodramatic score. Gluck's radical objectivism forbade that a single tone be shortened or held a little too long by arbitrary singers. He insisted on the proper setting of tempo. He did not tolerate the employment of an appoggiatura, trill, or run in the wrong place. In short, he threw overboard whatever would jeopardize the dramatic effect. The contemporary remark above quoted, concerning Gluck's abandonment of the *castrati*, cannot be taken literally. He was not altogether prejudiced against them, and entrusted the title part of the famous *Orfeo* performance in Vienna to the *castrato* Guadagni. In the Paris version, the alto part was transposed for tenor. Since the nineteenth century, interpretation has alternated between these two registers. Berlioz preferred the alto, Liszt the tenor range. An attempt was even made (at the instance of Abert, in 1917) to employ a baritone in the same role, to obviate the use of female registers altogether, simultaneously rejecting the tenor quality as unsuitable to the character of Orfeo. Yet today the alto seems again to have become the general choice, in this country as well as anywhere in Europe where this music drama is performed.

In this connection, it is well to point out that Mozart, like Gluck, and certainly more than one would surmise from many modern presentations of his works, stressed to the utmost the importance of the action on the stage. If Mozart's singers, no matter how celebrated, were lacking in acting ability, he held them in contempt, and was always ready to admonish them with very profane language. Along with the expressive element in his melodic declamation, Mozart insisted on con-

cordance between acting and singing at the historic performances under his direction, such as those of *The Abduction from
the Seraglio* in Berlin, *Don Giovanni* in Prague, and *Idomeneo*
in Munich and repeatedly in Vienna, when he was in charge
of the production.

GESAMTKUNSTWERK BEFORE
WAGNER

IN THEORY

It is only the truly creative composer who can bring to
life, through the production of his score, those gray theories
that would remain nebulous and be soon forgotten were it
not for their shining manifestation in a great living art work.
It is justifiable that the artist should reap glory from such
theories and reforms, even if they are not specifically his own.
Thus, the famous theory of the *Gesamtkunstwerk* (unity of
poetry, music, and action) is generally associated with Wagner
and his Bayreuth style of musicodramatic interpretation.

If we were to read from the pages of a certain treatise called
Versuch einer Ästhetik des dramatischen Tonsatzes, in ignorance of its author's name, we would be fully convinced that
its theories had been formulated by Wagner: they promulgate
ideas of totality in music drama identical with the Bayreuth
concept. This book on musical aesthetics, however, was written
in 1813, the year of Wagner's birth. Its author was the musicologist Ignaz Mosel, the previously mentioned friend of
Beethoven. Mosel, as an ardent admirer of Gluck's music
drama, anticipates Wagner in every important point. Reaf-
firming Gluck's idea that opera is not a playground for silly
singers, but a dignified spectacle with musical accompaniment,
he rejects performers without histrionic ability, no matter how

beautifully they sing. In bitter words, akin to the biting prose of Wagner's essays on the same topic, Mosel fights the conversion of opera performances into concerts in fancy costumes. He declares that music itself is the best producer. Thus it is shown how certain "singing virtuosi, who never before had betrayed any signs of acting talent," suddenly turned into able actors— namely, when interpreting Gluck. To their own amazement and that of their followers, the true dramatic Gluck style had also changed their whole interpretative personalities.

Another case in point is a work by Jean Georges Noverre, published in Lyons, France, in 1760. In his *Lettres sur la danse et sur les ballets,* the author prophetically envisions the musical theater as a unity of all forces. One century before Wagner, the art of ballet is promoted to a *Gesamtkunstwerk,* the production of which touches the intellect as well as the eyes and emotions. Called by Sachs the "Gluck of the ballet," Noverre coordinates all the features of music and stage—performers, *décor,* costumes—in the effort to create a total drama.

IN PRACTICE

If the modern opera enthusiast is accorded an opportunity to visit backstage on a rehearsal day, he will notice a blackboard near the entrance. Here the members of the company find their weekly schedule. The singers are informed about everything concerning their preparation for performance, from the first assignment with the coach, through ensemble practice, to the final dress rehearsal. This entire system, taken for granted throughout the world of opera today, was in its modern elaboration the work of Weber. Of course, there had always been methodical rehearsals. But it was the composer of *Der Freischütz,* in his capacity as opera director in Breslau, Prague, and Dresden, who in his rehearsals organized the routine procedure into a precise system unifying drama and music. Weber's method is described by himself in a notebook, dated October, 1816, upon his departure from Prague.

While nobody can claim that the opera of today suffers from an overabundance of preparation, Weber's notebook shows not only numerous musical rehearsals, but a minute dissection of various other meetings for the purpose of co-ordinating music and drama—including rehearsals exclusively for text reading and for the technical setup of the stage work. Weber also gave introductory lectures to his performers on the subject of the true interpretation of new operas in their repertoire. He wrote the scenario and supervised the stage down to the smallest detail, as did Gluck before him. Nothing was left to chance. Unquestionably, the executive opera interpreter who kept so closely in touch with the different departments of his production—overseeing the work of every individual member of the cast, from prima donna to the last stagehand—was bound to achieve in his performances the highest degree of musicodramatic homogeneity. Historically, Weber's accomplishments mark the midway station on the direct route from Gluck to Wagner. With the *Gesamtkunstwerk* anticipated by Gluck and Weber, Mosel and Noverre, Wagner's greatest contribution to musical interpretation is, as we shall see, the elaboration of a system concerned with the whole realm of music, and not limited to the performance of opera alone.

THEATER ORCHESTRA

In the foreground of the many problems of opera performance that Weber solved, was his reorganization of the orchestra. He set definite standards of size and proportion during his activities as conductor in Breslau, Prague, and Dresden.

The arrangement of the Dresden orchestra, which we described in its earlier stage under Hasse (p. 171), now, under Weber, shows the following personnel:

4	first violins	2	clarinets
4	second violins	2	bassoons
2	violas	4	French horns
2	violoncellos	2	trumpets
2	double basses	3	trombones
2	flutes		percussion
2	oboes		

This setup already resembles our modern arrangement. Still, the number of strings is small. Only eight violins (counting the first and second sections together) performed the famous parts in *Der Freischütz* and other classical operas that Weber directed. How different they must have sounded from our present-day performances, in which we hear usually four times as many violins, and other instruments multiplied in similar proportion.

WAGNER'S METHOD

First and foremost, pay attention to the scene.—WAGNER
ADDRESSING THE CONDUCTORS

Wagner's famous essay *On Conducting* is a paradox: while, notwithstanding its title, it contains hardly anything on the technique of the baton, it presents, on the other hand, infinitely more than its heading promises. The essay gives a complete theory on interpretation—in fact, with that of Berlioz' *Traité*, the most important one to appear in print during the nineteenth century. It is paradoxical also in a second sense. Founded upon the purpose of establishing an attitude of loyalty toward the misinterpreted great masters of the past, by seeking to rediscover ingeniously the composers' hidden will, the essay reflects free, subjective interpretations of virtually all the examples given.

Taking literally Beethoven's word that "tempo is the body of performance," Wagner demonstrates how the technique of correct interpretation centers around the setting of the right tempo, and clarifies this point as follows:

> Briefly, the question of correct execution of a musical work may be expressed thus: Has the conductor established the true tempo? The way he sets and maintains the tempo is as eloquent as his grasp of the content of the composition. Performers are guided to a correct rendition by the tempo, which, at the same time, reveals the extent of the conductor's knowledge of the composition. But the difficulty of finding the right tempo becomes manifest when we realize that only thorough and detailed acquaintance with the work will yield this vital knowledge.

Musicians of early times understood this so well that Haydn and Mozart usually designated their tempi by broad terms, such as "allegro" and "adagio," with a few common modifiers —these comprising all they considered necessary for the purpose.

NAÏVE AND SENTIMENTAL TEMPO

In Bach, we seldom find the tempo given at all; Wagner considers this the best method in the real musical sense. For further specification, Wagner employs two terms in allegiance to the aesthetics of Schiller. According to the great poet's noted dissertation on naïve and sentimental poetry, Wagner distinguishes between Mozart's naïve and Beethoven's sentimental tempo. The true adagio can hardly be played too slowly; the naïve allegro is usually a quick *alla breve*. Fastest of all is the closing allegro. Between the forte and piano sections in such an allegro, no allowance is made for emotional interpretation. It is the truly naïve tempo. In contrast to the naïve allegro stands the allegro of Beethoven. This second type, governed principally by its basic melody, has much in common with the adagio, thus acquiring that "sentimental" quality that sets it apart from the earlier naïve allegro. Wagner's examples are taken from the first movement of the *Eroica* and from certain themes of Mozart.

How can the right tempo be discerned? The genuine sense of tempo comes only from proper understanding of the melos: the two elements are interdependent. "I have never," Wagner says, "met a German *Kapellmeister* who could really sing a melody, whether his voice was good or bad. Music to them is a mixture of grammar, mathematics, and gymnastic exercises." The credit goes to France, when Wagner ascribes his own enlightenment concerning tempo to the Paris conductor Habeneck, referred to in connection with Berlioz as a "corrective" interpreter (p. 264). A performance of Beethoven's Ninth Symphony by the orchestra of the Conservatoire under Habeneck in Paris, in 1839, caused "the scales" to fall from Wagner's eyes. The essence of the problem was at once revealed to him when he realized that Beethoven's melody was known to the orchestra in every measure: "Thus was the secret laid bare—and by a musician with no claim to genius. Habeneck discovered the tempo simply through proper interpretation of the melos."

After considering the problem of *tempo primo,* Wagner approaches that of tempo modification, bitterly complaining that the technique of time variation was utterly unknown to performers. But to his mind this very factor was the vital principle of all music-making. How modification should actually work is shown in several examples. For the modern interpreter, the composer's own illustration of the proper rendering of his *Meistersinger* prelude, in a flexible four-four time, is most important. Here modifications serve the purpose of exposing discriminately the diverse themes as interwoven in the polyphonic web. At the first performance, in a private circle in Leipzig, the overture proved a triumph, yet the same performers under Reinecke's baton were hissed at the Gewandhaus. But Wagner points out to whom the blame should go. After he had learned what beat the conductor had taken, no further explanation was necessary. He explains it to us: the prelude bears the tempo heading, *sehr mässig bewegt*. No tempo requires or is capable of more modification than such an *allegro maestoso*. When a moderate allegro continues for some time, and particularly if the thematic subjects are stressed episodically, the breadth of four-four is very well adapted to modifications of this kind. It could be interpreted (after the scherzando part) as *alla breve*, then taking up the grave andante as used especially in church music. A constant modification of the main tempo is the secret of a faithful performance of this prelude.

AGAINST MUSICAL TEMPERANCE

Wagner's freedom in modification of tempo is a further elaboration of a technique we encountered with Liszt. We remember also that this performing style was diametrically opposed to that of the Mendelssohn school—which Wagner caustically refers to as "classical playing," exemplified by an undeviating performance of a Beethoven symphony without modification. To show how it should be done, the *Eroica* is again given as an example. Wagner demands tempo changes in the course of the opening movement; yet this was generally treated by conductors as a single unit. In such undeviating execution, Wagner sees a danger of going to extremes. He dubs Mendelssohn's classical school a "musical temperance union," an assembly of "eunuchs of classical chastity." Later he refers to Brahms in a similar way.

An analogy between Wagner's theory of tempo modification and the *Affektenlehre* becomes apparent. The eighteenth-century doctrine advocated similar fundamentals of performance: a quick figuration in the *alla breve*, a sustained tone in the adagio, a naïve and sentimental tempo—all of which must be realized according to the underlying programmatic idea. The Bayreuth style demands a relaxing for quiet, dreamy thoughts, a going ahead in parts of happy, excited mood. These are typical exemplifications of the *Affektenlehre*.

NOT SOULLESS PEN MUSIC

In his article "The Virtuoso," Wagner asserts:

> The first rule of interpretation is to convey the composer's intention with scrupulous fidelity, . . . to transmit his thoughts without any change or loss. The greatest merit of the virtuoso consists in imbuing himself completely with the musical perception of the score, without introducing modifications of his own.

Yet apparently this end be accomplished only by reading between the lines and behind the notes. For without the interpreter's imagination, the score script remains forever "soulless pen music—nothing more." To clarify his conviction, Wagner recalls how Mozart directed his men in rehearsals, by word of mouth, expecting the orchestra to be capable of executing his wishes without written instructions in the music. Mozart did not feel the necessity of writing very many details into the parts; he was most exacting about his songlike motifs during rehearsals. The case is different with Beethoven, whose scores have more detailed instructions and more involved thematic design.

But here too the interpreter's fantasy is indispensable. According to Wagner, Beethoven's interpretation did not cope adequately with his ideas, because of the master's deafness. From such premises, Wagner concludes that the performer not only has the right, but the clear duty, to add his intuition in the performance of great scores. His re-scoring of Beethoven's Ninth Symphony is but the logical outcome of such beliefs. Wagner's approach to numerous historic works always shows an analogous corrective attitude. This can be seen in his spirited analysis of the *Freischütz* overture. Here Wagner's genial personality stood in the way of a truly objective reading of Weber's manuscript. Unquestionably, Wagner's comments are brilliant. His deep insight into the dramatic workshop of his operatic predecessor is astonishing. Yet, if we compare the Weber script with Wagner's essay on how the overture should be interpreted, the strong wilfulness in Wagner's approach becomes strikingly obvious.

Summing up, we realize that Wagner's interpretative ideology is that of his age. All the traits of Romanticism are embodied in this one great mind: extreme subjectivity seeks the strange company of a passionate striving for extreme loyalty. The Bayreuth creator, in whose life-work German Romanticism culminated, appears likewise as the climax of Romanticism in interpretation.

VERDI AND ITALIAN OPERA

Once one had to tolerate the tyranny of the prima donna; now, also that of the conductor.—VERDI TO HIS PUBLISHER, RICORDI

The interpretative differences between Wagner and Verdi are obvious. A singing style, shaped to fit the many consonants of the German language, does not suit the cantilenas in which the southern vocal ideal, from Palestrina to Bellini and Donizetti, lives traditionally on. Evidently, the *bel canto* melody of Desdemona must vary from Isolde's dramatic exclamations, and naturally the comedy of *Falstaff* calls for a different theatrical approach from that appropriate to the German humor of *Die Meistersinger*. Verdi, who put into music the Shakespearean scenes of *Macbeth, Othello,* and *The Merry Wives,* was certainly closer to the realities of the theater than was Wagner with his long-bearded heroes and spear-shaking gods. Thus, the performer's attitude to Italian operas will necessarily be more realistic, human, and theatrical than the superhuman and powerful gestures of the Bayreuth style.

However, all these differences in the style of the two greatest nineteenth-century masters of the opera do not necessarily connote a difference in the basic interpretative approach to their respective scores: the idea is still in vogue that, while one may interpret Verdi's operas freely in respect to vocal parts, one must adhere with pedantic strictness to the Wagner score. That the turn from Wagner to Verdi, from the Bayreuth music drama to the Italian opera, involves interpretative freedom, is one of those fairy tales that seem to enjoy immortality in the international world of the opera theater.

The fact is, Verdi went even farther in emphasizing radical objectivity of rendition than did Wagner. Not torn like the latter between antagonistic ideologies (of work-fidelity on the one hand, and the claim to the interpreter's right to re-create on the other), Verdi was most tyrannical in demanding unconditional obedience to his scores. In 1871, he states his refusal to concede either to singers or conductors the freedom to interpret "creatively." In a letter to his publisher, Ricordi, in 1872, he complains that, while once one had to tolerate the tyranny of the prima donna, now there is that of the conductor, who indulges in senseless liberties along with the singer. "Never, never, never," Verdi raves, "did anyone succeed in culling from the score all the effects as I intended them." And his assaults on the Italian *maestri* read like Wagner's on the German *Kapellmeister*.

It is noteworthy that this insistence on objectivity was not an outgrowth of Verdi's later operatic style. As early as 1847, Nini Barbieri, leading lady in the Florentine *Macbeth* production, relates how exacting and resolute the composer was in the pursuit of his aims. The baritone Varesi refusing to go over a scene as he had rehearsed it one hundred and fifty times, was told by Verdi: "You will put on a coat and rehearse it the one hundred and fifty-first time." There are countless episodes of this kind throughout Verdi's entire career, showing him to have been, like Lully, Gluck, Spontini, and Weber, a despotic tyrant in his productions, putting vain coloratura sopranos, tenors, lazy baritones, and arbitrary conductors in their places.

The idea that the singer can dispense with the script of the Italian opera and consider it as a pleasant vehicle for his vocal parades, proves to be only the vicious tradition of the inferior performer. The times have gone in which a man like Jacopo Peri, one of the first creators of opera, was obliged humbly to thank his singer, Vittoria Archilei, for "having condescended to interpret his music." With Verdi, the note script of the Italian opera has become as binding as that of the German music drama. Tosi, in his *Opinioni de' cantori*, mentions the most celebrated singers of his time as models of rhythmic discipline. The distrustful Rossini wrote ornaments and coloratura passages in full to confine the extravagances of his prima donnas. A singer who indulged in vocal pyrotechnics, who tried to break the world's record for the longest shake on the highest tone, was considered a nuisance in the serious Italian opera style of any period, from Monteverdi and Lully to Spontini and Verdi. Spontini, as Berlin *Generalmusikdirektor*, evoked the admiration of Wagner for his despotic drill of performers. The latter felt in Spontini's dramatic ideals a kinship with his own Bayreuth tenets.

One lesson must be learned from all these examples: discipline, not arbitrariness, emerges as the watchword of artistic interpretation in Italian opera. Let vocal wilfulness go where it belongs—through the trapdoor of the opera stage.

XI. Between Two Epochs

The Absolute Ideal

THE TRAIN of thought in nineteenth-century interpretation, which proved most prophetic for the development of our time, emanated from the aesthetics of the greatest man in German philosophy—Immanuel Kant. It was on Kant's *Critique of Pure Reason* that Eduard Hanslick based his famous treatise, *The Beautiful in Music.* This revisal of musical aesthetics, published first in 1854, stood and still stands as the manifesto of objective interpretation—as the defense of absolute subject matter in music. Inspired by Kant in principle and formulation, Hanslick shows that the investigation of music must, above all, consider the art *object* and not the perceiving *subject.* In analogy to the other arts, so in music, too, the objective mode of procedure must be adopted. The task is to realize music clearly as a self-sufficient form. This form and its content, as proven in the *Critique,* must always be in complete harmony. Like the song of the birds, music has no subject matter; it is the art of the beautiful play of sensations.

With the existence of any extra-musical subject in the score wholly denied, the interpreter's question as to what is to be expressed in his performance with the material at hand is answered categorically: Musical ideas—nothing else! Without any extraneous material as a premise, the executant is obliged to think exclusively in terms of sound, as did the composer be-

fore him: "Music is to be played, but is not to be played with."
The interpreter is never to look for a nonmusical subject beyond
the tonal form, for even the most romantic, poetic ideas in
music, as we saw in Schumann's case, can speak only through
the medium of sound. Interpretation deals with the *absolute*
intrinsic beauty of tonal combination as an end in itself. Therefore, the most important quality of the interpreter is what Max
Schoen calls "form-mindedness." Such sensitivity to form, however, must not be confused with the executant's external knowledge of structure. Following the structure is an intellectual
game. But the composer's experience of form must be felt and
re-created by his interpreter. Thus, the *absolute ideal* in musical
performance does not mean a cold, soulless rendition. On the
contrary, it calls upon the interpreter to pursue his artistic goal
with warmth and identification with the art work.

Musical aestheticism based on these ideas was bound to lead
to a rejection of Wagner's theories in the realm of absolute
music. Small wonder then that two schools rose in open battle
against each other: Brahms found himself in the center of this
battlefield very much against his will, owing to the fact that
the grim Wagner-hater Hanslick had become generally accepted as the staunch exponent of the Brahms school. Only
the warning of friends not to take unnecessary chances with the
influential critic and Vienna university professor finally prevented Wagner from using the name of Hanslick, corrupted
to "Hans—lick," for the ridiculous figure of the faultfinder,
Beckmesser, in *Die Meistersinger*. In other ways, Wagner was
vituperative in attacking Brahms not only as a composer but
also as an interpreter:

> Herr Brahms's readings of masterworks as well as of his
> own variations show that he does not understand any jokes.
> His performances caused me so much distress that I would
> have given anything to see his technique moistened with a

little oil of that school [referring to the Liszt school]—an oil that appears not to exude from the keyboard itself but must be dropped from at least a more ethereal sphere.

What did Wagner miss in the Brahms performance besides the Lisztian oil? The answer is given when Wagner further assails Brahms's "woodenness and primness." "I hold by the man who gives something of his heart, and makes it really touch our ear and feeling," stated Wagner in rejecting a Brahms apostle, Joseph Joachim, for the post of director of the Berlin Academy. Wagner, the dramatist, who did not write symphonies (discounting attempts in his youth), and Brahms the symphonist, who did not write operas, were at different poles. Who could expect an affinity in their interpretations? A *rapprochement* between the theatrical pathos of Wagner's heroic music and the formalistic inwardness of Brahms's lyricism is inconceivable.

An example taken from the First Symphony of Brahms will further demonstrate the difference in approach between the two schools. In the finale, a choral theme appears twice— the first time in the andante introduction, fifteen measures before the entry of the *allegro ma non troppo*, the second time sixteen measures after the *più allegro* close to the end. While the first appearance of the theme is performed *piano dolce*, played by three trombones, the bassoons, and the double bassoon, the second appearance is fortissimo in full scoring. The majority of conductors render this second occurrence with a retard of differing degree, varying from a slight *rallentando* to a complete change of the speed toward *maestoso*.

Such modification of time would be well suited for the musicodramatic style of Wagner. The Brahms style, however, does not permit interference with the unity of the form. But even if the interpreter of the First Symphony wishes to give the poetic idea ascendancy over the absolute idea, he should not ignore the score script: obviously the second version of the motif above quoted implies a different meaning from the first. Perhaps Brahms's music symbolized here a glorious victory over the adversity of life, and thus the motif, now so differently instrumentated, must appear in a more tempestuous character. Absolute or poetic idea—if Brahms had wanted alteration of time, he would have indicated it, as he so carefully did in other passages in the same symphony, in fact in the same movement.

CHAMBER MUSIC

The absolute ideal of transparency and formal clarity has always found its most adequate medium in chamber music. Concentration upon only a few performing parts calls for expressive economy. Obviously, the spirituality of counterpoint, the basis of all classical chamber music, is no vehicle for sheer emotionalism or virtuosity. It is primarily in chamber music that the absolute, the unprogrammatic, and the intrinsic musical content should guide the interpreter. Einstein observes that as early as the seventeenth century the chamber duet and *concertante* music reached noble heights of purity, never meant to be represented dramatically or naturalistically; the performance of such music must be within the limits of lyrical unity. The chamber music of the classical era likewise fulfilled the pledge implicit in its name: it is truly music for the *Kammer*, the intimate room, an abstract style of noble expression, in contrast to the world of theatrical effects.

Beethoven's chamber music demanded a new kind of performer, capable and willing to devote his life's work to the study of the new style and its phenomenal development from Haydn's *divertimento* type to the abstract polyphony of the last quartets. The protagonists of this new chamber music were the members of the Rasoumowsky quartet. Their memory lives on, not only in Beethoven's dedication of his Opus 59 to Prince Andreas Rasoumowsky, who sponsored this organization and played the second violin, but also because of their artistic courage (and their patience with the composer, who was not always too appreciative of their interpretation). Schuppanzigh, the leader of this group, became the godfather of modern quartet playing.

The greatest quartet player of the century, however, was Joseph Joachim. He and his partners brought the Beethoven tradition to the threshold of our century. Brahms was their guiding star, after Joachim's association with Liszt and the Weimar circle was severed. In the Brahms-Joachim interpretation of chamber music, the emphasis is not on emotionalism or dramatic tension, but is in affinity with the above-described historical ideals of chamber music style.

Freedom of meter, as generally advocated by the Liszt school, can be tolerated only as an exception, as in the recitative-like passages of the later Beethoven quartets. While a contrast between an energetic first group of themes and a lyrical second group is still distinctly felt, it must not be achieved, as in Wagner's case, by a dualism of tempo, i.e., by differentiation of naïve and sentimental allegri. Instead of the Wagnerian scheme of time modification, there is a unity of tempo throughout the movement. It is the interpreter's task to find a superior main tempo to suit them both, rather than to indulge in the Wagnerian device of yielding, in time, to the individualistic nature of each theme.

In the chamber music of Brahms, perhaps more than in any other of his scores, there is a glorious realization of the Kantian axiom of harmony of form and content, offering the players the most perfect opportunity for absolute music-making—for a formful interpretation along classical lines. And even in his art songs, Brahms sometimes superimposed his formalistic and intrinsically musical ideal upon the poet's word. Such hidden feelings beneath a disguise of beautiful form remained an enigma to many of his contemporaries. Among them was Tchaikovsky, who showed himself irritated that such a "self-conscious mediocrity should be recognized as a master." And the great man of Russian emotionalism, who wore his heart on his sleeve, called his melodious countryman, Rubinstein, a genius in comparison with Brahms!

DUSTING OFF OLD WORKS

Vacillating between the Brahms and Wagner camps, the most significant liaison officer of the subjective trend from Wagner to our time was Hans von Bülow, a pianist and conductor of outstanding gifts. Much admired for his opera conducting in Munich, concertizing with the Meiningen orchestra, he was one of the first traveling star conductors in history. If we judge his interpretative position not from enthusiastic contemporary accounts, but from his editing of piano works, we find a picture of excessive subjectivity, in complete opposition to Joachim's work-fidelity. No doubt Bülow, with his wilful approach, was a strange anomaly in the Brahms circle.

"Bach's harpsichord works," says Bülow convincingly, "are the Old Testament; Beethoven's sonatas are the New. We should believe in both." Bülow believed, however, in a third power also, namely, in himself. And so he sails in completely subjective waters, recklessly changing eternal words, such as Bach's *Chromatic Fantasy*, and showing, in his editing of Scarlatti or Beethoven, his own theatrical showmanship rather than a true historical approach. "Old works must be given a dusting," Bülow warns, "a public that does not care for sonatas must be accommodated." Thus Bülow deteriorated from spir-

itual beginnings to a musical headwaiter, eager to serve the
à la carte taste of his illustrious clientele.

FIN DE SIÈCLE

America reflects lightly upon memories of the last decade
of the romantic century. Still today, the "gay nineties" (which
were in reality quite turbulent times) conjure up, on the stage
and in the movies, the smiling shades of an era's happy ending. America had not found its musical bearings; the men who
are now its musical leaders were then unborn, or children
playing their first tunes. In Europe, however, the nineties
marked a period of extreme productivity. We may marvel at
the upward spiraling in musical evolution, without sharing
the pessimistic view of many who see here the last rise of
musical art before its downfall.

A survey of the main creative forces during this period
would reveal the following highlights. First, there was the
ascendancy of Richard Wagner's power, felt both in the composition of new and in the interpretation of old works. As the
Wagner school dominated in Europe, its apostles, Muck, Rich-
ter, Bülow, and Nikisch were sent as ambassadors of Bayreuth
to England and America. In Munich, a second Richard, son of
the anti-Wagnerian French-horn player Strauss, but himself a
promising Wagner conductor, continued in the orchestral polyphony of *Tristan* and *Die Meistersinger* in symphonic poems
from *Don Juan* to *Thus Spake Zarathustra*. The late roman
tic Wagner harmony prevailed in the Austrian world of the
Lieder of Hugo Wolf, and Wagner's instrumentation, solemn
and mystical, found its place in Bruckner's gigantic symphonies. A superb interpreter, loyal to Wagner's *Festspiel*
idea, Gustav Mahler, elevated the standards of the opera
houses in which he directed to those of Bayreuth. As a com-

poser, Mahler did not eschew the Wagnerian media. He transformed them, however, into his own highly personal idiom of orchestral expression. Among the young generation, Mahler's favorite, Arnold Schönberg, had to his credit, among other scores, the sextet *Transfigured Night*. Outside the Bayreuth realm stood Brahms in lofty independence. The imperturbable Bohemian, Dvořák, believing in both Wagner and Brahms, finally escaped from the clash of hostile schools safely to the United States. In Italy, Wagner's greatest antithesis, Verdi, with his *Falstaff*, proved the immortality of Latin opera melody, subordinating the accompanying orchestra, and opposing Bayreuth's operatic symphonism. Puccini's *La Bohème* had already been a signal success. In Russia, Tchaikovsky had written his swan song, the *Symphonie pathétique*. Young minds were being influenced by Rimsky-Korsakoff; Stravinsky was yet to come in contact with him. In the north, two scores from Finland, *En Saga* and the Symphony in E Minor, introduced Sibelius to the musical world. Reviewing the phenomena of the last decade in Europe, one can better neglect other names than those of Elgar, Scriabin, Grieg, and Johann Strauss.

But it was neither central Europe, eastern Europe, nor Italy that became, with the turn of the century, the cradle of a new style of performance. The focal point of progress shifted to France, where men were enjoying the rare privilege of peaceful life after the nation had been defeated in the Franco-Prussian War. Of course, the Bayreuth sphere of influence did not end at Germany's southwest boundaries. Wagner enthusiasm easily traveled the few hours from Strassbourg—where it was legal—to Paris, where it was unpatriotic to enjoy arch-German performance. But just as "love is a child of Gipsyland" in Carmen's philosophy, so the Parisian infatuation for Wagner also "careered wherever it chose." Bizet, who with his chef d'oeuvre, *Carmen,* suffered so tragic a defeat in his own country, was posthumously compensated by its triumph in Germany. What a confusion of taste! The quintessence of Latin opera spirit spurned, the Teutonism of the *Ring* cycle hailed. And all this in Paris—the fortress of simplicity and rationalism, the homeland of Rameau, Bonnet, and Rousseau, whose watchwords "simplicity," "clarity," "humanity," and "back to nature," became the keynotes of French interpretation. With the same force with which the French earlier had denounced Wagner as a romantic caricature of Gluck, they now in their traditional hate-love of the German music, compelled their artists to do everything "à la Wagner."

ARS GALLICA

In the year of the humiliation of the Bismarck peace, France had a victory on another front. The *Société Nationale de Musique* was founded. Romain Rolland, calling it "the sanctuary of French art," asserts that "without the *Société* the greater part of the works that are the honor of our music would never have been played; perhaps they would never have been written." The slogan of the society, *ars Gallica,* indicates its aims in general but clear terms. The best-known French composers have taken part as performers in its concerts, among others Franck, Saint-Saëns, Massenet, Bizet, D'Indy, Fauré, Chabrier, and Debussy. The spirit and activities of the *Société* were greatly responsible for the reawakening of national ideals. These ideals had been expressed for centuries in French master scores as well as in French theories. It is in Rameau's theories that we find a summary of the true goals of French music. In his *Code de musique pratique,* he makes a plea, with the wisdom of his long life, for "thought, sentiment, and the passions as the essence of interpretation." Significantly, thought is given first place. And his contemporaries likewise realized that Rameau's work displayed "order, reason, light, clarity, and simplicity."

Rameau's doctrines are anticipated in other important theories of the French. Highly representative of the traditional French ideology is *L'histoire de la musique*, by Jacques Bonnet. Here we find, in 1725, the musical application of the axiom that aesthetic pleasure can consist only in a right proportion and correspondence between the object and the senses, a thought of obvious meaning for interpretation in times to come. Emphasizing further the difference in national styles of performance, Bonnet draws a distinct line of demarcation between the French and Italian taste. Italian music is charged with a lack of expression and with profusion of ornaments. Artificiality is denounced as its capital fault. In contrast, the chief attributes of the French style are called *naturelle, vive, et juste*. Love of the Italians for extraordinary song, their habit of suddenly changing from one fashion of execution to another, proves that they lack the most important quality, naturalness.

SIMPLICITY

The natural is called "the source of all beauty in music." An interpretation that permits a repetition of a word for a quarter of an hour is an absurdity. Logic and good taste must dominate in every branch of musical performance. And also within the confines of church performance, the French succeeded in preserving these ideals. Finally, we have the leading motif of the French style expressed in a single phrase—*La simplicité, deuxième perfection de la musique*.

What the French musicians, at the end of the nineteenth century, learned from the rebirth of their national ideals was, once more, to strive for perfection by seeking simplicity. If, in the eighteenth century, French interpretation opposed the Italian style, then the *ars Gallica* movement of the nineteenth century was directed against the German influence. Of course, there were factors other than musical ones—spiritual, political, economic forces—which helped at the *fin de siècle* to reshape the artistic destiny of France. In literature, two main trends are in evidence—the naturalistic, which springs from Balzac, Flaubert, and De Maupassant, with Zola later as its leader, the other centering around Mallarmé and Verlaine, searching for the principles of a pure and absolute aestheticism. It is the latter group that turned out to be so meaningful for music.

A chief laboratory for artistic research was the Paris apartment of Mallarmé. Here artists assembled whose work in poetry, music, and painting was to make history. André Gide describes the atmosphere of these gatherings *chez* Mallarmé: "One entered the room. It was evening. And silently, insensibly, and of its own accord, the conversation would rise to heights of almost religious solemnity." Musical interest remains focused on a certain loyal member of that circle—Claude Debussy. His adaptation of Mallarmé's *The Afternoon of a Faun,* and his setting to music of sixteen poems by Verlaine, are only the tokens of this affiliation with the *literati;* his first compositions were issued by a literary publisher at the Librarie de l'Art Indépendant, of which Gide, Louÿs, and Regnier were members. Debussy was active also as a writer on music. He did not contribute heavy treatises on interpretation like Berlioz or Wagner, but, like Schumann, with whose music he has many bonds, he wrote fine poetic essays. The study of Debussy's thoughts on interpretation may follow either road: what he left us in prose, or the music in his scores. We shall trace both.

DEBUSSY

*Remember the word "impressions"—
for I insist on keeping my emotions free
from all parasitic aesthetics.*—DEBUSSY

The strains of Schubert's *Unfinished Symphony* permeated the hall. Arthur Nikisch was directing a symphony concert in Paris. Suddenly a number of unexpected visitors arrived: some sparrows perched on a window sill. But the conductor "had the grace not to demand their expulsion." Thus reads the comment of Claude Debussy, the music critic, and in countless reflections like this lies a clue to his world of interpretation. In Debussy's mind, the little birds and a symphonic concert were not incongruous. Nikisch appeared a better conductor because of his disdain of formality and pomposity. The whole scene—the informal conductor, the birds, the audience—was unified by the deep humanity of Schubert's music. As Debussy felt it, a performance that falsified life, that was not humane and true to nature, was meaningless. Mere virtuosity provoked only his contempt. In this vein his writes:

> The attraction of the virtuoso for the public is very much like that of the circus for the crowd. There is always hope that something dangerous may happen. M. Ysaye may play the violin with conductor Colonne on his shoulders, or M. Pugno may conclude his piece by lifting the piano with his teeth.

The simple human truth of expression and performance became Debussy's dogma. His statements draw a perfect picture of his interpretative convictions. Just as Bonnet's musical conception in the early eighteenth century reacted violently against the artificiality of the Italians and their affected expression, so Debussy rebelled against the nineteenth-century hypervirtuosity and its Wagnerian pathos, the tone language of gods and superbeings. At the same time he rejected the impending mechanization of musical forces. In *La revue S.I.M.*, we read his comment:

> At a time like ours, in which mechanical skill has attained unsuspected perfection, the most famous works may be heard as easily as one may drink a glass of beer, and it only costs ten centimes, like the automatic weighing machines. Should we not fear this domestication of sound, this magic that anyone can bring from a disk at his will? Will it not bring to waste the mysterious force of an art which one might have thought indestructible?

Thus we see Debussy fighting simultaneously on two fronts, against the maxims of both the nineteenth and the twentieth century—a true son of the *fin de siècle*. His rejection of anti-French idols turned into the embodiment of a magnificent new art. *Pelléas and Mélisande,* his only opera, demonstrates, more strikingly than his work in any other genre, Debussy's mission of reawakening French ideals. Here a counterrevolution against the revolutionary Wagner is consummated. In fact, the pages of this score disclose one of the most curious paradoxes in musical history. While the *Pelléas* interpretation on the stage must display the ideological inversion of the Wagner style, it fulfills at the same time Wagner's basic principle of music drama—predominance of the drama. This Debussy accomplished at the expense of the music.

Pelléas music without the drama is incomprehensible. In 1906, Debussy canceled an already accepted invitation to conduct the orchestra of the Philharmonic Society in London, when he learned that excerpts from *Pelléas and Mélisande* were on the program. "Not only is it impossible to give *Pelléas* at a concert," he protested, "but the composition of the work is such as to make extracts utterly impossible." The great music of *Tristan und Isolde*, detached from the stage, is successfully accepted in concerts today (Wagner himself repeatedly conducted excerpts of his music dramas), and it may continue to live in this way, even though posterity may not appreciate it as a five-hour music drama.

HUMAN TENDERNESS

The modern interpreter can learn a great lesson from a little scene in Debussy's only opera score: it is the scene where Mélisande confesses to Pelléas, "Je t'aime aussi," in low voice, whispered in four syllables, all on the low C. Obviously, the singer must suggest emotions rather than display them heroically as in Wagner's music. Romain Rolland shows how Debussy's Latin sense shuns the great scenes of endless melodious chains of sobbings and lamentations when Tristan and Isolde embrace each other. In contrast, Debussy's contempt for display of emotions leads to moments of utmost intensity. An uncanny sense of timing blends and balances every detail of the drama, with clocklike precision, in perfect subordination to the music. While Debussy did not feel the need to write a programmatic explanation of his interpretative tenets, like Caccini and Gluck, he still guides his interpreter, on his way to human tenderness and emotional restraint, by the unmistakable meaning of his music.

The mistake is frequently made of describing the difference between the *Tristan* and the *Pelléas* conceptions as a deep-seated difference between German and French styles. But there are glorious instances in German music and literature of a related inwardness and expressive restraint. In music, one has only to think of Bach's interpretations of the Passions. In literature, the farewell in Goethe's *Iphigenie* concludes this five-act classical drama with a single and simple "Farewell," with which the greatest German poet created a scene of eternal symbolism: in which human beings seem for the first time to love, to bid farewell, and to part forever.

LANGUAGE OF FINE SHADES

Gluck, so deeply admired by Wagner, wrote, in 1772, an *Iphigénie* score, a French adaptation of Racine's tragedy. This great contribution to the purification of French opera style was not acknowledged by Debussy. In an open letter to Gluck, he sarcastically addresses the long-dead master: "Between ourselves, your prosody was very bad; at least you turn the French language into an accented language, when it is, on the contrary, a language of fine shades." This certainly seems a coup of lesser glory on the part of Debussy, but understandable in terms of its milieu. After all, Paris is an old battleground where fighting and quarreling about the unification of prose and music has been the traditional pastime of musicians. As Bonnet's example shows, the French have always indulged in a jealous defense of their "language of fine shades" and have opposed any foreign infiltration. Rousseau had attacked the recitatives of Lully who, in his French master scores, never completely forgot the Italian inflection of his youth. Yet, as a musician, Rousseau trapped himself in a contradiction with his own rationalistic philosophy. In keeping with his general back-to-nature principle, the conclusion became inevitable that the words should guide the melody, instead of melody dominating the language. At the same time, Rousseau was too much of a real musician to overlook the necessity of a concise rhythmical structure in the recitative, Italian or French. Thus, a dilemma existed in Rousseau's mind between the instinct of a musical performer and the theory of a philosopher, a conflict which no one in the eighteenth century seemed able to resolve. The solution occurred one and a half centuries later, when Debussy created the *Pelléas* score. Here, the laws of a language of fine shades and a music of human tenderness are blended into a most typical French score, which transcends national boundaries, and has become, by international acclaim, the representative music drama at the turning point of our century.

CHARMING RIDICULE

> *I herewith forbid reading of the text aloud during the performance.*—SATIE

No revolution is complete without its sideshow. That there should be rebellion against or at least satires on Debussy was just as inevitable as that there were parodies on Wagner. The Viennese Johann Nestroy's parodies and Offenbach's unsurpassable operettas, satirizing so magnificently the pompous opera style, are independently great art.

Thus it is not surprising to read in a piano piece of notation without bars, like medieval music, called *Idylle à Debussy,* the following text:

> What do I see? The rivulet is all wet and the woods are inflammable like matches. But my heart is very small. The trees resemble crooked combs, and the sun has pretty gilded rays. But my heart has a cold in the back. The moon has quarreled with her neighbors and the rivulet is wet to the bone.

Is this biting ridicule by a man on the opposite side of the fence? No, Debussy is only being amicably teased by one of his close friends in life and art, Erik Satie, the *enfant terrible* of the modern French school. Today, opinions differ on the quality of Satie's musical material, in spite of the pleas of Debussy, Ravel, or Stravinsky in behalf of Satie's merits as a composer.

In the history of interpretation Satie demands special attention, for he represents one of the most original influences in modern performance, at least in its happy byroad humor. He was capable of amusing himself and others by appearing at a recital wearing a fireman's helmet. Lockspeiser, Debussy's biographer, sensed in this form of musical exhibitionism a case for a psychoanalyst. Be this as it may, Satie was obviously an iconoclast of performance. Countless effects that later reached the musical stage (Satie died in 1925) were fully anticipated in his charming ridicule. The fun of the Satie performance starts with a funny title. His captions, in their associations with impressive music, puzzle even the well-disposed listener. Jean Cocteau, the poet who, like the painter Picasso, collaborated with Satie in several stage performances, explains how these titles protect Satie's music against people who are prey to the "sublime," and allow those who do not see their import to laugh. Indulging in comic appellations, Satie stands on traditional French ground. One has only to open a volume of Couperin's music to be amused by headings such as *Les coucous bénévoles* or *Le tic-toc choc ou Les maillotins*.

Satie's scores are full of directions such as, "Like a nightingale with a toothache," "For a dog," and "If the good Lord could see that, he would be furious," and, in the piano piece *Sur un vaisseau*, "The captain wishes a very pleasant voyage." In *Sur une lanterne*, it is suggested, "Don't light it yet; you still have time." These remarks can be read by the pianist during the performance, yet in *Heures séculaires et instantanées*, a long story about a Negro who is "bored to the point of dying of laughter," the composer finally adds a footnote: "To whom it may concern: I forbid reading the text aloud during the musical performance. Failure to comply will entail my just indignation against the transgressor."

If one reads the list of instruments intended to be used for background noises in the performance of Satie's ballet *Parade* —sirens, typewriters, airplanes, dynamos—it becomes clear that our machine age has fully entered the realm of performance.

But Satie, with his texts, had no "program" in mind—he obviously was one of the first musical Surrealists. He combined his compositions in tone and observations in words, not on the basis of an apparent realistic relationship, but as free association of different psychic strata. His remarks, "For a dog," or, "If the good Lord could see that, he would be furious," betray how he combined an extremely naïve, somewhat childlike and at the same time fanciful expression. Our time, perhaps, is better equipped than that of Satie to appreciate Surrealism. Its trend has been broadly accepted, to the point of commercialization, as shown by the fact that its leading exponent in painting, Salvador Dali, was commissioned to decorate the windows of a New York shop. This was so well received that now every provincial department store, to prove that it is up to date, has a display à la Surrealism, combining the idea of *épater les bourgeois* with an invitation to buy.

End and Beginning

ROMANTIC OBJECTIVITY

"Slow, dragging, like a sound of nature"—with such opening directions in Mahler's First Symphony, the interpreter finds himself once more in the old realm of Romanticism. Poetic instructions appeal to his fantasy; at the same time, he is directed in a most precise manner by Mahler's score. For instance, after eight bars, there is a change of the initial tempo to *più mosso*. From here, a gradual fluctuation of tempo occurs. *Più mosso*, after two measures, is changed to accelerando, and altered at the end of the next bar by a ritardando, which is enlarged to *molto ritardando* in the succeeding bar. Two more measures, and *tempo primo* is resumed. We see how the composer has carefully planned and written out, in a meticulous time-table, the intended variations of the main tempo. What is this main tempo? In spite of Mahler's painstaking and detailed orders for his rubato, no metronome marks appear. Thus the conductor must find for himself, subjectively, a *tempo primo* that will best lend itself to the later objectively indicated modifications. Wagner's conviction, that nothing is gained by setting a mathematical standard at the beginning, lives on. It is only the correct interrelationship of the different tempos that secures a sensible performance. Instead of restricting the performer with a metronomic bond, Mahler chooses to help him discover the right modification of time.

We recall Wagner's tempo discipline as the crux of his whole system of interpretation. That Mahler should have continued where Wagner left off is logical. He grew up in the Wagner atmosphere of Prague, Leipzig, and Hamburg, he was sponsored by such Wagner apostles as Angelo Neumann, Seidl, and Bülow. In opera, Mahler became one of the most convincing conductors of Wagner. In concert, his keen sense of the secrets of the orchestra tended toward a corrective approach in works like Schumann's beautiful but inexpertly scored symphonies. As a composer, seeped in the romantic world of one of the loveliest examples of German folk poetry, *Des Knaben Wunderhorn*, Mahler was bound to incorporate a certain degree of subjectivity in his interpretation, which can never be fully divorced from the general conception of Romanticism.

This subjectivity, however, does not mean arbitrariness. On the contrary, Mahler scores, in spite of their last integration of Wagnerian devices, point most distinctly into the future of objectivity. Thus, we read in the First Symphony: "Remark for the conductor: This lowest A must be played *very distinctly* through *pp*." Trumpets, entering after the figure 1, are set at a great distance. The clarinet is admonished to imitate the cuckoo's call. And here are a few more directions from the opening of the First: "All accents very delicately"; "Shakes without *Nachschläge*"; "Pizzicato divided"; "A dominant chord in the harp must not be broken"; "*pp.*, weaker and weaker"; "The clarinet, playing a fourth (D to A downward) imitates the cuckoo."

The examples speak for themselves. The trend is unmistakably to reinforce the binding precision of the script to an extreme by adding a multitude of verbal directions. Thus, Mahler's script becomes a score for study in the real sense of the word. Specific directions for entering and leaving the stage are given in the Second Symphony for those players who perform in the backstage orchestra. The score has become a musical scenario, taking into consideration the most minute directions for everything that has to be done and may happen, not only during the performance, but also during rehearsals.

Mahler's interpretative ideology is explained by his most forceful disciple, Bruno Walter. The composer's watchword— "What is best in music is not to be found in the notes"— emerges as the desire to discover the spirit behind the letter, an objectivity of the intended effects rather than of printed symbols.

PART FOUR

THE OBJECTIVE PRESENT

XII. Historical
═══ Correctness ═══

THE PRINCIPLE of historical correctness, one of the most significant trends in modern interpretation, had its beginning long before the dawn of the twentieth century: we have only to recall the work-fidelity of the romantic era to realize that the objective approach is not an achievement of our age. Just as, in the nineteenth century, earlier romantic forces gradually gained the upper hand until their aims found consummation in Wagner's life-work, so the forces of historical and objective interpretation, latent long before, became strongly dominant in the twentieth century. Supported by great scores, important ideologies, undreamed-of technical accomplishments, the trend to correctness in musical rendition is now an established principle. Loyal publications of old masterworks, standardization of pitch and instruments, and new electric media of performance are but the milestones on the modern highway to an interpretation guided by the road sign: "Correctness."

OBJECTIVE PUBLICATION

Mendelssohn's objective revival of the St. Matthew Passion led eventually to imposing projects of editing the collective works of great masters. As early as 1850, which was marked by the centenary of the death of Bach, the complete publication of his compositions was started; this was followed nine years later by similar publication of the works of Handel. Editions of Orlando di Lasso and Palestrina (the works of the latter numbering 950) joined the growing list of printed monuments of the old masters. Before 1900, editions of Mozart, Schütz, and Purcell appeared. By 1909, the year of the Haydn centenary, the classical series was completed.

Instead of the previous corrective tendency in the editing of masterworks, the new historical movement tends toward the opposite pole: toward accuracy of publication and elimination of subjective modification on the part of the editor. It is true that some of the collective editions are still far from perfect, and improvements toward stricter adherence to the manuscript are imperative. The all-important feature, however, is the policy of editing with fidelity to the original text. An outstanding example of such a correct approach is Friedrich Chrysander's collective edition of Handel's music, in one hundred volumes, completed in 1894. Philip Spitta's editions of Schütz, Buxtehude, and Bach follow similar ideals.

With such a general turning to the past world of music, emphasis on a legitimate old style of performance is but the logical consequence. If baroque scores are to be played with historical correctness, then the historical instruments actually used in readings by their composers, and not our modern ones, must be employed. The historical approach to old music is demonstrated as an artistic necessity by Sachs in the final chapter of his *History of Musical Instruments*, where the problem in music is compared with that in painting: "An outline drawn by Raphael could not be colored with Cézanne's palette. Only the old instruments, the original ones, can express the eighteenth-century sound ideals with appropriate colors; harpsichords, gambas, and ancient organs are needed." This points the way that can claim veracity in the interpretation of old music. Not only the need for the return to the old sound ideal, but simultaneously the absurdity of certain modern arrangements is indicated: it is historically incorrect to substitute the modern orchestra palette for the old one, since "the sensual tone of the violoncello will destroy the delicate line of a gamba composition; a cross-string piano suffocates the unemotional melody of a harpsichord piece."

This principle of correctness has occasionally been labeled an old-fashioned pedantry of musicologists. Responsible for many aesthetic miscomprehensions, Friedrich Nietzsche's denunciation of historical accuracy lives on as the battle cry of subjective interpreters today. "Should we put our soul," asked Nietzsche half a century ago, "into the older works according to their own soul? Not at all! Only in approaching them with our soul are old works capable of surviving. It is only our blood that makes them speak to us. The really historical performance would talk to ghosts." Unquestionably, Nietzsche's words are taken only too literally today. The genuine historical interpreter has hardly any chance to raise his voice loudly enough against those orgies that dress up the old spiritual polyphony in the shining masquerades of an orchestration à la Till Eulenspiegel, plus some undeniable jazz effects. Paradoxically, Nietzsche served the cause of the objectivists too. His argument, so typical of the "blood and soul" ideology of the period in which it was written, proves that the fanciful arranger, who proudly boasts of his modernity, does not know how hopelessly old-fashioned he really is. Instrumental streamlining of baroque façades is in reality reactionary—a return to the bombastic interpretative ideology of the nineteenth century, with its "corrective" pretentions and "superhuman" staging. The truly modern artist is one who can see eye to eye with the old masters.

BAROQUE ORGAN REAWAKENED

The clash between the extreme subjectivity of Romanticism and the new correctness was bound to make itself felt violently in relation to organ performance. This is in part due to the fact that the organ played today in churches, halls, and schools is altogether different from the baroque and prebaroque model. Opposition to the romantic organ was manifested in 1906, when Albert Schweitzer reawakened the sound ideals of the Bach organ with a reconstruction of the Silbermann instrument. (The Silbermanns were a family of organ builders for several generations, Gottfried Silbermann being especially noted for his association with the work of Johann Sebastian Bach.) An attempt to reconstruct a still older type of organ was that made by Willibald Gurlitt, a musicologist who worked from the plan of an instrument described in *Syntagma musicum* by Praetorius (1619). Today, the task of reconstructing old organs has been continued in the United States. We can hear and see such historical instruments at the Westminster Choir School in Princeton, and at Harvard University; in Cleveland, and in certain churches in the east, as in Groton, and the Church of the Advent in Boston, and at St. Mark's in Philadelphia. These instruments are designed to serve the baroque performing ideals of transparency and polyphonic clarity, as opposed to the romantic color orgy and desire for dynamic power. The twentieth-century organist is again given an adequate instrument for the purpose of correct historical interpretation.

The objectivist movement in organ performance in this country is most significant, because the United States is definitely a land of organists. Here organ playing outside of church walls is more popular than anywhere else in the world. The baroque "queen of instruments" has for the past generation been serving a useful purpose: it has acquainted music-loving people with the wide scope of nineteenth-century music, at a time when orchestra concerts could be heard in only a few cities, and of course only by those with ability to pay. Here the organist stepped in. In the days prior to records and broadcasts, his playing substituted for orchestral performance. Free recitals promoted knowledge of the literature, forcing the average organist to undergo a metamorphosis from church musician to jack-of-all-trades. Thus it became the organist's task to play not only music written specifically for his instrument, but also, in arrangements, anything in the whole range of music, ecclesiastical or secular, orchestral compositions or vocal scores. It is an open secret that not all organists (among whom are many fine scholars) are wholeheartedly in sympathy with such a practice. But the musical mores of bygone days still compel them to imitate the brass fanfare of the *Light Cavalry* and the sighing strings of the *Liebestod* in an effort to emulate as much as possible the multicolors of the orchestra palette. On the other hand, we cannot overlook the limits of the baroque organ. It is not possible to perform on it the works of later periods, such as the important literature of the French school, which calls for a different equipment.

TRANSCRIPTIONS

It is clear that the organ performer can never successfully compete with the sound ideal achieved by the heterogeneous medium of the modern orchestra. On the other hand, the orchestra can well reproduce the contrapuntal web of an organ score. It can even extend its polyphony beyond the limits imposed on the composer by the organ keyboards and pedals. This is the reason why it will always be more convincing to hear an orchestra play the transcription of an organ piece than to listen to the organ performance of an originally orchestral composition. Transcriptions of organ music for orchestra enjoy great popularity today. The quality of these interpretations is decided exclusively by the style in which they are done. If the transcriber loses sight of the intrinsic spirituality and the absolute polyphonic forces of the old score, and reduces them to a mere display of instrumental virtuosity, Mannheim stunts in dynamics, and Wagnerian brass power—then his transcription no longer can claim to be interpretation of Bach or Handel.

How the task of genuine transcribing may be accomplished with artistic discrimination is shown by quite a good authority —namely, Bach himself, who in his own examples of arrangements solved this interpretative problem so magnificently that their standard can never be surpassed.

As an illuminating instance, we may turn to his arrangement of Vivaldi's D Major Concerto for violin, orchestra, and harpsichord. The formal structure of Vivaldi's work is faithfully guarded. However, the technique of violin performance is imaginatively transposed to the keyboard of the harpsichord. The record collection of *Anthologie sonore* contains both versions, Vivaldi's and Bach's, and offers the student an opportunity to analyze, measure by measure, note for note, Bach's technique of transcription. One can follow the actual steps of the master who set the model for all times and all arrangements to come.

RESCORING

The mere use of original historical instruments by no means solves the problem of correct execution. After all, we have been learning of so many instances in which the old manner of playing differed fundamentally from our modern approach; the fingering of the virginalists, the rhythmic alterations of Lully, are such examples. The modern violin of longer neck length is not played with the technique of Corelli. Obviously, the interpreter of today has to do more than just get his hands on the old instruments and scores, if he really wants to play in genuine historical style. We must also bear in mind that, since the days of Handel or Mozart, orchestral instruments have been enormously improved. This very fact lends opportunity to a subjective trend: taking the amelioration of instruments into account, the modern interpreter is confronted with the possibility of readjustments that can be made in the old scores by virtue of the later improvements of the instruments. Among the classics, Beethoven scores are favorite subjects for instrumental readjustment on the part of modern conductors. Wagner's rescoring of Beethoven's Ninth Symphony became the model. After 1900, not only the so-called Wagner school of conductors, but the vast majority of performers, took a re-orchestration of Beethoven's orchestral works for granted, differing only in the degree of their instrumental retouching.

OBJECTIVITY OF SPIRIT

These changes are easily justified. The Classicists created an era of great instrumental development. Mozart first heard the effect of the clarinet in Mannheim, Haydn probably in London. Thus the lack of clarinets in the wood-wind sections of the earlier scores is explained. After his Mannheim experiences, Mozart himself rescored some of his symphonies, adding, to the older setup of two flutes, oboes, and bassoons, a pair of clarinets. Much more complex than the problem of clarinets is the scoring for the French horn. In Beethoven's time, valves had not yet been introduced. This explains the apparent inconsistency in his use of the horn. Probably the best-known example is found in the opening movement of the Fifth Symphony. In the fifty-ninth measure, the theme is given to the horns; the analogous passage of the recapitulation, however, is given only to the bassoons. Why Beethoven resorted in the second version to bassoons is obvious: since he could not use the stepped notes of the E flat horn for the expressive power of this phrase in C major, the only alternative available was to substitute bassoons for horns. With the advanced technique of the instrument today, conductors do what Beethoven could not have done in 1805, and use the horn in both cases, relieving the bassoons from a task for which they are not well suited.

Does such a procedure imply a subjective approach? Yes and no. It is subjective in the sense that it changes the original instrumentation of the composer. But it may claim objectivity in its final goal: to re-create the author's unmistakably intended effects by means which he would doubtlessly have used had they been available. We have here objectivity of spirit rather than of the letter. Why did Weber, Beethoven's contemporary, score the horns in a much more elaborate way, as in the *Freischütz* score, where the two pairs of horns are handled in a manner anticipating future possibilities? What was it that kept Beethoven from reaching Weber's mastery in the treatment of the horns? Obviously, his deafness. At least, Wagner feels that

> after the period of deafness had begun, Beethoven's mental conception of the orchestra grew fainter in proportion as the dynamic conditions of the orchestra became less familiar to him; and these conditions lost their distinctness just when they were becoming most indispensable, namely, at a time when his conceptions needed a constantly changing manipulation of the orchestra.

OBJECTIVE PITCH

Tuning of instruments is a phenomenon familiar to everyone who has ever attended an orchestral performance. Assembled on the orchestra platform or in the opera pit, the players of all the sections gather a few minutes before the beginning of the performance to adjust their instruments to a certain pitch, sometimes from a special tuning fork, but usually from the a' of the oboes. This procedure is often supervised by the concertmaster, as the quality of every performance depends to a high degree on the careful tuning of the instruments. The standard pitch accepted today is 435 double vibrations per second. This standard did not exist before the nineteenth century, a fact of obvious meaning for interpretation. We have only to recall that eighteenth-century music was supposed to be interpreted on the basis of certain connotations that musicians attributed to the different keys. Yet, whatever symbolic meaning the scale of F major might have had to the mind of the performer around 1750, it is only when the pitch of the old tone row called F virtually corresponds to the pitch of our modern F that the consideration of such aesthetics in the service of today's performance can make sense.

As a matter of fact, the modern pitch and the old one are far from being identical. Many misrepresentations of pitch are demonstrated by Sachs. We learn that the pitch of the baroque organs varied no less than from 347 to 567. This amounts to a deviation from f' sharp to c'' sharp in comparison with the standard a' of today. Thus it emerges that when either Bach or Handel played in C major or A minor, it was not the same key that is designated by that name today. What is true of the organ likewise applies to the piano. The fork used in 1780 to tune Mozart's piano had a frequency of 422 vibrations. Mozart played on an instrument between a quarter and a half tone lower than ours. Could he hear a pianist play the *Turkish March* from the A Minor Sonata, he might cry out: "But why do you play in B flat?" And the *Jupiter Symphony* would seem to his ear as being performed in C sharp, provided the instruments of his orchestra had the same pitch as his piano had.

The French government, to cope with the disorder in tuning, in 1858 appointed an investigating committee, which included Halévy, Berlioz, and Meyerbeer. It was this group that decided on the standard of 435. Yet today pitch is still rising; thus the final word does not seem to have been spoken yet. Furthermore, the general tuning to 435 does not secure complete unity of pitch in ensemble performance of instruments. A listener's discriminating ear discerns quite a few discrepancies in tuning, even in the performance of fine organizations. This is chiefly due to the difficulty, even impossibility, of tuning a variety of instruments to the same frequency. Furthermore, the specific intonation of the string instruments differs from that of other instrumental groups. To mention only one instance, the sensitive string player will make a fine discrimination in the way he plays an F sharp as a leading tone for G, playing it slightly higher than he would play the G flat on a descending scale, such as B minor. It is obvious that the wood winds and the brass can hardly encompass such highly refined adjustments.

A tuning problem unknown in former periods presents itself with the performing of music on records. Playing a record at different speeds alters the pitch of the reading. Some gramophones have a handy speed control at the disposal of the player; others permit adjustment inside the machinery. At any rate, only if a disk revolves in the key of the original rendition, can the proper tempo and therefore the proper interpretation be obtained. For the average music lover this question is not supremely important; but for the musician who is turning more and more to recordings for study, it is necessary to make sure that his machine is tuned to pitch.

In *a cappella* renditions, the preservation of initial pitch has been a problem to performers from Palestrina to Schönberg. Every practical musician knows the danger lurking in unaccompanied singing—the inevitable lowering of the pitch. *A cappella* singing seems to follow the law of gravity—with a tendency to fall. This fact has been gradually taken into account in modern score writing: Gustav Mahler, who as the infallible routinist, anticipated in his scores every problem of performance, provided in the finale of his Second Symphony a discreet instrumental accompaniment to protect the *a cappella* chorus from falling in pitch at certain spots. This is so skilfully done, that the *a cappella* character of the *Resurrection* chorus is preserved. Likewise, Schönberg suggests, for his *a cappella* chorus *Peace on Earth*, the use of one or two clarinets for the soprano and alto section each, and one or two bassoons for tenor and bass. These wood winds provide a means for maintaining the pitch throughout the performance. Apparently, more time will have to pass before the audacious modulation of the score will be sung with impunity by the average *a cappella* chorus.

New Subjectivity

SYMPHONY REVISED

The proneness to "correction" in the nineteenth-century tendency found a corollary in the twentieth-century tendency to re-orchestrate. Works of older periods were revised for the new media of a highly developed orchestra. In a much more arbitrary way, the phenomenon of the correction of Beethoven, discussed above (p. 318), is repeated in the case of Bruckner. His original scores and parts are obtainable only with great difficulty, so fully entrenched have the revisions become. These revisions are not limited to instrumentation alone, but include very drastic corrections involving actual changes of harmony and form. Ferdinand Löwe, the editor of the Bruckner scores, certainly had no selfish motive for changing the music of his adored master, and he did what he sincerely felt was best. He reasoned that Bruckner, as a church organist and counterpoint teacher, had little experience with the orchestra. And so Löwe, the routine *Kapellmeister*, considered himself indispensable in elevating the orchestration of Bruckner's music to the standards of modern scoring.

OPERA REVISED

Shifting from symphony to opera, the most characteristic example of changing ideologies in modern interpretation is represented in the various versions of Mussorgsky's masterpiece, *Boris Godunoff*. The arrangement in which the opera is familiar to thousands is that of Rimsky-Korsakoff. As an unchallenged connoisseur of instrumentation, the latter made two versions of Mussorgsky's opera, one as early as 1896, the other in his last year, 1908. However, it was not until recently that the fundamental changes in which Rimsky-Korsakoff indulged were recognized. The severe, long-bearded, bespectacled professor of composition had a complex about his disciple's Asiatic wildness, and so did away with some of the most strikingly original music that ever emanated from Russian soil. He deleted, added, and diluted. He changed rhythm, harmony, and form according to his own conventional standards. Finally, the big red pencil of that academic censor, Professor Rimsky-Korsakoff, scratched out the magnificent and so typically Russian scene in front of the Church of St. Basil, in which Boris begs the idiot to pray for his soul.

In 1941, another prominent Russian composer, Dmitri Shostakovich, came forward to meet once more the challenge of revising the score of *Boris Godunoff*. Other interpretative lines, however, are now the goal. Olin Downes in the *New York Times* explained Shostakovich's approach, and quoted him as saying:

> In my orchestration of the opera, I wished to keep it on another plane, to bring out, as far as possible, those traits of affinity with the Soviet epoch. I strove toward a more symphonic development of the opera, toward making the orchestra a more important factor than a mere accompaniment for the singers.

XIII. The Objective Revolt

N O ONE could have done more to clarify ideas on interpretation than Stravinsky. In his autobiography, he says: "An executant's talent lies precisely in his faculty for seeing what is actually in the score, and certainly not in a determination to find there what he would like to find." So we have, in the composer's own words, a definition of the interpreter's task, and the sum total of what the Stravinsky memoirs contribute to the problem of performance amounts to a virtual revolt against arbitrary rendition. Nineteenth-century ideologies and false aestheticism are challenged as the *raison d'être* of subjective interpretation. Objectivity no longer connotes one of two ways in performance; it now becomes the only kind of interpretation that makes sense. Moreover, the final step must be taken and the whole matter of "interpretation" thrown overboard. The idea of interpreting music is rejected *per se*, since interpretation reveals the personality of the performer rather than that of the composer. "Who can guarantee that such an executant will reflect the author's vision without distortion?" asks Stravinsky. To qualify for the task of competent performance, one must, above all, transmit the composer's thoughts without ever falsifying them by personal, wilful interpretation.

Stravinsky's own musical material lends itself perfectly to this type of objective rendition. Yet, ever since his works were first performed, they have given rise to very emotional discussions regarding the extent to which emotionalism can really be excluded from musical rendition. Opposed to Stravinsky's dogma is the age-old idea that claims music to be primarily an art of the feelings, through which its effects must be derived. We have only to recall certain eighteenth- and nineteenth-century ideologies discounting the idea that music can be appreciated objectively by the ear alone. Be this as it may, Stravinsky's actual musical material will provide better information than aesthetic discussions, which in any case often boil over into quarrels about terminology and definitions. So let us make a short-cut to those characteristic innovations that have connected Stravinsky's name with the history of musical progress. A token of these innovations is the change in setup of the orchestral apparatus from the postromantic monster orchestra to the miniature ensemble, where economy, not luxury, is the goal.

SCULPTURED IN MARBLE

For the performance of *L'histoire d'un soldat*, seven musicians are required—one violin and one double bass, in addition to a clarinet, bassoon, trumpet, trombone, and a percussion set. In *Les noces* the chorus is accompanied by four pianos and a diversity of percussion instruments. The *Symphonie des psaumes* calls for flutes, oboes, trumpets, horns, piano, cello, and double basses. The orchestral setup has once more undergone a radical change. The abandonment of the strings as the backbone of the orchestra would have been unthinkable in the romantic era. Obviously, Stravinsky's novel orchestra is not meant to balance in the sense of Wagner or Strauss. The conductor cannot approach the performance of the Stravinsky score with the classical sound idea in mind. He must realize that Stravinsky's use of an orchestral palette is different in quality, shading, and density from that of the romantic era. He appeals to the senses through primitive patterns and forms—not balanced, not beautified, but true to their nature. "Sculptured in marble" is Stravinsky's own way of putting it.

THE NEW RHYTHM

The nineteenth-century struggle for greater freedom of the meter, as exemplified in the interpretation of Liszt, remained in the experimental stage. Rhythmical elasticity emerged primarily as a device for the performer rather than as an integral part of the composition. In contrast, Stravinsky has employed a type of meter comparable either to the interpretation of the *a cappella* period or to the metrical technique of the Greeks. His melody, likewise, flows in strict allegiance to the accents of the language. This, in turn, is made possible by the employment of shorter, elastic, movable motifs in preference to the traditional type of four- or eight-measure themes that served the Classicists. Stravinsky's measure consists of small units. Phrasing now depends upon this rhythmical unit rather than upon the broad melody of the nineteenth century. This procedure takes the minimum unit instead of the maximum. Whereas the conductor's baton, in the performance of a work like the *Meistersinger* prelude, charts the main rhythm in a simple four-four beat, expecting the orchestra players to make their own subdivisions, a heterogeneous technique often becomes necessary in the polyrhythmic Stravinsky performances. Here the conductor either gives his beat on the basis of a minimum unit of the bar, or must resort, especially in the case of counterrhythm, to more complex diagrams to be determined individually by the score.

PRIMEVAL FORCES

Stravinsky interpretation is unthinkable without full realization of what has actually taken place in his workshop. The composer has returned to primeval natural tonal forces. He has, as Bekker puts it, "replaced the expressive power of music by its motor power." It is this "rude treatment" of the material that has been shocking audiences ever since the first performance of *Le sacre du printemps.* Yet the Stravinsky interpreter must tenaciously hold to the type of sound that Schloezer describes as "a disdain for everything that charms or pleases, stinging brutalities—all of which were necessary for the destruction of sentiment and subjective emotion, and to make things act directly and by themselves." This impersonal objective attitude does not change with the diversity of Stravinsky's material. Thus, whether he cites (as he does in *Jeux de cartes*) Johann Strauss or Rossini, or whether (as in *Baiser de la fée*), he is inspired by the muse of Tchaikovsky, Stravinsky's music always exhibits objective elements in a way that is unmistakably his. The subjective element, which Stravinsky would like to see eliminated from music-making, is characterized in the autobiography: "Most people like music because it gives them certain emotions, such as joy, grief, sadness, an image of nature, a subject for daydreams, or—still better— oblivion from 'everyday life.' "

But Stravinsky insists that people must learn to love music for its own sake, listen with other ears, and not to care for music because it gives them subjectively certain emotions. Here the last remnant of a romantic perspective is dispelled. That such a view is by no means one solely of theoretic speculation, but has far-reaching practical consequences for the performer, need hardly be restated. This is demonstrated by an example relating to dynamics. Since the employment of crescendo and decrescendo, the diversity of dynamics has become an ever increasing factor in orchestral expression. During the nineteenth century, dynamics became a paramount feature of performance —a romantic device par excellence. Today certain concerts are merely exhibitions of dynamic stunts. Essential points of the score, such as balance and proportion of form, are often sacrificed for the sake of irrelevant dynamic pyrotechnics. The tricky conductor easily submerges the basic features of the score in the hyperromantic flood of dynamic thrills. Without being really and intrinsically precise in performing, he somehow manages to impress the musical dilettante enormously, plunging him into an ocean of tone waves in which the important details have been engulfed. Stravinsky explains why, in a rendering of the *Soldat* with an orchestra of only seven musicians, all playing as soloists, there could be no question of fooling the public by means of the dynamic effects. With so small a number of instruments, it is impossible to conceal what an adroit conductor could have made to pass unnoticed in a large orchestra. On the other hand, for genuine understanding of his style, Stravinsky cites, among leading conductors in this country, Fritz Reiner, who "has the score in his head and not his head in the score," and Serge Koussevitzky, the traditional exponent of all Russian music.

SCHOOLING THE YOUNG INTERPRETER

Yet the whole complex of objective playing and listening still seems to be a hope for times to come, when musical enjoyment will be of a higher order and audiences able to judge it on a higher plane, realizing the objective values of musical interpretation. It is impossible to secure such an attitude as long as teaching is inadequate from the very beginning. "One has only to think," complains Stravinsky, "of all the sentimental twaddle so often talked about Chopin, Beethoven, and even about Bach—and that in schools for the training of professional musicians!" It is shown that the tedious commentaries on the side issues of music not only do not facilitate understanding, but, on the contrary, are a serious obstacle that prevents the understanding of its essence and substance.

For the schooling of the young interpreter, Stravinsky's suggestion is noteworthy that it would be wiser to start the education of the young musician by first giving him a knowledge of what is, and only then tracing history backward, step by step, to what has been. How much truth there is in this suggestion of Stravinsky, no one should be better able to judge than those who have had an opportunity to work on the problem of interpretation with American college students. They are fresh in their appreciation of modern music, free from prejudice, and amazingly adjustable to its most complex problems. Every progressive teacher has discovered, in classroom or rehearsal hall, that problems are best elucidated from the modern point of view, past by present and present by past. It is no exaggeration to claim that such a modern approach is the one that most appeals to young minds and the one through which they will readily participate in work even on seemingly obsolete problems, otherwise just textbook "stuff" to them. Thus, a not too welcome part of the music student's required assignment is now turned into living and forceful material. And both have gained, the old music and the new.

Schönberg

Schönberg grew up in the Mahler sphere of influence. Returning from the first world war, he was still in soldier's uniform when he took over the presidency of a unique musical club housed in the gymnasium of a progressive private school for girls. Under the rather unassuming title of Society for Private Musical Performances, an institution was developed the importance of which can best be judged from the fact that it became the model for similar organizations throughout Europe. Schönberg's club was designed from its very beginning for this dual purpose: to give modern music of all styles an opportunity to be heard in the right interpretation, and to provide the club members with the chance for full appreciation even of the most complex progressive scores.

Taking for granted that the difficulty in understanding new music can be overcome only by repeated hearings and study, a specific system of performances was devised. Through regular renditions, the problematic and unclear attitude of the audience was to be changed by repeated performances of high interpretative standards. To insure a thorough study, repetitions were given in proportion to the difficulty involved in the composition. All that was considered harmful to the educational end in view was avoided. No applause or hissing was permitted, no critical comments on the concerts appeared in papers or journals, nor was any publicity attempted. Since the repertoire was kept secret, nobody stayed away from the presentation of a work because of dislike of or prejudice against a particular style. True, such a practice might yield less entertainment, but its educational value is evident. Among the performers were artists, many of them now acknowledged interpreters in this country, who were not interested in virtuosity or other externalities, but in the idealistic aim of the club. The end of the society's activities was forced by the European inflation of 1921, when the Austrian crown become a million overnight—insufficient to defray even the cost of lighting the rented hall for an evening.

NEW NOTATION

There was no better way of getting acquainted with Schönberg as interpreter than in the countless rehearsals of the club. Schönberg interprets objectively in the sense that he gives each note the very place it should have in the construction of the whole work—every note receiving its precise share. Likewise, each phrase is carefully adjusted to its function in the totality of the composition. To insure an unmistakable picture of the structure of the score, Schönberg resorts to a method of punctuation described in the preface to his Fourth String Quartet. Here the composer explains that:

1. H͞ means principal part ⎱ the ends of which have been
   N͞ means secondary part ⎰ marked with the sign ⏋
   These indications are for the purpose of making clear to each performer his specific and varying role. He retires into the background of accompaniment if his passages are unmarked

2. ╱ and ╱ mean accented, like a strong beat
   ∪ means unaccented, like a weak beat

3. In the notation of short notes, a distinction has been drawn between the hard, heavy, *martelé* notes and the light, elastic, thrown ones. The first have been indicated by the sign ▌, the latter by the sign •
   — means that the note should be lengthened (*tenuto* and *portato*). When the mark is placed above the dash (╱), the note should be accented and lengthened. When it is the staccato dot that is placed above (⸱⸻), the note is to be well sustained and yet separated from the next by a slight pause or interruption
   ∧ means "do not allow this to weaken" and often "bring out." (It is mainly up-beats that have been marked thus)

4. *col legno battuto* means struck with the stick of the bow
   col legno tratto means drawn with the stick of the bow

5. The metronome marks must not be taken literally—they merely give a suggestion of the tempo
6. Trills must always be played without after-beats
   Appoggiaturas should be regarded as up-beats

In such notation, Schönberg, integrating a few historical devices into his own original method, achieves a high degree of objectivity. The need for additional signs supplementing the score script was already felt by Frescobaldi. He, too, marked on certain manuscripts the entrances of themes with words or numbers, in order to clarify the polyphonic texture. Like the modern master of the twelve-tone system, the great seventeenth-century Italian composer was most progressive in his attitude toward harmony.

By this system, a note script otherwise complex to the contemporary eye is elucidated. An elaborate method of phrasing, likewise, does justice to the melodic polyphonic element which Eduard Steuermann calls the very essence of Schönberg's music. He explains that "a classical melody, if interpreted with inadequate phrasing, may lose something of its beauty, whereas Schönberg's would be downright incomprehensible."

In the third of his five orchestral pieces Opus 16, Schönberg specifically warns the conductor not to emphasize certain parts that he, the interpreter, deems of thematic importance. When a part is prominent, the composer has taken care of his intentions by way of the instrumentation. On the other hand, it is the task of the conductor to see that every instrumentalist plays precisely the degree of dynamics prescribed by the score. All this leads to the very core of objective interpretation: emphasizing the musical thoughts of the composer rather than the mood or the feeling of the performer. The picture of the Schönberg score is not a musical tableau lending itself to the subjective caprices of the executant, but a blueprint of the architecture of the music. This does not imply, as is often contended, the absence of the human element in the Schönberg performance. Characteristic is the composer's remark (see 5 in synopsis above) concerning metronomization: the marks must not be taken literally, but merely as a suggestion of the tempo. Neither is this type of performance "emotionless." However, it is unnecessary to add the performer's own emotional attitude, since the score has already absorbed the mental and emotional features surrounding its creation. The romantic interpreter who gets his result by mere temperament, by a display of fire, sadness, or agitation, is, as Rudolph Kolisch remarks, at a loss with Schönberg. The romantic method necessarily consists of a heightening of the surface luster, rather than what Schönberg demands—balance and symmetry of presentation, where true insight into the construction governs the outline as well as all the details of the interpretation.

SONG SPEECH

We have seen how composers, in three centuries, have experimented with the fusion of prose and music. No one has proved as persevering as Schönberg in seeking new media of vocal expression. As early as in the *Gurrelieder*, "song speech" (*Sprechgesang*) appears as a specific means of expression. In a later work, *Pierrot lunaire*, Schönberg directs his singer's understanding of this novel type of recitative as follows:

> The melody indicated for the speaking voice by notes (apart from a few specially indicated exceptions) is not meant to be sung. The reciter has the task of transforming this melody, always with a due regard to the prescribed intervals, into a speaking melody. That is accomplished in the following way:
>
> 1. The rhythm must be kept absolutely strict, as if the reciter were singing; that is to say, with no more freedom than he would allow himself if he were just singing the melody.
> 2. To emphasize fully the contrast between the sung note

and the spoken note, whereas the sung note preserves the pitch, the spoken gives it at first, but abandons it either by rising or by falling immediately after. The reciter must take the greatest care not to fall into a singsong form of speaking voice. Such is absolutely not intended. On the contrary, the difference between ordinary speech and a manner of speech that may be embodied in musical form is to be clearly maintained. But, again, it must not be reminiscent of song.

Song speech is likewise employed in the stage work *The Lucky Hand*. This time it is entrusted not to a solo voice (a man in the *Gurrelieder*, a woman in *Pierrot lunaire*), but to a small choir of six men and six women. This ensemble assumes a part comparable to that of the chorus in Greek tragedy, to which it is almost equal in number (fifteen being the Greek average). Half singing, half speaking, *The Lucky Hand* chorus becomes the sympathizing commentator on the action, somewhat in the ancient manner of the choruses of Euripides or Aeschylus. In either case, the audience's reactions are projected against the experiences and suffering of the hero. This background function becomes evident in the song-spoken words of the chorus.

LIGHT SCALE

Schönberg, who also wrote the words to the score of *The Lucky Hand*, accentuates the symbolism of its interpretation through a unique application of light. A characteristic example is the scene where the woman leaves the man with another lover. This moment is followed by a crescendo in light and wind that gradually increases in violence. A touch of red light passes through brown into a mottled green; from this into a dark blue-gray, followed by purple. This is followed by an intense dark red that becomes brighter and more glaring. From this it passes, through orange and bright yellow, to blinding light.

The introduction of the light scale in *The Lucky Hand* does not mark the first instance of a blending of tonal and lighting effects in musical interpretation. There were the attempts of Scriabin, much discussed at the time of the first performance of *Prometheus*, the poem of fire (1911). Written for orchestra, piano, organ, choruses, and the keyboard of light (*clavier à lumières*), an accumulation of such fanciful tone-light effects did not prove to be a lasting contribution of the otherwise most stimulating Russian. It is only on the opera stage, with its action, that the interpretation can be aided by the language of light. In absolute music, it is a distraction.

The Lucky Hand, with its great variety in performing technique, has been referred to as a "psychological pantomime." This, however, is not too happy a term, because the actual singing precludes pantomime, although it must be conceded that the line of demarcation between the genres opera, music drama, symbolic oratorio, pantomime, becomes tenuous. Whatever its appellation, the symbolism that Schönberg brought to the musical stage has close ties with much that has since appeared.

If *The Lucky Hand* has hardly any story, Schönberg's other stage work, *Erwartung*, has none. The whole action revolves around the shock to a human being in a moment of highest tension and intensity of feeling. A woman searches for her lover in the deep gloom of the nightbound forest until she finds him—dead. This is the only incident in the psychological drama, the protagonist of which is the music. Schönberg's style is particularly adept in symbolizing the hidden sources of the conflict. The music of *Erwartung* is as abstract as the human subconscious, as free in form as a dream. The monodrama thereby becomes the life-history of an emotion interpreted in the language of music.

XIV. New Gateways == of Interpretation ==

There's music in all things if men had ears;
Their earth is but an echo of the spheres.
—BYRON

MUSICAL conditions have changed to a degree that the most radical iconoclast of former times would not have considered possible. Beethoven, who could play only to the limited visible audience, would have loved the idea of people all over the world listening simultaneously to the *Ode to Joy*, his musical manifesto of humanity and brotherhood. Revolutionary electromechanical inventions have opened new gateways for performance—of old music as well as of music still to be written. Good old Quantz, could he have witnessed the new type of performance, would have been the first to investigate thoroughly the new interrelationship of technical and artistic conditions. And just as Quantz started his research with seeming trivialities, so the modern survey of new performing conditions must not exclude the "extraneous" factors surrounding the electric performance. It is these very factors that impose new interpretative conditions on the musical executant.

A NEW PERFORMER

Electric performances are the result of teamwork. Not only the musician but also the engineer contributes to the execution

336

of a musical score. It is hardly necessary to explain why the result of the broadcast or the record rendition depends on the "close harmony" of their performance. The performing musician is somewhat at the mercy of the engineer at the control board. No matter how delicate the touch of the Chopin player or the harmonics of the violinist, a rough handling by the controlling engineer would nullify these effects. Vice versa, the full volume of an orchestra would quickly become a neutral *mezzo piano*, over which the players and conductors would have no control.

The larger broadcasts are more extensively rehearsed and handled with relatively more care as regards the teamwork between musician and engineer. The smaller and unheralded ones (which may not be less artistic or less conscientious in interpretation) are frequently left to chance. Much remains to be done in the improvement of such performances. Heretofore the man at the control board has been too much the mechanic and not enough the musician. A new type of performer, however, is in the making: the musical sound engineer, a technician who will be fully versed in musical discipline and score reading, whose technical and artistic qualities will supplement those of the musical performer. The ideal sound engineer, as collaborator in interpretation of the score, would rehearse with the performer, note for note, bar for bar. His sound-control machinery would supplement the performance as an accompanist supplements a soloist. In such a case, the performing musician would have the full sympathy and understanding of the accompanying engineer. Thus, electric performance will bring forth a type of performance that will be democratic not only in the technical sense but also in its ideology of co-operation. Neither of the two—the musical sound engineer nor the performing musician—can alone reach the ultimate goal.

TIMBRE AND TRANSMISSION

The history of electric performance will have to be constantly rewritten as technical improvements are made. Today's
technical shortcomings may be eliminated tomorrow. In the
meantime, however, performers are faced with general difficulties of "pickup" and transmission, which must be met as
well as possible. Such is the case with the problem of carrying
the dynamic extremes. The softest pianissimo or the over-
powering fortissimo, which in concert or opera becomes a
source of romantic thrill, is not always satisfactorily transmitted
by record or broadcast. Tchaikovsky's five and six *p*'s in the
clarinet and bassoon parts of the *Symphonie pathétique*, Verdi's
extremes in opera scores like *Othello*, the terrifying fortissimi
of Berlioz and Wagner, are a constant worry to the engineer.

Likewise, the performer is perhaps disappointed by the
absence of many of his subtle details, which in the transmitted
version become vague generalities. The consequence is clear.
The performer must give way and keep a smaller margin of
dynamics, or be subdued by the sound technician, especially
if their respective ideas of good audibility differ. In addition
to the problem of dynamics, the new electric media reproduce
true timbre only in the case of certain instruments; the roll
of the timpani, the brass in fullest power, certain types of
chorus music, still present problems in transmission. On the
other hand, one can find little if any fault with other timbres
in transmission, such as that of the wood winds. Instruments
with distinct transmitting qualities, such as the saxophone,
which was a novelty when introduced by Bizet in the incidental
music to *L'Arlésienne*, have become an integral part of scoring
for electric music.

TIMING

Timing of electric performances is another extraneous factor affecting transmitted renditions. In the nontransmitted reading, a certain latitude is allowed. After all, it does not make a great deal of difference whether a concert program is over at 10:30 or 10:35. But with the electric performance, a complete change in timing considerations has come about. To realize the consequences of imposed timing, one has to bear in mind that frequently the tempo in which a work is performed must be adjusted to the exclusive purpose of completing it on a given number of disks. If a number which takes perhaps ten minutes to play must be recorded on two sides that allow only nine minutes of playing time, obviously the whole tempo must be accelerated to fit this time limitation. Here a completely extraneous factor is imposed on the reading of the score.

What is true of records applies also to broadcasting. Once the numbers have been timed for a program, the performer must adhere to the original tempo and cannot afford to yield to a momentary mood that would alter the prearranged schedule. He must carefully watch the studio clock to make sure that he plays in accordance with the rehearsed timing. Some interpreters are blessed with an infallible sense of tempo that could be termed "absolute time," in analogy to absolute pitch. This capacity for governing tempo and all its modifications in the performance accounts for the fact that certain conductors or soloists hardly ever deviate in their total timing when performing a given score. They have, as it were, an inbuilt metronome. With the absolute space and time limits of disks and broadcasts, the importance of interpreters with such qualities is self-evident.

On the other hand, the highly romantic type of interpreter discussed at length in earlier chapters, becomes an anachronism in connection with the new media. The romantic performer who follows the impulse and inspiration of the moment and is unwilling to and perhaps incapable of confining his emotions within the split-second requirements of the chronometer, is out of place in the modern studio.

CONTROVERSIAL ATTITUDES

Different attitudes toward the technical limitations of the new media are apparent. One group of interpreters awaits perfection with the gradual development of the apparatus. They believe that, with the perfection of the electric media, their transmitted performances likewise will improve. They do not acknowledge a need of changing their usual style of presentation for the sake of a mechanical medium. They see no reason to adjust the reading of a Beethoven score to the limits of the microphone.

The other group of interpreters, realizing that the experience of performing in the studio will necessarily differ from performing in the concert hall, regardless of how perfect the electric media become, takes the above-mentioned differences of microphone performances into account. While both groups are eagerly awaiting the perfection of the technical apparatus, it is the interpreter in the second group who tries to adapt himself to the microphone in order to get the best musical results. Notwithstanding his respect for the intrinsic musical texture of the score, he may be willing to compromise for the sake of the best transmission effects. He also knows that there are certain results that can be attained by mere maneuvering before the microphone. A singer's voice, for instance, can be reproduced in varying force merely by moving nearer to or farther from the microphone.

This problem is illustrated by Howard Taubman, who relates that

> Caruso made a recording of the quartet from Verdi's *Rigoletto*, with Galli-Curci, Perini, and DeLuca. When the record was played back, only Caruso was heard. It was suggested that the powerful tenor keep his voice down. He did, while the others let loose with all they had. This time the result was better, but Caruso still dominated the quartet. The problem was finally solved by placing Caruso five feet behind the others.

Transmitting conditions have definitely improved since Caruso's day, yet problems of voice balance must still be considered. On the opera stage, the conductor can blend voices of considerably different quality and volume only by adjusting the dynamics relatively. In a broadcast rendition, performers confronted with the same problem may resort to purely mechanical adjustments. Again, a crescendo from piano to fortissimo can be accomplished by the controlling engineer alone, without orchestral indulgence in the famous Mannheim effects. Berlioz' "crescendo like a fire that sets the sky aflame," for which he required sixteen French horns, ten timpani, and twelve trombones, can now be achieved in different ways— perhaps with a fraction of that number of instruments playing into the microphone.

ELECTROGENIC SCORES

If it is assumed that the electric reproduction of music not written for the new media will, at least for the time being, only approximate the original, in spite of remarkable achievements and progress made every day, the next logical step is special scoring and composing for the individual conditions of mechanical reproduction. Works specifically conceived and composed for radio and record performance have already been commissioned by various organizations. Composers start planning their scores with a consideration of imposed time limits and timbre limitations, and go from such vantage points to the other structural problems of composition.

Roy Harris' *Time Suite*, especially written for broadcast, shows such consideration for the new media on the part of a modern composer. Harris explains that he "made a study of exact time periods as the prescribed forms in which complete musical organism could be molded." The six movements of the *Time Suite* "are as follows, in order of sequence: one minute, two minutes, three minutes, four minutes, five minutes, four minutes." Again, Harris' overture *When Johnny Comes Marching Home*, written specifically for recording, had its first "public" hearing not in a hall, but in the private homes of the various buyers of the record, after the protagonist of the new medium, Eugene Ormandy, had completed the recording in the studio.

The scope of performing opportunities and the dangers presented by electric devices cannot yet be estimated. We have only to think of the possibility of an apparatus that will permit the composer to transmit his music directly into a recording medium without the help of the middleman interpreter. So far, there is only a theory about such an apparatus. If it should materialize, it will have the most far-reaching effects, and, obviously, the present task of the interpreter will be automatically eliminated.

INTERPRETATION STANDARDIZED

One of the direct consequences of recordings is the means they provide for improving the average interpretative standards. With the renditions of the great musicians available on disks, the mediocre performer has a priceless opportunity to orientate himself by model performances. Persevering, he may so familiarize himself with an interpretation along the lines of a great reading that a certain degree of correctness may be injected into his performances. But there is another side of the picture: such a second-hand interpretation, accomplished through imitation, is bound to lack the conviction of a personalized conception. The student, before the convenient availability of the gramophone, was forced to acquire his knowledge of a masterwork by direct study of the score, playing it on the piano, or just reading it. This approach sharpened his ear and imagination. Without the comfortable short-cut of a record player, the student had to transpose carefully for certain instruments, and to figure out every chord combination. The reproduction of the music occurred only in his brain or on the keyboard.

The listening connoisseur can unfailingly detect the difference between an imitated reading and one that arises from a thorough knowledge and spiritual comprehension of the score. While it is not necessary to point out the dangers involved in a performer's depending on a "canned" interpretation, it would be a great mistake to overlook its educational advantages. Clearly, major pitfalls in interpretation may be avoided by the student's use of authoritative records as a basis of his approach. By comparing the various records of reliable performers, he may perhaps find his own musical bearings without, at the same time, trapping himself in the role of a musical parrot.

INVISIBILITY OF AUDIENCE

Schumann writes of a Liszt concert: "I had heard him before, but an artist is different in the presence of the public. The brilliant lights, the elegantly dressed audience, the wide hall— all this elevates the spirit of giver as well as receiver." Such interaction of artist and audience does not exist in the case of the electric rendition. Neither is the interpreter before the microphone stimulated by an audience, nor can the listener to a record or a broadcast performance be influenced beyond the aural sensation. From these premises emerges one fact: the convincing electric interpretation is the one based on formal lucidity, clarity, concise tonal balance, not too extreme dynamics, and embodying other features that have become the *conditio sine qua non* of electric performance. It is not the one that stresses improvised nuances and sudden dynamic changes that are effective in the concert hall.

Surrounding this problem are countless psychological ramifications, such as what Schumann describes as Liszt's and Paganini's power to subject, lead, and elevate an audience, or the fact that one interpreter may be immensely stimulated by the presence of an audience and shiver in front of a "cold" microphone, or the reverse situation, where a performer is relieved by the solitude of the studio and gives his best, owing to the absence of the very conditions that inspire the first interpreter.

TELEVISION

Whatever has been said of invisibility as a factor influencing interpretation becomes outmoded the moment television becomes generally available to the public. Television will, of course, bring precious vistas to the home: one will not only hear *Don Giovanni*, but will also see the demonic seducer in the ghostly churchyard scene inviting the governor's stony statue to dinner. Likewise, in the concert performance, television will restore the lost category of visual impressions. To what degree the visual will be emphasized, is a question for the future. It remains to be seen, in the literal sense, how musical broadcasts will be projected.

There are infinite possibilities. Will one see, in a televised symphony broadcast, the entire orchestra, or will the focus be on the conductor, or on the conductor's hands? If the emphasis turns again on the performers' antics, then the streamlined magic box of the twentieth century might take us back to the romantic days. Like Schumann in his description of Liszt and Paganini, so the music lover of tomorrow may be hypnotized (in the privacy of his own home) by the demonic appearance as well as by the performance of the supervirtuoso. Will this start or close a historical vicious circle? Time proves how its new media promote new styles of musical performance. Yet these very media are apt to revert musical interpretation to the styles of bygone days. Such a phenomenon, if viewed in historical retrospect, proves an eternal law: the constant spiraling of heterogeneous styles throughout the ages of history.

MOVING PICTURES

The story of musical performance in the movies from the "mood man" to the theater orchestra, and finally to the development of the sound track, is a familiar one. Today, as in the earlier years, the problem can be viewed from the movie producer's angle or from the musician's point of view. The old problem of co-ordination, associated with the opera since its birth, appears again in a streamlined variation. We recall how this question has been answered, either in favor of the drama or of the music, throughout history, from Monteverdi to Debussy. Musical interpretation in the moving pictures is faced with analogous problems of priority. In the correspondence between Mozart and his father (from which we culled so much valuable information on the interpretative problems of the eighteenth century) special reference is made to George Benda's theatrical score *Ariadne auf Naxos* (1775). Here a constant change between the spoken word and musical passages occurs, a tone language found also in certain scores of Rousseau (*Pygmalion*), of Beethoven's teacher, Christian Neefe, and in Mozart's unfinished *Zaïde*. The term used for this type of stage play with music is "melodrama." While on the legitimate stage no important contributions have been made to this form since the prison scene in *Fidelio* and the wolves' glen in *Der Freischütz*, the motion picture producers experiment a great deal with this hybrid type of performance, in attempts to avoid the conflict between word and tone, to emphasize the action and yet not lose the valuable background factor of the music.

In our own day, composers like Schönberg and Shostakovich have written scores intended to accompany motion pictures. Toch, Copland, Eisler, Korngold, and others working for the films remind us of the historical fact that in the past too it was the acknowledged composer and not just a specialized craftsman who made the important musical contribution to the theater. Beethoven's incidental music to Goethe's *Egmont*, Mendelssohn's to Shakespeare's *A Midsummer Night's Dream*, and Bizet's to Daudet's *L'Arlésienne*, live on and are being interpreted as independent concert music. Whether movie music can be effectively interpreted apart from the screen is questionable, especially if the score is intrinsically linked to the action of the sound film. Music such as Copland's *Our Town*, when played in concert presentation, may perhaps lend itself with a certain elasticity to "absolute" performance, since the score was written as a general background for the picture. But in music for a prescribed scene, the original conception must be slavishly adhered to, especially in tempo. If a person walks sedately across the screen to the accompaniment of music, a different tempo in performance would make the actor saunter or run. In a case like this, there exists only one interpretation of the action, and thus of the music. The performance is objective, as is the music, which has been literally measured, in small units of time correlated with film space: music of minutes and inches as well! Everything is synchronized to the utmost, the best example of this being perhaps the cartoon production.

The sound film offers infinite possibilities for new musical ventures. Music has been little used as a medium for psychological enhancement. When Siegfried is welcomed by Hagen with the hypocritical "Hail, Siegfried, bravest heart!" (*Götterdämmerung*, Act I, scene 2) the music we hear is the curse motif. Thus the theme implies that Hagen is contemplating the murder of the guest whom he is greeting. Again, when King Mark finds his bride, Isolde, in the arms of Tristan, and no reply is given to the old man's despairing question, "The unexplained and hidden cause of all my woes who will to us disclose?" the orchestra alone supplies the answer: it plays the love motif.

Certain German piano scores of Wagner's operas contain a table of motifs in which every theme is numbered and classified according to its psychological implication. Thus the operagoer, in following the action, can constantly refer to the motif table in order to understand the opera in all its ramifications. While this certainly is not a very natural approach to the *Gesamtkunstwerk*, the film, with its infinite visual possibilities, is truly better equipped than the opera to supplement the psychological implications of drama and music. In fact, Herbert Graf stresses unlimited opportunities offered by the music film for opera production, and calls the moving pictures the answer to many of the difficult problems of opera.

XV. The American Scene

CRUCIBLE OF MUSIC

WORLD events are placing new emphasis on the art of the Western hemisphere. Music, like the other arts, reflects a change of spirit and substance, as the interpretation of American ideals replaces the imitation of the European heritage. While culture and tradition have been destroyed abroad, a young and independent art is being formed from the United States to Mexico, Brazil, Argentina, and all the other nations to the south. America no longer goes to Europe for its musical education. The best of musical Europe, composers, interpreters, musicologists, are in the Americas. The finest performances anywhere now take place in our midst. The Western hemisphere has become the musical world.

All this is bound to sharpen our self-examination as regards the new direction and definition of American interpretative ideals. We have only to think in terms of geography to realize this diversity. As W. D. Allen convincingly demonstrated, it would be necessary to study American music, "state by state, with a tolerant enjoyment of the contribution each has to offer, in order to secure a combined history of music of the United States." There are the English, Scotch, and Irish elements spread throughout the country. In the Northeast, the French Canadian element is dominant. Going down the Atlantic coast, there are Slavs, Swiss, Armenians, Syrians, Italians, Germans, Swedes, Finns, Dutch; finally we reach the South, with its large and musically important Negro population. In Louisiana, there is the French Creole element, in California, the Spanish Mexican influence. On the Pacific coast, one can hear any folklore from the European Finnish and Portuguese to the Asiatic Chinese and Japanese. That San Francisco incorporates the largest Chinatown outside of the Far East is undoubtedly a factor in the music-making in that great western port, and interaction with American music has already resulted (as in the case of Edgar Stillman Kelley). Last but not least, the native Indian element has greatly influenced some of the most important composers. Edward MacDowell, born in New York, the metropolis of more musical dialects than any other place in the world, resorted to the Indian music, the only true earthy idiom of the American soil, amalgamating it with late-romantic European elements.

In an American city like Pittsburgh, the home of Stephen Foster, one may hear, in addition to the English, Scotch, and Irish strains, a great deal of German music, as well as Italian, Croatian, Serbian, Jewish, Greek, Russian, Bohemian, Hungarian, and French tunes. Here Foster heard frequently the imported German *Ländler* (which lives on in songs like *Beautiful Dreamer*); farther south, he listened to the Negro ballads and slave songs, the flavor of which prevails in Foster's music and has exerted a marked influence on American music in general. It is particularly in the Negro spiritual, with its touching primitive quality and its naïve mood, that the interpreter from other parts of the world will find clues to the American way of expressive simplicity.

FOLKLORE

Much of American music grew out of a variety of folkloristic forces. While these have been at work since the early days of colonization, their modern style integration can readily be demonstrated by a panorama of contemporary scores, chosen for their quality as well as frequency of performance. Opening our survey with a composer as deeply steeped in folklore as Roy Harris, we realize that his technique of folk song integration is infinitely more sophisticated than that of his predecessors. His interpreter may look for historic parallels concerning the rhythmic freedom and other artistic premises of folklore in the style of the *a capella* period, certain madrigal types, and the interpretative tenets of the *nuove musiche*. Douglas Moore, with his opera *The Devil and Daniel Webster*, established a lyric style of American background. In the *Overture on an American Tune*, he presents a musical portrayal of the average citizen in a small town—as American in spirit as Sinclair Lewis' *Babbitt*, which inspired the score. In Randall Thompson's *Americana*, life's realities are embodied in what may be called a secular American cantata. Yet the composer's choral writing copes with the superb standards of the old polyphonic era. Virgil Thomson's ballet *Filling Station* depicts humorously typical American scenes in variations on familiar tunes. However, in this American sense of humor, one may detect a flair for the charming satire of the French. Here, as in Thomson's numerous other scores, the key to the American quality can perhaps be found in the truly cosmopolitan experience of the composer. Harl McDonald explains how the last movement of his Symphony No. 1, the *Santa Fe Trail*, "represents the many influences—Hispanic, Nordic, and American Indian—that combined to build the spirit and substance of the Southwest." And so it is with many of the best American scores—they so often combine the spirit and the various musical substances of the great country, without expressly resorting to one specific type of folklore. Again, if Aaron Copland, as vital and versatile as his city of New York, enjoys an excursion down the Rio Grande (in his *El salòn Mexico*) then his music sounds as genuinely

Latin American as Ravel is truly Spanish in his *Rapsodie Espagnole.*

SOUTH OF THE RIO GRANDE

The music of Mexico is of Indian and Spanish background. However, its quality is not altogether derived from its folkloristic make-up. "The existence of many new local factors—historical, geographic, and ethnic circumstances," Carloz Chavez, Mexico's leading musician, asserts, "work directly on the artistic phenomenon." Thus, emphasis is not laid on a return to past sources. On the contrary, a most progressive attitude on the part of the Mexicans toward the problem of the new media of interpretation is a salient feature in their musical life. It is no coincidence that one of the best studies on this subject has been written by Chavez himself, who, as teacher of a whole generation of Mexican musicians, placed his school in the *avant-garde* of interpretative progress.

The farther south we go, the more obvious it becomes that the Latin American music world cannot be tamed by standards that draw distinct frontiers between the realms of popular and of serious art. Music-making is undertaken for the sheer elementary enjoyment to be drawn from it. In Brazil, the charming folklore of that coffee-growing country, when appearing in symphonic garb, suggests to northern neighbors the carefree atmosphere of the café itself, the sociable milieu of tropical relaxation, without too much concern for the intellectual problems of structure and style. This carefree element of Brazilian music is not, however, without a melancholy counterpart, designated by the term *saudade.* Gilbert Chase traces this quality back to the natural sad tendency of "Portuguese lyricism, intensified by the conditions colonists had to face in this immense country with its wild jungles and manifold dangers." The music of Heitor Villa-Lobos, Brazil's outstanding composer, is full of kaleidoscopic changes of mood. And in the variety and color of these scores, the interpreter faces a musical microcosmos of southern life. He must follow through wholeheartedly a seeming montage of styles that is proving to be one of the most vitalizing musical forces on the American scene.

TANGO: STYLE TRANSFORMATION

Interpretative experiences, as described in our section on dance types (p. 119), are reflected in the style transformation of dances from South America. Like the old Spanish saraband, so the American tango and habanera have undergone changes in the course of time. We have only to remember that, when Bach wrote his sarabands, he did not "refine" the wild dance for the execution of which people in the sixteenth century went to jail. He wrote sarabands as time had brought them down to him, entirely different from the forerunner type, developing them in a purely musical sense and in terms of his own style. Likewise, the reading of the tango in symphonic surroundings does not have to adhere to the original Buenos Aires outdoor style. Diversity of performance is inevitable, depending on geography and, of course, on the purpose of the performance. The Cuban habanera in the opera of Spanish milieu, *Carmen*, breathes the spirit of Paris, because of Bizet's French treatment of the ensemble. It was perhaps only Ravel, born a few miles from the Spanish border in a little Basque town, who was able to evoke the Spanish spirit of the dance in his French scores. Naturally, then, Ravel's style is held in high esteem in Latin America: Argentina is strongly affiliated with the musical spirit of her motherland. The fact that Manuel de Falla, the greatest living Spanish composer, is now making his home in Argentina, will doubtless cause further interaction between the old and the new Hispanic countries. And the fate of men is reflected in that of their music: migration results in transmutation of styles. The very dance types we have used as our examples, the tango and the habanera, have traveled back and forth across the Atlantic between the old and new worlds, assuming new characteristics, creating hybrid forms, and, of course, varying in the manner of their performance. In the words of the Spanish historian Adolfo Salazar, now in Mexico, "the tango of Cadiz, mixed with African and Cuban influences, has engendered nearly the whole South American music."

JAZZ: A RETURN TO IMPROVISATION

The terpsichorean spirit of Latin America has vitalized the music of the Western hemisphere. A growing list of colorful and fiery southern dances is being integrated into modern symphonic music, just as the old dance types were incorporated into the eighteenth-century instrumental suite. Harl McDonald's *Rumba Symphony* indicates a general trend. This tendency of employing popular music as raw material for more serious expression is manifested in the style amalgamation of jazz. As Douglas Moore points out, we must acknowledge "popular forces, such as jazz, as typical American music products, which, despite their divided allegiance between commerce and art, are of much greater cultural value than the average American suspects." George Gershwin's premature death prevented us from seeing how his refreshing employment of the jazz element and the Negro folk tune might have further developed into different channels of American music. However, he showed the way that many young Americans are following. In addition, the popular American musical element has flourished in the scores of European composers now in this country: jazz or South American dances appear in some form or other in the music of Stravinsky, Milhaud, Hindemith, Krenek, Weill, Eisler, and others.

From the interpretative outlook, the most significant feature in jazz is its improvisation. In the extemporaneous performance of certain instruments in the jazz band, we are facing a new counteraction against the objectivity of the modern performing style—an escape from the binding script, and a return to a status that our century seemed to have left behind forever. We may skip five hundred years if we want to trace back certain habits of a streamlined jazz band in its own atmosphere of dance accompaniment. When the two main forms of old dancing, the stepped and the leaped, merged into a single unit, it became unnecessary to invent another melody for the so-called afterdance. The band did not repeat the first tune literally, it improvised a variation of the tune. Fiddlers played their extempore just as our saxophones or clarinets improvise, more or less contrapuntally against the dance tune.

Turning from the historical example to speculation on future interpretation, jazz may prove to be a springboard on the road back or forward (depending on the point of view) to the old practice of extemporaneous performance in serious music. This would mark another instance of the eternal spiral winding forward and backward between extremes of musical interpretation. And the striking talent for improvisation of the American band musician, now limited to the dance hall and often wasted on the silly task of paraphrasing Tchaikovsky or Mozart melodies, may find a more sensible function in the musical performance of the future.

Cosmopolitan Trends

A large portion of the music written in the Americas is quite detached from the folklore of the Western hemisphere. Many

South American composers take their guidance from the impressionistic world of Debussy or Ravel; we have already shown that leading North Americans choose from cosmopolitan elements for the material of their expression. Deems Taylor feels that "national characteristics are not nearly so clear-cut and important as we have deluded ourselves into thinking." His scores, of course, re-echo such convictions. Philip James has many interests: in his suite *Station WGZBX* he takes the radio medium as his theme. It is self-explanatory that his music on Goethe's *Iphigenie* or *The Overture in an Olden Style on French Noels* is beyond national classification. Howard Hanson, in his *Northern Symphony*, reflects reminiscence of his Scandinavian ancestry. Horace Johnson's orchestral scores conjure up the spirit of Florence and India. Folklore of native origin or from overseas is built into American scores in varying degrees, ranging from the borrowing of literal quotations to fine montage on a high technical level. Thus the interpreter must realize that while many American composers may use the same grammar, most obviously their idiomatic expressions or techniques of folklore adaptation are entirely different.

AMERICANISM: HUMANITY

The historian of a distant future will probably evaluate American music as an entity that to our day is still indiscernible. However, if he looks for a historical analogy to the American crucible, he will find it in the musical history of the old Austrian empire. Austrian music developed into a classical style without any ideological support, out of a diversity of national elements. Close to the Hungarian border, in a Burgenland hut, was born the man who wrote the Austrian national anthem. Called derogatorily "the Croatian," he worked on the estates of Hungarian counts and used in his music tunes ranging from Italian to Bohemian, from South Slav to German, and fused them into the precious idiom that, in a single word, was called "Austrian," and that, as such, has become universal. His name, of course, is Joseph Haydn; on certain manuscripts in his own handwriting, it is Giuseppe Haydn. We see that the greatness of Haydn, the good patriot, the friend of many folklores, the arch-Austrian of obscure extraction, the composer of the Austrian national anthem, lies in his musical genius and great humanity, neither of which is dependent upon nationalism in the political or geographic sense.

Likewise, musical chauvinism, the use of Sioux Indian tunes, and accumulation of folklore, will not make great American music. Misuse and misconception of national ideals have played their part in the destruction of the musical culture of Europe. We in America may follow the lead of Roger Sessions, who concluded an address to American musicologists and music teachers in Pittsburgh, in 1937, with these words: "Being American involves, after all, first being human; and what Americanism can have any ultimate value, except as the specific and inescapable inherent coloring of humanity?"

Epilogue

The writer has reserved his closing words for a discussion of our national anthem: the piece of music most frequently performed in this country today reflects many interpretative problems discussed in previous chapters. It is heard in a multitude of readings, which is perhaps surprising even to the average listener, who may expect a more standardized interpretation in the performance of music of such meaning. Even erudite musicians differ widely in their reading of *The Star-spangled Banner*, particularly in regard to tempo. The Army and Navy have their own style. Conductors vary in their instrumentation. Recently Igor Stravinsky published a new arrangement of the anthem. Since *The Star-spangled Banner* is still in process of being polished and revised, it might prove fruitful to look at its background in order to see whether any clues can be found as to its proper interpretation. It merits such historical investigation not only because of its renewed significance today, but for the striking example it affords of interpretative metamorphosis.

Who would suspect, without knowing the facts, that these lines—

> Our toast let it be:
> May our club flourish happy, united and free,
> And long may the sons of Anacreon entwine
> The myrtle of Venus with Bacchus' vine.

were the original text of the tune that is now used for the American national anthem? Obviously, such lyrics could hardly serve as the fighting song of a country at war, although they fulfilled the original purpose well enough as the drinking song of a comfortable club in London back in the 1770's. Its members must have had a merry time dining, wining, and singing —a gay variation of the typical old English after-supper singing, as described in our discussion of madrigals (p. 50).

Oscar Sonneck and others have traced the composition of the tune to an able member of the club, the versatile John Stafford Smith, an organist, singer, composer, and antiquary. His song, called *To Anacreon in Heav'n*, soon became a favorite in England, and reached this side of the Atlantic with the British settlers. The process of conversion must have started early, since by 1797 the music had already lost its original words and had turned into a song of patriotic significance. With this change in words, a change in interpretation naturally followed. The same tune would inevitably be sung in a different manner when it extolled a country's freedom instead of the pleasures of Bacchus and Venus.

The life-story of the American anthem is another demonstration of the plastic nature of music—of how time and environment can so alter a tune that the original connotation is completely lost. To recall how frequently music has been employed as an expression of diametrically opposed meanings, we may think of the fate of secular tunes adapted for church service (chap. i). Handel in his *Messiah* uses, in the first part of the chorus *For unto us a Child is born*, the music of a madrigal of erotic content composed for Princess Caroline of Hanover. The tragic duet *O Death, where is thy sting?* also proves to be the music of another madrigal, *Se tu non lasci amore*. The pastoral number in Bach's Christmas oratorio was borrowed from some of his secular cantatas and was perfectly adapted to its religious environment.

In each of these cases, the music retains its identity, while the change in words necessitates a modified interpretation.

Likewise, when Key's impassioned words, inspired by the bombardment of Fort McHenry, were set to the drinking tune of *To Anacreon in Heav'n*, their spirit compelled an emotional interpretation of the music expressive of the mood and hope experienced by the poet. Here we have a possible first clue for the spirit of the interpretation: it is this very mood of patriotic passion and hope that should constitute the basis of our contemporary performance, notwithstanding the numerous adjustments in harmony and form that have been made and are still being made.

In 1911, a specially appointed committee, which met in Boston, attempted to standardize the performance of four national songs, and succeeded in doing so, at least for years to follow. As to *The Star-spangled Banner*, the pitch decided on, by a close vote, was B flat, while the version adopted was the one that permitted changes of the stanzas to accommodate the words. However, the War Department, on April 2, 1942, officially announced that the United States Army, Navy and Marine Corps had agreed upon an A flat version of the anthem. This lowering of the pitch, of course, is designed to bring the high notes farther down for the average singer.

The next question to be answered is that of tempo. Recalling once more Beethoven's dictum that "tempo is the body of performance," we, too, can hope to get at the crux of the problem by setting the right timing in which *The Star-spangled Banner* should be sung and played. Toward this end, we must bear in mind that the song is a national anthem. An anthem calls for dignity, and dignity, musically speaking, calls for moderation of speed. One hears the tune frequently played quite rapidly (M.M. $\quarternote = 96-108$). This might suggest a military spirit, and a substitute for the march rhythm that, of course, the three-four meter of the song cannot offer. In contrast, a middle-course timing, fast enough to denote fighting spirit, yet sufficiently moderate to retain solemnity, is convincing. A metronome setting between 80 and 88 is perhaps the most suitable timing for chorus and community singing in large halls. This, in fact, is the tempo that has become most popular with some of our leading orchestras. It makes for a more coherent reading, quite appropriate when played as the overture for concert programs.

The problem of interpretation of the middle section centers around the fact that while the music of this part seems to lend itself well enough to a cantabile rendition, the words from "and the rockets' red glare" to "our flag was still there," scarcely permit such modification toward a lyrical rendition. However, many performers, in their desire for variation, invariably tend to endow this part with a lyrical quality. Historically, since the tune stems from the eighteenth century, its performance should follow the doctrine of affections, which holds that every phrase should be sung with strict adherence to the meaning of the words. Such a stylistic demand is violated if the middle section is sung lyrically. Obviously, the lyrical quality must be sacrificed for the sake of the words. The prevailing manner of playing the middle section should be discontinued in order to permit of adequate dramatic expression.

The cadence is always rendered with several ritardandi and pauses (*fermatas*). Such a slowing down is certainly in keeping with everything that we know about historical readings of this type of music. Since no standardized version indicates the retard, we clearly cannot employ objective interpretation. (After all, no original manuscript exists; even if it did, it could not serve as a guide for the reading of *The Star-spangled Banner*, because of the metamorphosis of the song in texture, meaning, and spirit.) A modified ritardando is suggested, gradually culminating in a majestic close. Therefore the initial tempo cannot be too fast, otherwise the final ritardando will become disproportionate. With a moderate beginning, a natural and logical development of the anthem evolves—a correct employment of *tempo rubato*.

In conclusion, we strike, for the last time, the theme which, like that of a rondo, has recurred through all the preceding chapters of this book—the theme we called objectivity of spirit. The true interpretation of *The Star-spangled Banner*, like that of every piece of music, does not hinge on setting the metronome slider at 80 or 88, or on any of the other objective musical conditions into which the conscientious interpreter must fit his rendition. After he determines the background of the work and all matters relative to its performance, which he can ascertain by research and study, there is still that intangible quality of emotion that makes the difference between a great and an ordinary performance. Through the ages, we see, it is not alone the musical material, but what we can do with it, that decides the destiny of an art work. Interpretation is the great force that brings to life what otherwise, as Wagner says, is "soulless pen music." The performer of the anthem must "glow, and feel," in the words of Berlioz, with the great emotional meaning behind the song. After all, there is no greater force than a people's voice for freedom.

BIBLIOGRAPHY
and REFERENCES

The bibliography is a selective one, composed of those main references that guided this investigation of interpretative problems. In addition, a few works are listed—ad libitum—for their value as collateral reading. A reference pertaining to more than one Part is listed only under the part to which it relates first.

PARTS ONE AND TWO

ADLER, G.: *Handbuch der Musikgeschichte*, Berlin, 1930

Archives, Papal Library, Vatican City

BACH, P. E.: *Versuch über die wahre Art das Clavier zu spielen*, Berlin, 1753

BUKOFZER, M.: "On the Performance of Renaissance Music"; *Proc. M.T.N.A.*, 1941

BURNEY, C.: *A General History of Music*, London, 1789

————: *The Present State of Music in France and Italy*, London, 1771

CACCINI, G.: *Le nuove musiche*, Florence, 1601; reprinted, Milan, 1919

CARSE, A. A.: *History of Orchestration*, New York, 1925

CAVALIERI, E.: *La rappresentazione di animo e di corpo*, Rome, 1600

CENCI, L.: *Madrigals* (Preface), 1647

CHRYSANDER, F.: *Georg Friedrich Haendel*, Leipzig, 1858–67

COATES, H.: *Palestrina*, London, 1938

COUPERIN, F.: *L'art de toucher le clavecin*, Paris, 1701

DIRUTA, G.: *Il Transilvano*, Venice, 1593

DOLMETSCH, A.: *The Interpretation of the Music of the 17th and 18th Centuries*, London, 1915

DURANTE, O.: *Maniera di cantar*, Rome, 1608

EINSTEIN, A.: "Das Madrigal," *Ganymed*, III, 1921

FINK, H.: *Practica musica*, Wittenberg, 1556

FINNEY, T.: *A History of Music*, New York, 1933

364   BIBLIOGRAPHY and REFERENCES

FRESCOBALDI, G.: *Toccate* (Preface), Rome, 1614–16

GOLDSCHMIDT, H.: *Die italienische Gesangsmethode des 17. Jahrhunderts*, Breslau, 1890

HAAS, R.: *Aufführungspraxis*, Potsdam, 1932

HARDING, R.: *Origins of Musical Time and Expression*, London, 1938

HEINICHEN, J.: *Der Generalbass in der Komposition*, Leipzig, 1728

HOWES, F.: *William Byrd*, London, 1928

JEPPESEN, K.: *Counterpoint* (transl. by G. Haydon), New York, 1939

JUNKER, K.: *Einige der vornehmsten Pflichten des Musikdirectors*, Winterthur, 1782

KINKELDEY, O.: *Orgel und Klavier in der Musik des 16. Jahrhunderts*, Leipzig, 1910

KUHN, M.: *Die Verzierungskunst in der Gesangsmusik*, Leipzig, 1902

LACH, R.: *Studien zur Entwicklungsgeschichte der ornamentalen Melopöie*, Leipzig, 1913

L'AFFILARD, M.: *Principes très-faciles pour bien apprendre la musique*, Paris, 1705

LANDOWSKA, W.: *La musique ancienne*, Paris, 1908

LÁNG, P.: *Music in Western Civilization*, New York, 1941

LOULIÉ, E.: *Éléments ou principes de musique*, Paris, 1696

MARPURG, F.: *Die Kunst das Clavier zu spielen*, Berlin, 1750

MATTHESON, J.: *Das neu eröffnete Orchester*, Hamburg, 1713

————: *Der vollkommene Kapellmeister*, Hamburg, 1739

MERSENNE, M.: *Harmonie universelle*, Paris, 1736

MONTEVERDI, C.: *Orfeo* (text of first performance), Mantua, 1607

MORLEY, T.: *A Plaine and Easie Introduction to Practicall Musicke*, London, 1597; reprinted, London: E. Fellowes, 1937

MOZART, L.: *Gründliche Violinschule*, 1756; facsimile ed., Vienna, 1922

MUFFAT, G.: *Florilegium*, 1695; also in *Denkmäler der Tonkunst in Österreich*

MYLIUS, W.: *Rudimenta musices*, Mühlhausen, 1685

PERI, J: *Euridice* (Preface), Florence, 1600

PIRRO, A.: *L'esthétique de J. S. Bach*, Paris, 1907

(POPE) PIUS X: *Motu proprio*, Rome, 1903

PLAYFORD, J.: *Briefe Introduction to the Skill of Musick*, London, 1655

PRAETORIUS, M.: *Syntagma musicum*, Wolfenbüttel, 1614

PRUNIÈRES, H.: *Vie illustre et libertine de Lully*, Paris, 1929

QUANTZ, J.: *Versuch einer Anweisung die Flöte traversière zu spielen*, Berlin, 1752

RAMEAU, J.: *Traité de l'harmonie*, Paris, 1722

————: *Pièces de clavecin*, Paris, 1731

REESE, G.: *Music in the Middle Ages*, New York, 1940

REICHARDT, J.: *Vertraute Briefe*, Berlin, 1809

ROLLAND, R.: *Handel* (*Les maîtres de la musique* . . .), Paris, 1910

————: *Voyage musical au pays du passé*, Paris, 1920

ROUSSEAU, J. J.: *Dictionnaire de musique*, Amsterdam, 1768

SACHS, C.: *History of Musical Instruments*, New York, 1940

————: *World History of the Dance*, New York, 1937

SCHENKER, H.: *Ein Beitrag zur Ornamentik*, Vienna, 1908

SCHNABEL, A.: *Ludwig van Beethoven: Piano Sonatas* (complete ed.), New York, 1935

SCHNEEGASS, C.: *Isagoges musicae*, Erfurt, 1591

SCHUBART, D.: *Ideen zu einer Aesthetik der Tonkunst* (posthumous ed.), Vienna, 1806

SCHÜNEMANN, G.: *Geschichte des Dirigierens*, Leipzig, 1913

SCHWEITZER, A.: *J. S. Bach* (Eng. transl.), London, 1912

SPIESS, M.: *Tractatus musicus*, Augsburg, 1746

SPITTA, P.: *J. S. Bach*, Leipzig, 1873

SPOHR, L.: *Grosse Violinschule*, Kassel, 1835

STRAUSS, R.: Berlioz: *Traité d'instrumentation* (Ger. ed.), Leipzig, 1905

SULZER, J. G.: *Allgemeine Theorie der schönen Künste*, Leipzig, 1792

TANS'UR, W.: *A New Musical Grammar*, London, 1746

ZABERN, C.: *De modo bene cantandi*, Munich, 1500

PART THREE

ABERT, H.: *Robert Schumann*, Berlin, 1903

BELLERMANN, H.: *Der Kontrapunkt*, Berlin, 1862

BERLIOZ, H.: *Memoirs* (Eng. transl. by R. and E. Holmes), London, 1894

ENGEL, C.: *Alla Breve, from Bach to Debussy*, New York, 1921

GRAF, H.: *The Opera and Its Future in America*, New York, 1942

GLUCK, C.: *Alceste* (Preface), Vienna, 1767

GUHR, K.: *Über Paganini's Kunst die Violine zu spielen*, Mainz and Paris, 1829, 1831

HANSLICK, E.: *Vom Musikalisch Schönen*, Leipzig, 1854

HIPKINS, E.: *How Chopin Played*, London, 1937

HOFFMANN, E. T.: *Musikalische Dichtungen und Aufsätze*

ISTEL, E.: "The Secret of Paganini's Technique," *Musical Quar.*, 1930

KAMIENSKI, L.: "Tempo rubato," *Archiv f. Musikw.*, I: 1

KAUFMAN, S.: *Mendelssohn*, New York, 1934

LISZT, F.: *Gesammelte Schriften*, Leipzig, 1880

MENDELSSOHN, F.: *Reisebriefe*

MOSEL, I.: *Versuch einer Aesthetik des dramatischen Tonsatzes*, 1813, new ed., 1910

ROLLAND, R.: *Musiciens d'aujourd'hui*, Paris, 1908

SCHUMANN, R.: *Music and Musicians* (Eng. ed.), London, 1877

WAGNER, R.: *Prose Works* (transl. by W. A. Ellis), London, 1892

WEBER, C. M.: *Notizbuch* (1816)

WERFEL, F., and STEFAN, P.: *Verdi; The Man in His Letters* (transl. by E. Downes), New York, 1942

PART FOUR

ALLEN, D. W.: *Philosophies of Music Histories*, New York, 1939

ARMITAGE, M.: *Schönberg*, New York, 1937

BARTOK, B.: *Hungarian Folk Music*, 1931

BONNET, J.: *L'histoire de musique*, Amsterdam, 1725

CHASE, G.: *Music in Spain*, New York, 1942

CHAVEZ, C.: *Towards a New Music*, New York, 1937

COPLAND, A.: *Our New Music*, New York, 1942

DEBUSSY, C.: Prose writings

————: *Monsieur Croche, the Dilettante Hater* (Eng. transl.), London, 1927

HARRIS, R., and EVANSON, J.: *Singing through the Ages*, New York, 1940

HAYDON, G.: *Introduction to Musicology*, New York, 1941

HILL, E. B.: *Modern French Music*, Cambridge, 1924

HOWARD, J. T.: *Our American Music*, New York, 1939

KANT, I.: *Die Kritik der reinen Vernunft*, Berlin, 1790

KRENEK, E.: *Music Here and Now*, New York, 1939

LOCKSPEISER, E.: *Debussy*, London, 1937

MOORE, DOUGLAS: *From Madrigal to Modern Music*, New York, 1942

NIETZSCHE, F.: *Gesammelte Schriften* (posthumous ed.), 1909–11

PISK, P.: "Schoenberg's Twelve-Tone Operas," in Armitage, M.:
    Schönberg, New York, 1937

SCHÖN, M.: *Art and Beauty*, New York, 1932

SCHÖNBERG, A.: *Harmonielehre*, Leipzig and Vienna, 1911

SLONIMSKY, N.: *Music since 1900*, New York, 1937

SONNECK, O.: *The Star-spangled Banner*, Washington, 1914

STEUERMANN, E.: "The Piano Music of Schönberg," in Armitage, M.:
    Schönberg, New York, 1937

STRAVINSKY, I.: *An Autobiography*, New York, 1936

THOMPSON, O.: *Debussy, Man and Artist*, New York, 1937

WEINGARTNER, F.: *Ratschläge für die Aufführung von Beethoven's
    Symphonien*, Leipzig, 1906

WELLESZ, E.: *Die neue Instrumentation*, Berlin, 1929

Index

NORTON PAPERBACKS ON MUSIC

Norton/Haydn Society Records

MASTERPIECES OF MUSIC BEFORE 1750
Three 12-inch 33⅓ RPM Long-play records to supplement Parrish and Ohl, *Masterpieces of Music Before 1750*.

A TREASURY OF EARLY MUSIC
Four 12-inch 33⅓ RPM Long-play records to supplement Parrish, *A Treasury of Early Music*.